From Balaam to Jonah
*Anti-prophetic Satire in the Hebrew Bible*

Program in Judaic Studies
Brown University
BROWN JUDAIC STUDIES
Edited by
Ernest S. Frerichs
Shaye J. D. Cohen, Calvin Goldscheider

Number 301
From Balaam to Jonah
*Anti-prophetic Satire in the Hebrew Bible*

by
David Marcus

# From Balaam to Jonah
## *Anti-prophetic Satire in the Hebrew Bible*

by

David Marcus

Scholars Press
Atlanta, Georgia

# From Balaam to Jonah
*Anti-Prophetic Satire in the Hebrew Bible*

© 1995
Brown University

**Library of Congress Cataloging-in-Publication Data**
Marcus, David, 1941–
  From Balaam to Jonah : anti-prophetic satire in the Hebrew Bible /
by David Marcus.
    p.    cm. — (Brown Judaic studies ; no. 301)
  Includes bibliographical references and index.
  ISBN 0-7885-0101-1 (cloth : alk. paper)
  1. Satire in the Bible. 2. Bible. O.T. —Language, style.
3. Prophets. I. Title. II. Series.
BS1199.I7M37    1995
221.6'6—dc20                              95-6409
                                         CIP

Printed in the United States of America
on acid-free paper

# Table of Contents

# Preface

The purpose of this book is to examine in detail four satires in the Hebrew Bible which appear to be critical of prophets, and which may be called anti-prophetic satires. Three of the satires occur in the Pentateuch and the Former Prophets: the satires of Balaam and his donkey (Num. 22:21-35), of the boys and the bald prophet (2 Kgs. 2:23-25), and of the lying prophet (1 Kgs. 13). The only satire that occurs in the Latter Prophets is the book of Jonah.

In chapter one we discuss the implications of satire for biblical research, and suggest reasons why satire has not been recognized before. We note the regular use of satire by the classical prophets, and why these four anti-prophetic satires represent an inversion of the norm. In the second chapter we describe how one can identify a text as satire, and outline the characteristic attributes of satire. Illustrations from other biblical satires are given for these features which include absurdities, fantastic situations, grotesqueries, distortions, ironies, ridicule, parody, and rhetorical features. Since satire, as a genre, is thought to have originated in Greece and Rome, the question is raised whether it is legitimate to call these stories satires and, if so, to what type of formal genre they belong.

The second part of our study deals with the three anti-prophetic satires in the Pentateuch and Former Prophets. Chapter three examines the story of Balaam and his donkey as related in Num. 22:21-35. The purpose of this satire is to belittle Balaam, a non-Israelite seer, and expose him to ridicule. Through the satire it is demonstrated that Balaam, supposedly the best of his profession, is not such an expert after all, and therefore cannot be relied upon as a legitimate source of the divine word. The fourth chapter focuses on the satire of the boys and the bald prophet (2 Kgs. 2:23-25). A satirical reading of the story enables one to posit an alternate interpretation to the standard didactic one: that the story is a warning to people to respect the prophets. In a satirical reading, the criticism is not directed at the boys, but at the behavior of the prophet (Elisha). The satire represents a criticism of the abuse of prophetic power by a prophet who invoked an atrociously severe curse for a seemingly mild offense.

The fifth chapter deals with the curious story of the lying prophet in 1 Kgs. 13. This satire differs from the first two in that it targets not one prophet, but two. Once again, a satirical reading of the story enables one to posit an alternate interpretation to the standard ones: that the story is etiological, that it has to do with competing revelations or with obedience and disobedience. A satirical reading indicates that the principal concern of the story is to satirize its targets, the man of God and the prophet of Bethel. They are satirized because of their behavior: for lying, foolishness, and concern with petty values.

The longest and most well-known of our anti-prophetic satires is the book of Jonah. The curiosities in the book are noticed, and the fantastic situations, distortions, and the host of ironies found in the book are listed. Also the many cases of ridicule and parody in the book are examined in detail, and a brief survey of the book's rhetorical techniques is provided. In chapter seven, we discuss the implications of reading the book of Jonah as a satire in regard to the interpretation of the book, its genre and its purpose. It is suggested that the message of the book is not any of the standard ones usually advanced (universalism, repentance, prophecy, God's mercy, tension between God's justice and God's mercy, or some combination of these). Rather it is held that the book is not advocating any particular philosophy or point of view. The purpose of the book is to satirize the prophet for behavior thought to be unbecoming to a prophet. Thus this satire is in accord with the three other anti-prophetic satires discussed in the previous chapters. All these prophets are satirized, not for ideological reasons, but for their behavior.

In an Afterword we sum up the common features of these four satires. They are all biographical, they all show prophets travelling, they all feature animals who do something extraordinary, and they all contain satirical features. This chapter also deals with the question of whether it is possible to identify the prophets who are the subjects of our satires, and whether these prophets were false prophets. Lastly, we offer some suggestions as to when and why these satires may have been written, and how these stories got accepted into the canon.

# Abbreviations

| | |
|---|---|
| AB | Anchor Bible |
| ABD | *The Anchor Bible Dictionary*. 6 vols. Ed. D. N. Freedman. New York: Doubleday, 1992. |
| AOAT | Alter Orient und Altes Testament |
| ATANT | Abhandlungen zur Theologie des Alten und Neuen Testaments |
| ATD | Das Alte Testament Deutsch |
| BibOr | Biblica et Orientalia |
| BKAT | Biblischer Kommentar: Altes Testament |
| BZAW | Beihfete zur *Zeitschrift für die alttestamentliche Wissenschaft* |
| CAD | *The Assyrian Dictionary of the Oriental Institute of the University of Chicago*. Eds. A. Leo Oppenheim, Erica Reiner, *et al*. 16 volumes. Chicago: Oriental Institute, 1956-. |
| CBC | Cambridge Bible Commentary |
| CBQ | *Catholic Biblical Quarterly* |
| EHAT | Exegetisches Handbuch zum Alten Testament |
| ExpTim | *Expository Times* |
| GKC | *Gesenius' Hebrew Grammar*. Ed. E. Kautzsch. 2nd English ed. Trans. A. E. Cowley. Oxford: Clarendon, 1960 <1910>. |
| HAR | *Hebrew Annual Review* |
| HBD | *Harper's Bible Dictionary*. Ed. P. J. Achtemeier, et al. New York: Harper & Row, 1985. |

| | |
|---|---|
| HUCA | *Hebrew Union College Annual* |
| IB | *Interpreter's Bible.* 6 vols. Ed. G. A. Buttrick. Nashville: Abingdon, 1956. |
| ICC | International Critical Commentary |
| IDB | *The Interpreter's Dictionary of The Bible.* 4 vols. Ed. G. A. Buttrick. Nashville: Abingdon, 1962. |
| IDBSup | *The Interpreter's Dictionary of The Bible. Supplementary Volume.* Ed. Keith Crim. Nashville: Abingdon, 1976. |
| JANES | *Journal of the Ancient Near Eastern Society* |
| JAOS | *Journal of the American Oriental Society* |
| JBL | *Journal of Biblical Literature* |
| JJS | *Journal of Jewish Studies* |
| JNES | *Journal of Near Eastern Studies* |
| JPOS | *Journal of the Palestine Oriental Society* |
| JPS | Jewish Publication Society |
| JQR | *Jewish Quarterly Review* |
| JSOT | *Journal for the Study of the Old Testament* |
| JSOTSup | *Journal for the Study of the Old Testament,* Supplementary Series |
| JSS | *Journal of Semitic Studies* |
| KAI | H. Donner & W. Röllig, *Kanaanäische und Aramäische Inschriften.* Wiesbaden: Otto Harrassowitz, 1962. |
| NEB | New English Bible |
| NICOT | New International Commentary on the Old Testament |
| OTL | Old Testament Library |
| OTS | *Oudtestamentische Studiën* |
| PCB | *Peake's Commentary on the Bible.* Eds. M. Black & H. H. Rowley. London: Thomas Nelson, 1962. |
| RB | *Revue biblique* |
| SAT | Die Schriften des Alten Testaments |
| VT | *Vetus Testamentum* |
| VTSup | *Vetus Testamentum Supplements* |
| WBC | Word Biblical Commentary |

| ZAW | *Zeitschrift für die alttestamentliche Wissenschaft* |
| ZDMG | *Zeitschrift der deutschen morgenländischen Gesellschaft* |
| ZDPV | *Zeitschrift des deutschen Palästina-Vereins* |

# I

## Introduction

The implications of reading any text, and particularly a biblical text, as satire have important consequences for the elucidation of that text. This can readily be seen in the areas of exegesis, and of social history. In the area of exegesis, a satirical interpretation, like a figurative or parabolic one, means that the text being read is not to be taken literally. At times, this may help eliminate obvious problems. Features that were formerly considered to be problems like fantastic events, incongruities, or exaggerations do not now have to be explained away. For example, a talking donkey, a man inside a big fish for three days, or other remarkable and fantastic happenings can be quite reasonably attributed to the satirical nature of the text. In the area of social history, a satirical inter-pretation helps elucidate texts by recognizing that they do not have to be taken at face value, that is, as factual representations of his-tory. Just as it is recognized that Jonathan Swift's *Gulliver's Travels* (1726) and Voltaire's *Candide* (1759), being satires, do not reflect actual conditions of 18th century European society, so too, for example, the satirical stories in the Epilogue of the book of Judges (chapters 19-21) do not, as is often thought, illustrate the dissolution of Israelite society prior to the monarchy.[1] Being

---

[1] Consider, for example, statements such as that of A. D. H. Mayes that these stories reflect "the moral and spiritual degeneration of Israel" (*Judges*, 15-16); or that of Robert Alter who writes that these chapters are "a kind of

satirical, these stories cannot be regarded as factual accounts[2] and
used as evidence that they reflect norms of behavior in Israel in
the pre-monarchal period.[3]

Considering the importance of a satirical interpretation in
these areas alone, one might be surprised that biblical scholarship
has not been more energetic in attempting to identify satire as a
literary device in biblical narratives. It is true that this situation is
gradually being rectified, and today one can find a growing number of articles and books on satire or satirical elements in some of
the biblical narratives.[4] But, this development is a relatively recent
phenomenon and has been inspired, in part, by the renewed interest during the last twenty years or so in the study of the Bible as
literature. In the past, however, there were a number of reasons
why satire previously had not been widely identified in the Biblical narratives.

First, in the standard textbooks on satire, little has been said
about satirical techniques in the Bible. Two examples will make
this clear. In Leonard Feinberg's *Introduction to Satire* (1967), the
only two satiric elements from the Bible mentioned are ironies:
the irony of Haman being hanged on the same gallows he ordered
built to hang Mordechai,[5] and the irony of Elijah taunting the

---

coda announcing the general breakdown of political and moral order"
("Language as Theme in the Book of Judges," 1).

[2] George Foot Moore's observations in the International Critical Commentary
a hundred years ago (1895) concerning the historicity of the battle sequences
are just as cogent today: "This way of making war, in which the operations
are immediately directed by Yahweh through his oracle, and the fighting
interspersed with religious exercises, is not history, it is not legend, but the
theocratic ideals of a scribe who had never handled a more dangerous
weapon than an imaginative pen" (*A Critical and Exegetical Commentary on
Judges*, 431).

[3] So John L. McKenzie, *The World Of The Judges*, 159.

[4] See pp. 5-7 below, and especially the list of scholars we mention in our discussion of Jonah in chapter seven, pp. 146-47 below.

[5] P. 163.

priests of Baal.[6] Or consider Dwight Macdonald's observation, in his well known anthology of parodies (1960), that "parody seems not to have appealed to the ancient Hebrews or the early Christians; at least there is no trace of it in either the Old or New Testament."[7]

Second, because the Bible has been utilized as sacred scripture, there has always been a general attitude of reverence to it by all faith groups.[8] Hence, it was thought that humor or satire did not exist in the Bible,[9] and that the ancient Israelites were a "humorless lot."[10] However, over the course of time a noticeable difference emerged between Jews and Christians as to how solemn the approach to the Bible had to be. Whereas, Rabbinic and later Jewish exegesis could tolerate light-hearted and often humorous interpretations for the narrative parts of the Bible,[11] Christian exegesis, in the main, related to these texts with deep reverence.[12] This situation intensified with the rise of modern German Protestant scholarship[13] and, under its influence, a common mis-

---

[6] P. 180.

[7] *Parodies*, 562.

[8] Francis Landy, "Humour as a Tool for Biblical Exegesis," 99-100.

[9] Conrad Hyers, *And God Created Laughter*, 4.

[10] See Yehuda T. Radday, "On Missing The Humour in the Bible: An Introduction," 21-38; Landy, "Humour as a Tool for Biblical Exegesis," 99-104; and R. P. Carroll, "Is Humour Among the Prophets?" 169-70.

[11] Radday, "On Missing The Humour in the Bible," 35-37.

[12] Ibid., 34. In Christian typology many events in the narrative texts of the Hebrew Bible (the Old Testament) are said to prefigure later events in the New Testament. For example, many events in the book of Jonah are regarded as a precursor to events in the life of Jesus. Thus Jonah in the fish in New Testament typology refers to Jesus' death and resurrection (Matt. 12:40).

[13] Note E. Bickerman's comments about the founders of modern biblical scholarship of the 18th century: "The theologians of the *Aufklärung* [Enlightenment] took their official religion seriously. There was no flippancy. Radical as they could be in the realm of pure thought, these profes-

conception arose that the Bible is lacking in humor and hence devoid of satire.[14]

The third reason satires have not been identified in the Bible is because their characteristic satirical features were not identified as such. Since satire almost always pretends to be something other than what it really is,[15] it sometimes succeeds so well that readers miss the satiric intention entirely.[16] Children are completely unaware of the satire of 18th century England in *Gulliver's Travels*. To them it is just "a story of funny little men and funny big men."[17] Indeed, literary critics often debate whether certain works are satire or not,[18] and it often happens that the targets of the ironies, of the ridiculing attacks, and of the parodies, become lost or forgotten. Or sometimes changes in language make puns pointless and other witticisms meaningless.[19] With changing historical and social conditions, the new generation of readers is simply not aware of the allusions, the connotations, or the hints to

---

sors were assiduous churchgoers, pious in their own way, and docile to the authority, secular and ecclesiastic" (*Four Strange Books of the Bible*, 22-23).

[14] See the observations of Mary Ellen Chase, *The Bible and the Common Reader*, 196-97; Millar Burrows, "The Literary Category of the Book of Jonah," 95; and Samuel Sandmel, *The Enjoyment of Scripture*, 20-21.

[15] Gilbert Highet, *The Anatomy Of Satire*, 158.

[16] Ibid., 21; and Feinberg, *Introduction to Satire*, 3.

[17] D. Worcester, *The Art of Satire*, 45. There is the oft-cited legendary story that Swift claims in a letter to Pope that a Bishop in Dublin had read *Gulliver's Travels* and decided it was full of improbable lies--he hardly believed a word of it! This story is cited by both Highet (*The Anatomy Of Satire*, 15), and R. C. Elliott (*The Power of Satire*, 197).

[18] One of the more prominent debates was the one some years ago over whether or not the work of the French writer Rabelais was satire. On one side, Gilbert Highet stated that Rabelais was the greatest French satirist and, on the other side, John Cowper Powys held that Rabelais "was no more a satirist than James Joyce was a clown." See W. Victor Wortley, "Some Rabelaisian Satiric Techniques," 8.

[19] Feinberg, *Introduction to Satire*, 272.

which the satire refers.[20] The targets of satire soon become faded and forgotten. In short, satire goes out of date very quickly.[21] But a satirical form, like any other literary genre, is basically time-less,[22] and even if a story was misunderstood or reinterpreted later, the satirical form is a clue to its original interpretation.[23]

So these three reasons, the lack of treatment in general works on satire, the attitude of reverence towards the Bible, and the fact that the characteristic features of satire were simply not recognized, all combined in the past to inhibit the identification of satirical texts in biblical narrative. But, whereas, in the past, satire has not been recognized in biblical narrative, this is not the case with regard to the prophets. For it has long been acknowledged that rhetorical features characteristic of satire, such as irony, sarcasm, parody, and ridicule occur in the prophetic writings.[24] Indeed, already in his *Myth, Legend, and Custom in The Old Testament* (1969),[25] Theodor H. Gaster had observed that satire was one of the cardinal elements of the prophetic technique, and in his book on *The Art of Biblical Poetry* (1985),[26] Robert Alter designated satire as one of the three principal modes of prophetic poetry, the others being direct accusation and description of impending disaster. Other writers, such as W. F. Stinespring (1962),[27] C. Corydon Randall (1990),[28] and R. P. Carroll

---

[20] Highet, *The Anatomy Of Satire*, 17-18.

[21] Northrop Frye, *Anatomy of Criticism*, 224. Feinberg claims, probably justifiably, that "very few satires written before 1800 provide pleasure today for readers outside the classroom" (*Introduction to Satire*, 272).

[22] Ronald A. Knox, "On Humour and Satire," 57, 61.

[23] See the remarks of Carl R. Holladay, "the literary form of a text is often a clue to its meaning" ("Biblical Criticism," 131).

[24] See, for example, W. F. Stinespring, "Irony and Satire," 726-28; and E. M. Good, *Irony In The Old Testament*, passim.

[25] P. 630.

[26] P. 141.

[27] "Irony and Satire," 727-28.

[28] "An Approach to Biblical Satire," 132-44.

(1990),[29] have catalogued some prophetic passages containing elements of satire, and David Fishelov (1989)[30] has discussed some of the satirical techniques used by prophets. In his recent book *Satire in the Hebrew Prophets* (1990), Thomas Jemielity has shown that prophecy and satire are near of kin. Jemielity compares the prophets to satirists, like Horace, Juvenal or Pope, and focuses on some of the themes, strategies, and techniques that prophecy and satire share.[31] Since the purpose of satire is to expose to ridicule vice or folly,[32] hypocrisy,[33] painful situations,[34] or excesses,[35] one can easily see why the prophets, who also condemn these same imperfections, would use this device as a means of transmitting their message.

This book does not deal with every satirical text in the biblical narrative. Such a work awaits to be written. We have identified at least 14 satires in biblical narratives. These satires target foreigners, the "primeval objects of satire"[36] and Israelites alike. Examples of satires against foreigners are the story of the

---

[29] "Is Humour Among the Prophets?," 169-89.

[30] "The Prophet as Satirist," 195-211.

[31] Jemielity does not discuss any example of narrative satire in the prophets. Unfortunately, like his predecessors (particularly Randall), Jemielity does not discuss independent prophetic units, but draws on scattered verses of prophecy taken from a wide variety of places. Also, Jemielity frequently, and illegitimately, dips into non-prophetic material as support for his comparisons with the prophets.

[32] Elliott, *The Power of Satire*, 111; and W. V. Harris, *Dictionary of Concepts in Literary Criticism and Theory*, 355.

[33] Edgar Johnson, *A Treasury of Satire*, 8; A. B. Kernan, *The Plot of Satire*, 36; Matthew Hodgart, *Satire*, 30; and Feinberg, *Introduction to Satire*, 23-24.

[34] Highet, *The Anatomy Of Satire*, 18.

[35] "The excesses that we laugh at are usually inferior excesses: the fat man, not the strong man; the fool, not the genius; greed, not philanthropy" (Feinberg, *Introduction to Satire*, 6).

[36] Worcester, *The Art of Satire*, 148.

Tower of Babel (Gen. 11:1-9, against the Mesopotamians);[37] the story of Ehud (Judg. 3, against the Moabites);[38] and the satires in the Book of Esther (against the Persian king, and his anti-semitic prime minister).[39] Examples of satires against Israelites are in the story of Jephthah and the Ephraimites (Judg. 12:1-10, against the Ephraimites);[40] in the story of Micah and the Danites (Judg. 17-18, against the Danite sanctuary);[41] and in the stories of the Levite and his concubine, and the subsequent civil war (Judg. 19-21, against the Bejaminites).[42] Here we are concerned only with those satires in which prophets are involved as targets, that is anti-prophetic satires. In many respects, the stories studied in our book represent an inversion of the norm since, as we have just remarked, elsewhere in the Bible, the prophets themselves frequently use satire and satirical techniques. Our book deals with

---

[37] See U. Cassuto, *From Noah to Abraham*, 227, and most recently (1994) Nisan Ararat, "Genesis 11:1-9 as a Satire," 224-31.

[38] While they do not actually identify this story as a satire, many satirical elements have been noticed by Robert Alter (*The Art of Biblical Narrative*, 37-41) and Baruch Halpern (*The First Historians*, 39-75; idem, "The Assassination of Eglon---The First Locked-Room Murder Mystery," 32-41, 44).

[39] The best works to date showing satirical aspects of the book of Esther are those of D. J. A. Clines, *The Esther Scroll*, esp. 31-38; Edward L. Greenstein, "A Jewish Reading of Esther," 225-43; and Yehuda T. Radday, "Esther with Humour," 295-313.

[40] I have pointed out the satirical elements in this story in my "Ridiculing the Ephraimites: The Shibboleth Incident (Judges 12:6)," 95-105.

[41] On some of the satirical elements in this story, see my "In Defence of Micah: Judges 17:2: He Was Not a Thief," 72-80, and for a view of the story as a polemic, see Yairah Amit, "Hidden Polemic in the Conquest of Dan: Judges xvii-xviii," 4-20.

[42] The humor and absurd elements in these chapters have been noticed by Stuart Lasine, "Guest and Host in Judges 19: Lot's Hospitality in an Inverted World," 37-59, 1984; and Barry G. Webb has observed that these chapters contains satires on Israelite hospitality and on the Israelite assembly (*The Book of Judges*, 190-96).

four stories, all of which are satires against prophets, and which we term anti-prophetic satires. The first satire is that of Balaam and his donkey (Num. 22:21-35). Balaam is a foreign prophet or seer, and the purpose of the satire is to denigrate him and his supposed powers as a seer. This satire lays the foundation for the other three works which will also criticize prophets, but in these satires they are Israelite prophets. The second satire in our corpus is the story of the boys and the bald prophet (2 Kgs. 2:22-24). In this story, the Israelite prophet, Elisha, is the subject of ridicule and the target of satire because of his improper behavior. The third satire, the lying prophet (1 Kgs. 13), is much longer, and actually targets two prophets, a man of God from Judah and an old prophet from Bethel. In both these satires the prophets are ridiculed because of their behavior. The fourth and longest satire is that contained in the book of Jonah. We shall demonstrate below that the primary emphasis of the book is not on any particular message, such as repentance, prophecy, universalism, or God's mercy. Rather, the emphasis is on Jonah himself. In the light of the other three satires, we will show that Jonah is satirized, not for ideological reasons, but for his behavior. All four satires then serve the purpose of ridiculing the prophets for behavior which, to the authors (and readers) of these satires, was considered objectionable and unacceptable.

Before we analyze these satires, we must first demonstrate how a text may be recognized as satire. In the next chapter, we will thus outline the essential characteristics which must be present in a text before it can be classified as a satire.

# II

## The Characteristic Features of Satire

A text may be identified as a satire if it has a target which is the object of attack,[1] either directly or indirectly, and has a preponderance of the essential attributes of satire.[2] These latter consist of a mixture[3] of unbelievable elements (absurdities, fantastic situations, grotesqueries, and distortions),[4] ironies, ridicule, parody,[5] and rhetorical features.[6] It is not enough for

---

[1] Frye, *Anatomy of Criticism*, 224.

[2] Literary scholars debate whether satire should evoke in the reader certain emotions, such as uneasiness (P. M. Spacks, "Some Reflections on Satire," 363-64), amusement (Harris, *Dictionary of Concepts*, 358), or contempt. According to Highet, "it is the balance between the amusement and the contempt which differentiates satire from pure comedy, on the one hand, and invective or diatribe, on the other" (*The Anatomy of Satire*, 21, 149-50). Similarly, Stinespring, "Irony and Satire," 727. On the other hand, others maintain that invective is part of satire (Johnson, *A Treasury of Satire*, 7; Worcester, *The Art of Satire*, 13-38; and Feinberg, *Introduction to Satire*, 108-12).

[3] The word 'satire' comes from Latin word *satura* 'full' or "mixture full of different things." It was originally part of the vocabulary of food, and a recipe of a sort of salad was called *satura*. Other types of literature have been given food names, e.g., 'farce' means 'stuffing', see Highet, *The Anatomy of Satire*, 231.

[4] Ibid., 158; and Frye, *Anatomy of Criticism*, 224.

[5] According to Leonard Feinberg, the main technique of the satirist consists of a "playfully critical distortion of the familiar" (*The Satirist*, 7). Feinberg's definition has been criticized by Philip Pinkus on the grounds that it does not

9

these techniques just to appear in a work in an isolated fashion, they must dominate it by being the very essence of the work.[7] It is this domination which distinguishes a genuine satire from other works containing some satire. The latter may contain a few satirical techniques here or there, but if these techniques do not overwhelm the work it is not a true 'satire'. Hence, there are many texts in the Bible which contain absurdities, fantastic events, irony, ridicule, parody, and fine rhetorical techniques which are not satires because as a whole they do not have a preponderance of these features, only isolated examples.

## Fantastic events

Fantastic events are those which rationally seem impossible or highly unrealistic. Because of the unnaturalness of these events, some readers often term these situations miracles.[8] Satirists are fond of engaging in the fantasy of portraying animals or inanimate objects, such as trees or dead people, to be speaking. Some well-known examples are the speaking horses in Book IV of Jonathan Swift's *Gulliver's Travels*, and the talking animals in George Orwell's *Animal Farm*.[9] In biblical satire Balaam's donkey speaks to him (Num. 22:28), trees converse[10] and the dead talk among

---

fit many satires ("An Impossible Task? Review of Leonard Feinberg's *Introduction to Satire*," 165-66).

[6] Highet, *The Anatomy of Satire*, 18.

[7] For example, if the satiric elements were removed from Swift's *A Modest Proposal* it would change the very nature of the piece. It would just be a didactic essay and no longer a satire. On the other hand removing the satiric techniques from Shakespeare's *Henry IV, Part Two* would not change the general nature of the play because the satire in it is incidental (W. E. Haas, "Some Characteristics of Satire," 2-3).

[8] See Yair Zakovitch, *The Concept of the Miracle in the Bible*.

[9] "Satirists have often made animals serve as symbolic extensions of human beings" (Feinberg, *Introduction to Satire*, 53).

[10] The pines and the cedars of Lebanon are depicted as rejoicing over the death of the Mesopotamian king, "Even pines rejoice at your fate, and cedars

themselves[11] (in Isaiah's mock elegy, Isa. 14:3-21). Other types of fantastic situations occurring in biblical satires include: trying to build a tower to the sky (Gen. 11:4); Lot's wife turning into a pillar of salt (Gen. 19:26); the appearance of a heavenly army, and an entire enemy force being stricken with temporary blindness (2 Kgs. 6:17-18).

## Grotesqueries

All the great satirists (Rabelais, Juvenal, Aristophanes, Petronius, Voltaire, Cervantes, Gogol, and Swift) employ grotesqueries in their satires.[12] Grotesqueries consist of atrocities characterized by violent actions such as beatings, mutilations, killings, murder,[13] rape, incest, and cannibalism,[14] and vulgarities such as obscenity[15]

---

of Lebanon: 'Now that you have lain down, none shall come up to fell us'" (Isa. 14:8).

[11] The inhabitants of Sheol (the dead) talk among themselves while making preparations to greet the new arrival, "All [the inhabitants of Sheol] speak up and say to you, 'So you have been stricken as we were, You have become like us'" (Isa. 14:10).

[12] Feinberg, *Introduction to Satire*, 70; and Worcester, *The Art of Satire*, 60-70.

[13] "Almost every kind of human suffering is inflicted on the four chief characters in Voltaire's, *Candide*. There is exile, imprisonment, torture, and execution" (Highet, *The Anatomy of Satire*, 21).

[14] In Juvenal's *Satire XV*, Egyptians devour an enemy soldier, and in Petronius' *Satyricon*, the heirs of Eumolpus must eat his body before they can share his estate. In Voltaire's *Candide*, Turkish soldiers engage in cannibalism during a siege. A pet spaniel and a tutor are eaten in Byron's *Don Juan*, as is Basil's finacée in Waugh's *Black Mischief*. See Ronald Paulson, "The Fictions of Satire," 340.

[15] "The effect of obscenity in satire is to level all men, and to level them downwards, removing the distinctions of rank and wealth. The satirist's aim is to strip men bare and, apart from physique, one naked man is much like another" (Hodgart, *Satire*, 30).

and scatology.[16] The presence of these features in a story is primarily for shock value. According to Paulson, these are the parts of satire which readers remember. They remember extraordinary images, such as the copulation of an ass and a woman (Apuleius' *Metamorphoses*), the drowning of half the populace of Paris in a flood of urine (Rabelais' *Gargantua*), and the projected cooking and eating of children (Swift's *Modest Proposal*).[17] Biblical satires contain equally vivid scenes. The Levite's concubine is gang raped and mutilated (Judg. 19:25-29); the daughters of Lot sleep with their father (Gen. 19:30-38); two women eat a child during a siege (2 Kgs. 6:26-31); Eglon's death spasm causes the release of his anal sphincter and an oozing out of feces (Judg. 3); and the Philisitines are punished by a plague affecting their buttocks or genital area (1 Sam. 5).

However, repeated grotesqueries in a satire dilute their shock value, as the reader tends to get inured to this type of material. The grotesquery can become absurd when, for example, characters, who are killed, come back to life again. In Voltaire's *Candide*, the philosopher Pangloss is publicly hanged by the Inquisition yet turns up again 22 chapters later; and another character is twice killed yet also reappears in the story.[18] In one

---

[16] "It is commonplace for Aristophanes's characters to break wind or relieve themselves with fright, like Dionysus in *The Frogs*, while Swift's Yahoos are remarkable for their urine and dung" (Hodgart, *Satire*, 28). See also, Feinberg, *Introduction to Satire*, 71; and Kernan, *The Plot of Satire*, 54.

[17] Paulson, "The Fictions of Satire," 340.

[18] See Highet, *The Anatomy of Satire*, 21. Highet writes about the grotesqueries in Candide's *Voltaire*: "When these hideous disasters and cruelties are put all together into a sort of cacophonous fugue, the final effect is not tragic. It is not even sad. It is--satirical. We cannot quite call it comic; but it does not bring agonizing tears to the eyes or icy horror to the soul. The result of reading this short book which, in thirty chapters of accidents, narrates the humiliating collapse of four lives, is neither tears nor hearty laughter, but a wry grimace which sometimes, involuntarily, breaks into a smile" (*The Art of Satire*, 12).

biblical satire, the tribe of Jabesh-Gilead is supposedly massacred to obtain wives for the Benjaminites (Judg. 21:10-12). However, the tribe is very much alive at the very beginning of Saul's reign (1 Sam. 11).

## Distortions

Distortion, which consists of exaggeration and understatement, is one of the major techniques of a satirist.[19] Essentially it is the use of hyperbole. Many examples of exaggeration can be seen in the Book of Esther. The Persian Empire is said to have 127 provinces; the banquet lasts half a year; the search for a new queen was empire-wide and lasted four years; Haman promises to pay ten thousand talents of silver and the gallows he built were 75 feet high. An example of understatement for effect is the report in the story of Pharaoh and the midwives (Exod. 1:15-22) that there were only two midwives for such a large population of Israelites. Distortion is typically seen in battle accounts when the enemy is almost totally eliminated but the Israelites suffer none or extremely few casualties. For example, in the story of Ehud, Israelites are able to kill ten thousand of the Moabite enemy without suffering any corresponding casualties (Judg. 3:29).

## Irony

Irony is perhaps the most sophisticated weapon at the disposal of a satirist,[20] and it is found in abundance in all works of satire.[21] The feature which is common to all forms of irony is a contrast of appearance and reality. An ironist seems to be saying one thing

---

[19] Feinberg, *Introduction to Satire*, 105, 119.
[20] Douglas Colin Muecke, *Irony*, 80. Frye believes that satire is militant irony (*Anatomy of Criticism*, 223).
[21] Kernan, *The Plot Of Satire*, 81-82.

but is really saying something quite different.[22] There are many different types of ironies (such as dramatic irony, comic irony, romantic irony and tragic irony),[23] but the two most familiar are verbal irony and situational irony. Verbal irony is often defined as "a figure of speech in which the intended meaning is the opposite of that expressed by the words used,"[24] and situational irony as "a condition of affairs or events of a character opposite to what was, or might naturally be, expected."[25] These standard definitions have been held to be inadequate by some literary critics. In particular, it has been pointed out that irony does not always equal the opposite or reverse, but it can also have to do with incongruity and incompatibility.[26] Verbal irony occurs when a character says "It is a fine day today!" when it is actually raining. Hence one may describe a verbal irony by saying that so and so "is being ironical."[27] Situational irony occurs when the narrator, in remarking about the same rainy day says, "It was a fine day." Hence one may describe a situational irony by saying that "it is ironic that...."[28] In the Bible most verbal irony is found in the ironic statements of the prophets, and will occur in prophetic satire. Most situational irony is to be found in the narratives, and will occur in narrative satire.

One of the major problems with identifying irony in a text is that, unlike spoken irony which can use a wink or a nod, in

---

[22] Muecke, *Irony*, 30, 35.

[23] See Douglas Colin Muecke, *The Compass of Irony*, 4.

[24] *Oxford English Dictionary*, sub 'irony'.

[25] Ibid.

[26] Muecke, *The Compass of Irony*, 19-20, 42, 444; Norman Knox, "On the Classification of Ironies," 54; and Wayne C. Booth, *A Rhetoric of Irony*, 34-41.

[27] Muecke, *The Compass of Irony*, 42-43.

[28] Ibid. The distinction between the ironies is often a technical one because in a narrative setting it is the narrator, after all, who gives the character his lines.

literary irony there are no external indicators: irony is not indicated in the text with any special mark.[29] There are, however, various techniques for identifying irony in a text. For example, a classic ironic indicator is a clash of style. Thus, if a speaker's style departs notably from whatever the reader considers the normal way of saying a thing, or the way normal for this speaker, the reader may suspect irony.[30] Another indicator is conflict of belief. Here we are alerted to irony whenever we notice an unmistakable conflict between the beliefs expressed and the beliefs we hold *and suspect the author of holding*.[31] A third indicator is the juxtaposition together without comment of two contradictory statements, or two incongruous images, or two incompatible phenomena.[32]

Despite these formal indicators, it is still often very difficult to be sure that a text is really ironic. This produces the (ironic!) situation that ironists run the risk of having their irony go undetected.[33] This is as true of novelists of yesteryear as of modern newspaper columnists. In many an English Department there are still lively controversies about whether this or that novel is ironic,[34] and many a modern columnist has often complained

---

[29] Muecke records the suggestion made in 1899 by a certain Alcanter de Brahm for a special punctuation mark (ç) "le petit signe flegellateur" to advise readers that the author is using irony (*The Compass of Irony*, 56). But as Booth noted (presumably ironically!), this would still not be too helpful for the reader because "there would always be the possibility that the *mark* was being used ironically, and that the *words* should be taken straight!" (*A Rhetoric of Irony*, 55).

[30] Booth, *A Rhetoric of Irony*, 67.

[31] Ibid., 73.

[32] Muecke, *Irony*, 61. Other stratagems by which irony may be recognized include praising in order to blame, and its converse blaming in order to praise, pretended agreement, innuendo, internal contradiction, exaggeration, understatement, ambiguity, or other stylistic warning signals (like a rhetorical question). See Muecke, *The Compass of Irony*, 67-86; idem, *Irony*, 55.

[33] Muecke, *The Compass of Irony*, 56.

[34] Booth, *A Rhetoric of Irony*, 47-48. Cf., the similar debate regarding works

that an intended ironic column has been taken seriously.[35] At
times, even though we may be able to define the *formal* requirements of an ironical remark or an ironic situation, we still have to
ask of a remark, *Was it meant ironically?* and of a situation, *Do
you feel it as irony?*[36] Hence, irony is basically interpretative. It
depends on the stance of the reader and often exists only in "the
eye of the beholder."[37] The reader must make an interpretative
decision from the facts related in the text and from what he knows
from outside. Nevertheless, despite these limitations, it is possible
to identify many of the situational ironies inherent in biblical
satires.

One of the most frequent ironical techniques in the Bible is
that of a "measure for measure" irony. A "measure for measure"
irony occurs, for example, when a pickpocket, engaged in the act
of pickpocketing, has his own pocket picked. There is an aesthetic
balance in this type of irony.[38] Thus, in the satire of the Tower of
Babel, the very thing the people did not want to happen happened.
The people wanted to construct their building, "lest we be scattered all over the world" (Gen. 11:4), but it subsequently turned
out that "the Lord scattered them over the face of the whole
earth" (Gen. 11:9). Or, in the story of Lot (Gen. 19), there is
poetic justice in the fact that just as Lot had offered his daughters
to the men of Sodom to be assaulted sexually, these same
daughters were the ones who committed a sexual assault on him.

---

of satire, noted above pp. 4-5.

[35] Booth reports a personal communication from the humorist Art Buchwald
that almost every ironic column he writes produces a collection of angry letters from irony-blind readers (*A Rhetoric of Irony*, 60, n. 15).

[36] Muecke, *The Compass of Irony*, 14.

[37] Ibid., 100. Note Booth's cautionary advice that "no complex piece of
irony can be read merely with tests or devices or rules, and it would be a
foolish man who felt sure that he could never mistake irony for straight talk"
(*A Rhetoric of Irony*, 81).

[38] Muecke, *Irony*, 45-46.

Another rhetorical term often associated with irony is sarcasm.[39] Sarcasm is a very effective tool of criticism and can accomplish much more than direct language can.[40] For example, a retort, "You were really very smart to do that!" said to a person who has just spilled coffee all over himself, is a much more effective, and probably less hurtful comment than a direct "you were really dumb to do that!" would have been. But sarcasm is, in one most important way, different from irony. In irony, as we have noted above, there is a contrast of appearance and reality: a text has to have both an apparent and real meaning. However, in sarcasm there is no pretense. The underlying (the real) meaning is so obvious that it cannot be misunderstood.[41] Sarcasm is one of the most common rhetorical tools used by the prophets. Elijah's taunt to the devotees of Baal to "Shout louder! After all, he is a god. But he may be in conversation, he may have gone to the bathroom,[42] or he may be on a journey, or perhaps he is asleep and will wake up!" (1 Kgs. 18:27) is a classic example of prophetic sarcasm. The use of the sarcasm "Shout louder! After all, he is a god" is so much more effective than if the same senti-

---

[39] Highet, *The Anatomy of Satire*, 57. But some sarcasms are not ironical at all. Muecke gives the following examples: A teacher who says to a pupil, "Well, of course I didn't expect *you* to get the right answer" is being sarcastic but not ironical since the ostensible meaning is the intended meaning. A man who says angrily, "Well, you've made a fine bloody mess of it, haven't you?" is barely ironical because his tone of voice, and the other words almost totally obliterate both the praise implicit in 'fine' and the syntactical appearance of a question. He might almost as well have said, "Well, you've made a god-awful bloody mess of it!" (*The Compass of Irony*, 54).

[40] Muecke, *Irony*, 51.

[41] Highet, *The Anatomy of Satire*, 57; Worcester, *The Art of Satire*, 78; and Feinberg, *Introduction to Satire*, 180.

[42] For the evidence that the Hebrew words (שִׂיחַ and שִׂיג) used here denote urination and defecation, see Gary A. Rendsburg, "The Mock of Baal in 1 Kings 18:27," 414-17.

ment were expressed in direct language such as "Don't bother to shout because, after all, he is not really a god!"

**Ridicule**

Of all the satiric techniques none is less sympathetic to a target than ridicule because, by means of ridicule an author is able to portray a target unkindly with the intent of making fun of him.[43] He can make unkind observations about a target's name, his personal characteristics, or he can portray him in undignified or embarrassing situations.[44] The humor can come from reducing something high and noble to something low and mean,[45] or putting a high, classic character into a prosaic situation.[46] A satirist might, for example, represent Aeneas as a vagabond and Dido as a fishwife.[47] Ridicule, naturally, abounds in biblical satire. In the story of Lot (Gen. 19), Lot is ridiculed as one who goes to extreme and laughable lengths to honor the code of hospitality even as far as offering his daughters to the townsfolk to protect his male visitors. Indeed Lot himself is considered ridiculous, a 'joker' (מְצַחֵק, v. 14) in the eyes of his sons-in-law. His descendants, the tribal ancestors of Israel's neighbors, the Moabites and Ammonites, are ridiculed by being shown to have had a disgrace-

---

[43] Ridicule goes hand in hand, and is often synonymous with, burlesque (from Italian, *burla*, 'ridicule') and caricature (Macdonald, *Parodies*, 558). The object of all three is the same: to diminish and degrade the target (Feinberg, *Introduction to Satire*, 185).

[44] "The basic technique of the satirist is reduction: the degradation or devaluation of the victim by reducing his stature and dignity" (Hodgart, *Satire*, 115). As far as ridicule is concerned, Highet describes satire as "the literary equivalent of a bucket of tar and a sack of feathers" (*The Anatomy of Satire*, 155).

[45] Kernan, *The Plot of Satire*, 53.

[46] Macdonald, *Parodies*, 557.

[47] Worcester, *The Art of Satire*, 46.

ful origin, to be literally nothing more than the products of incestuous intercourse.

An example of ridicule against a personal characteristic is in the satire against Eglon, king of Moab (Judg. 3:12-30). Eglon is characterized as extremely fat and obtuse. His very name, which means either 'calf' or "round one," hence "King Fatted Calf" or "King Round One" is the object of ridicule, for the king is considered to be a fat, round head of cattle. We are told that Eglon was so fat that not only did the fat close up around the sword that assassinated him, but that the hilt, which normally would remain in the hand of the assailant, penetrated along with the blade.

## Parody

Another of the chief components of satire is parody. Parody imitates someone or something by distortion, thereby "evoking amusement, derision, and sometimes scorn."[48] The object of a parody can be a text, a genre, a person, or a behavior.[49] Parody occurs when traditional texts are used in a distorted fashion, as well as when a character does not conform to expected forms of behavior. Another form of parody is to use familiar quotations in an unfamiliar context. Parody, however, can work in two ways.[50]

---

[48] Highet, *The Anatomy of Satire*, 69. Similarly, M. Hannoosh, "parody is the imitation and distortion, or transformation, of a well-known work with comic effect" (*Parody and Decadence*, 13).

[49] Hannoosh, Ibid.

[50] Margaret Rose observes that there are two main theories about the nature of the attitude of the parodist to the text quoted: (1) imitation by the parodist of his chosen text has the purpose of mocking it, and that his motivation in parodying it is contempt; (2) the parodist imitates a text in order to write in the style of that text, and is motivated by sympathy with text. The first view sees parody as an umambivalent form of comic imitation, while the second acknowledges that the parodist has both a critical and an admiring attitude to his 'target' or 'model'. See her *Parody//Meta-Fiction*, 28; and her latest book (1993) *Parody*, 45-46.

A parodist may mock the original, or the original may be set up as a contrast so that the new creation is thereby mocked.[51]

There are various methods or signals of detecting parody. Some of these are linguistic. For example, because of linguistic alteration, it is easy to detect the parody in Dylan Thomas' phrases "Once below a time" or "The man in the wind and the west moon."[52] The reader has expectations about the text parodied and when, because of the parody, these are upset, a comic effect is produced.[53] This comic element is essential to parody and that is why the devices of humor, such as puns, paronomasia, exaggeration etc., all of which serve to effect some kind of distortion and deception of expectations, are common in parody.[54] Nevertheless, despite these linguistic clues, parody, like irony, has not always been recognized. The reason for this may be that the imitation of the original is just too good, and thus the parody is unsuccessful. Indeed, it has often been the case that some of the best parodies have been accepted by the unwary as genuine examples of the original author or style parodied.[55] Another reason for non-recognition of a parody is that the reader simply does not recognize the text being parodied[56] and, normally, only objects

---

[51] Hannoosh, *Parody and Decadence*, 13.

[52] In "Fern Hill" and "And Death shall have No Dominion." See G. Lee, *Allusion, Parody and Imitation*, 3-4, 16. Many other linguistic changes, such as semantic changes, changes in literal and metaphoric functions of words, syntactic change, changes in tense or persons, and other grammatical features, are listed by Rose, *Parody//Meta-Fiction*, 25-26; idem, *Parody*, 36-38.

[53] Hannoosh, *Parody and Decadence*, 13; and Rose, *Parody//Meta-Fiction*, 25-26; idem, *Parody*, 33, 41.

[54] Other devices are substitution, incongruity, anachronism, and repetition, see Hannoosh, *Parody and Decadence*, 26.

[55] "Sometimes it is difficult to detect that a work is indeed a parody, and the imitation may be taken as the real thing" (Highet, *The Anatomy of Satire*, 72).

[56] Rose, *Parody//Meta-Fiction*, 27. See her latest discussion of this question in *Parody*, 39-41.

which are familiar can be parodied successfully.[57] Parody thus ages faster than any other literary form: either the issues or the people are dead, in eclipse, or just plain forgotten.[58] If this is true for parody in general literature, how much more so in texts of antiquity, including the Bible.[59] But the failure by later readers, whether they were the canonizers or religious interpreters, to recognize a parody does not make it any less parodic.[60] The Book of Jonah is an example of a text whose parodies have largely been ignored by later readers yet, as we shall demonstrate below, these features are very much in evidence in the book.

A characteristically biblical type of parody occurs when an author has non-Israelites quote Hebrew scripture. A good example is in the story of the ark and the Philistines (1 Sam. 5-6). As a result of all the misfortunes that occur while the ark is residing among them, the Philistines are advised by their priests and diviners that the ark must be sent home with suitable gifts. The Philistine priests and diviners warn their people that they must not harden their hearts (תְּכַבְּדוּ אֶת־לְבַבְכֶם) as Pharaoh and the Egyptians did when the Israelites were in Egypt. At that time the God of Israel "made a mockery of them" (הִתְעַלֵּל בָּהֶם, 1 Sam. 6:6). The allusion here is to Exod. 10:1-2, where the Lord says: "Go to Pharaoh. For I have hardened his heart (אֲנִי הִכְבַּדְתִּי אֶת־לִבּוֹ) and

---

[57] Feinberg, *Introduction to Satire*, 185.

[58] "Knowledge that seems to one age to be graven in adamant seems to the next to have been written in the sand" (Macdonald, *Parodies*, xi-xii); "The *Batrachomyomachia*, or *Battle of Frogs and Mice*, finds a small audience today although it parodies Homer, the Bible of the ancient world" (Worcester, *The Art of Satire*, 42-43).

[59] "A modern reader who is unacquainted with Greek mythology or the Bible will obviously not recognize a parody of those worlds" (Rose, *Parody//Meta-Fiction*, 27).

[60] Rose argues that even if the readers do not already know the target text "they may come to know it through its evocation in the parody itself" (*Parody*, 39).

the hearts of his courtiers (וְאֶת־לֵב עֲבָדָיו)...that you may recount in the hearing of your sons and of your sons' sons how I made a mockery of the Egyptians (הִתְעַלַּלְתִּי בְּמִצְרַיִם)." The fact that the enemy Philistines are characterized as reciting an episode from Israelite sacred history, and that they use the exact phrases "to harden the heart" (לְהַכְבִּיד אֶת הַלֵּב), and "to make a mockery of" (לְהִתְעַלֵּל בּ), is clearly parodic. For these references would most certainly not be expected from such an alien source.[61]

## Rhetorical features

Since satire is the most rhetorical of all the kinds of literature,[62] a satirist will inevitably use a variety of rhetorical devices.[63] Good satirical writing is full of these devices,[64] and nearly every major satirist since Juvenal has been analyzed in rhetorical terms.[65] A satirist will use metaphor, hyperbole, hysteron-proteron, chiasmus, oxymorons, puns, rhymes, and unsuspected parallels in grammar and syntax.[66] Some satirists may use lists such as, for example, Rabelais's interminable lists of books, games, and parts of the body,[67] or Poins's catalogue of the contents of Falstaff's pockets, etc.[68]

---

[61] Other parallels with this text and the story of the plagues in Exodus have been noted by Moshe Garsiel, *The First Book of Samuel*, 51-54.

[62] Worcester, *The Art of Satire*, 8; and Kernan, *The Plot of Satire*, 25.

[63] M. C Randolph, "The Structural Design of the Formal Verse Satire," 373.

[64] Highet, *The Anatomy of Satire*, 103.

[65] Kernan lists a selection of words and verbs which occur most frequently in Pope's *The Dunciad* (spreds, sluices, creeps, drawls on, stretches, spawns, crawls, meanders, ekes out, flounders on, slips, rolls, extends, waddles, involves etc.). See *The Plot of Satire*, 106. For Swift, see Martin Price, *Swift's Rhetorical Art*; and Edward Rosenheim, *Swift and the Satirist's Art*.

[66] Kernan, *The Plot of Satire*, 26-27, n. 5.

[67] Wortley, "Some Rabelaisian Satiric Techniques," 8-15.

[68] "These minute details are not, as it were, in focus for a person of normal vision. They startle and upset our ordinary sense of reality, for they compel a shift in our point of view" (Worcester, *The Art of Satire*, 67).

Hebrew satire, no less than general satire, contains many typical rhetorical devices. In a Hebrew context this means the presence of key words, paronomasia, artful repetition of verbs, chiastic structures, etc. The nature of the Hebrew language lends itself admirably to the formation of homophones, homographs, and word play in general. Some good examples may be illustrated from the Tower of Babel story in Gen. 11. To explain why the gigantic ziggurats, of which the Babylonians were so proud, and from which they wished to "make a name for themselves" (v. 4), did not survive the vicissitudes of time, the narrator points out that these conceited Babylonians had used the wrong building materials. The Babylonians are ridiculed because instead of the proper materials of stone and mortar, they had used perishable mud bricks and bitumen--which every Hebrew knew were liable to disintegrate. For his satire he employs word plays on these building materials. There is the defective "mud brick" (לְבֵנָה), and the proper 'stone' (לְאָבֶן); the defective 'bitumen' (חֵמָר), and the correct material 'mortar' or 'cement' (חֹמֶר). In the same satire, the name of Babylon (בָּבֶל), the capital city of the Babylonians, is made fun of. In Akkadian, Babylon (bāb ili) means "gate of God." The Hebrew author, however, has derived it from a root bll, meaning "to mix up," because there the Lord mixed up the speech of the whole earth.

The biblical satirist, like his counterparts in other literatures,[69] in order to shock his readers, will sometimes resort to expressive language containing colloquialisms, obscenities, or indelicate expressions.[70] However, because of their uncommonness, some of these words only occur once, as *hapax legomena*.

---

[69] See Highet, *The Anatomy of Satire*, 20-21.

[70] "Most satiric writing contains cruel and dirty words; all satiric writing contains tribal and comic words; nearly all satiric writing contains colloquial anti-literary words" (Highet, *The Anatomy of Satire*, 18).

One such *hapax legomenon*, which occurs in the scene of Eglon's death spasm in the story of Ehud (Judg. 3), is הַפַּרְשְׁדֹנָה. While the final element of this word דֹנָה is unknown, the main element consists of the word 'dung' or 'excrement' (פֶּרֶשׁ). Hence, what occurred to Eglon in his death spasm was the oozing out of feces caused by the release of his anal sphincter. Another example of coarse language is in the story of the capture of the ark by the Philistines (1 Sam. 5-6). The word describing the epidemic that plagued the Philistines is written in the text with the consonants עפלם, which indicates some sort of swelling. This word was considered by the Masorites to be so improper that a milder word, טְחוֹרִים, was enjoined to be read in its place. However, the distinction between these two words is very slight.[71] The meaning of both is hemorrhoids, tumors, boils, or some inflammatory swelling in the groin or rectum area.[72]

Having surveyed the essential characteristics of a satirical text, we will demonstrate in the following chapters that our four stories contain these essential formal characteristics. But if these stories do contain the requisite number of satiric features, is it legitimate to call them satires? After all, satire as a rhetorical technique is thought to have originated in Greek literature, long after most of the first two collections of biblical books were canonized, and the very term 'satire' is Latin (*satura*).[73] Are we

---

[71] Robert Gordis, *The Biblical Text in the Making*, 167.

[72] The word occurs alongside שְׁחִין 'inflammation', גָּרָב 'boil-scars' and חֶרֶס 'itch' in Deut. 28:27. The root עפל means "to swell," perhaps indicating a swelling in the buttocks or genital area; the Aramaic root טחר means "to strain the rectum," perhaps indicating hemorrhoids as a result of excessive straining of the rectum during defecation. Myron Eichler ("The Plague in 1 Samuel 5 and 6," 157-65), and Lawrence I. Conrad ("The Biblical Tradition for the Plague of the Philistines," 281-87), believe that the most tenable explanation of the disease is that of bubonic plague.

[73] As exemplified by the oft-quoted statement of Quintilian: *satura quidem tota nostra est*, "Satire [as opposed to the elegy and other literary forms] belongs to us [Romans] alone." Quintilian was, of course, referring only to

not in danger of imposing on the Bible an alien structure? We
believe, however, that it is legitimate to use the term satire for the
following reasons. First, other rhetorical techniques such as irony,
allegory, parable, and parody are also said to originate in classical
times, nevertheless we customarily, and conveniently, use these
terms when describing these techniques in biblical and other pre-
classical literatures. Second, the use of a later term in no way
means that the rhetorical technique was not in use earlier. For
example, situational irony has been a staple irony of drama from
Aeschylus to the present day, yet no one called it irony until, at
the earliest, the late eighteenth century.[74] The phenomenon of
irony existed before it was named.[75] The Israelites may even have
had a name for that satire which we identify as formal verse satire
(see below). One biblical satire, Isaiah's mock elegy (Isa. 14:3-
21), is introduced by a specific term מָשָׁל which we can translate
as a "satiric taunt."[76] Thus, while we have no way of knowing
whether biblical authors were aware of satire as a genre, we
believe that it is perfectly reasonable to use the term satire for our
four stories which, as will be demonstrated in the following chapters, contain so many of the formal characteristic features of
satire.

---

formal verse satire, see G. L. Hendrickson, "*Satura Tota Nostra Est*," 46-
60, and Elliott, *The Power of Satire*, 3-99.

[74] The word 'irony' does not appear in English until 1502 and did not come
into general use until the early eighteenth century (Muecke, *Irony*, 15).

[75] Homer uses irony, yet did not use the term *eironeia* since it did not mean
"verbal irony" until the time of Aristotle when the term *Eironeia* is first
recorded in Plato's *Republic*. See Muecke, *Irony*, 14. The same is true for
parody. Hannoosh remarks, "the claim that parody was theorized only in the
last few centuries in no way prevents it from applying to works of other periods" (*Parody and Decadence*, 223, n. 2).

[76] The term מָשָׁל denotes many things in the Hebrew Bible: proverbs,
parable, by-word, poem, etc. In "Jonah: A *mašal*?," 137-58, George M.
Landes discusses whether the term is suitable for the book of Jonah.

Finally, when discussing the formal genre of satire, it is necessary to distinguish between two types of satire: formal verse satire and narrative satire. Formal verse satire is a poem in which a satirist speaks usually in the first person.[77] The best equivalent of formal verse satire in the Bible is in the prophetical writings.[78] Narrative satire, on the other hand, is constructed in the form of a narrative or ironic essay. This type of satire is usually called Menippean after Menippus, a third-century B.C. Greek Cynic.[79] Though this term was originally applied only to satire mixing poetry and prose, any extended satire that resists classification as formal verse satire is likely today to be regarded as Menippean. Hence, works such as Petronius' *Satyricon*, Shakespeare's *Timon*, Swift's *Gulliver's Travels*,[80] Voltaire's *Candide*, Twain's *A Con-*

---

[77] Formal verse satire is thought to have originated with Lucilius (180-102 B.C.), and reached its height in Roman literature in Horace (65-8 B.C.), the earliest satirist whose work has survived intact. See Highet, *The Anatomy of Satire*, 22. English verse satire from the end of the sixteenth century to the early nineteenth, as exemplified by Dryden, Hall, Butler, and Byron, was greatly influenced by, and often imitated, these Roman models (Worcester, *The Art of Satire*, 160-61). For the similarities, see Randolph, "The Structural Design of the Formal Verse Satire," 368-84.

[78] Prophetical satire is written in poetic form, and uses similar rhetorical techniques (distortion, irony, etc.). See Fishelov, "The Prophet as Satirist," 195-211; and Jemielity, *Satire in the Hebrew Prophets*, passim.

[79] Menippus wrote satirical pieces mixing prose and verse. In his comprehensive survey of the subject, E. P. Kirk lists the chief features of Menippean satire as unconventional diction, outlandish fictions such as fantastic voyages, dreams, visions, and talking beasts, and extreme distortions of argument. Furthermore, Menippean satire, being concerned with right learning or right belief, often ridiculed or caricatured some sham-intellectual or theological fraud (*Menippean Satire*, xi). According to M. Bakhtin, the most important characteristic of Menippean satire is that extraordinary situations are created in order to test philosophical ideas (*Problems of Dostoevsky's Poetics*, 94-97). See also, Frye, *Anatomy of Criticism*, 309-10.

[80] Although Swift's major satires lack the characteristic Menippean element of verse mixed with prose, in most other respects, they fit the pattern (Elliott, *The Power of Satire*, 188).

*necticut Yankee in King Arthur's Court*, and Huxley's *Brave New World* fall into this category.[81] All the satires in our corpus are narrative satires, but it is questionable whether they can be classified as 'Menippean'.[82]

We now turn to an analysis of these four narrative satires which are the subject of our book. The first anti-prophetic satire which we shall discuss is that of Balaam and his donkey (Num. 22:21-35). In this satire the target is the famous Aramaean seer, Balaam.

---

[81] Frye, *Anatomy of Criticism*, 308-12.

[82] Because only one (Jonah) has a mixture of poetry and prose, and only in Jonah could it be argued (in our opinion unconvincingly) that a philosophical idea is being tested (see chapter seven, below). See also George M. Landes' recent remarks on Jonah as a Menippean satire in his "Review of Lacocque and Lacocque, *Jonah*," 133.

# III

## Balaam and His Donkey

The first anti-prophetic satire in our corpus is the story of Balaam and his donkey (Num. 22:21-35). Balaam, an Aramaean seer[1] has been commissioned by Balak, the king of Moab, to curse the Israelites who are stationed on the border of Moab poised to enter their promised land. He saddles his donkey and starts on his journey westward to Moab. God, however, is angry that he is going and an angel of the Lord, with a drawn sword,[2] blocks his way. Balaam, who is depicted as riding a she-donkey, does not see the angel, but his donkey does and swerves into the field. Balaam beats the donkey to turn her back onto the path. Once again the angel of the Lord blocks the way, this time on a lane between some vineyards which had a fence on either side of the lane. In order to avoid the angel, the donkey has to swerve into the fence, and Balaam's foot gets squeezed against it. Balaam beats his donkey once more. But yet a third time the angel of the Lord blocks the way. This time it is in a very narrow area where there

---

[1] Balaam comes from Pethor (Num. 22:5) identified with Pitru on the Sajur River, a tributary of the Euphrates, south of Carchemish. He uses divination techniques like a typical Mesopotamian seer, but he is also a prophet of God by virtue of the fact that he communicates regularly with God and delivers His word. See Samuel Daiches, "Balaam--a Babylonian *bārû*," 60-70; and Jacob Milgrom, *Numbers*, 471-73.

[2] An angel with a drawn sword is a signal of God's anger. Cf., Gen. 3:24; Josh. 5:13, and see Julius H. Greenstone, *Numbers with Commentary*, 246.

was no room for the donkey to swerve to avoid the angel. So she
simply lies down with Balaam on top of her. At this point, Balaam
is furious with his donkey, and beats her with his stick.

Now, the Lord opens the donkey's mouth and she asks
Balaam why he has beat her these past three times. Balaam
responds that it is because she had mocked him, and that if he had
a sword he would have killed her. The donkey protests. Was she
not his donkey that he has been riding for years? Has she been in
the habit of doing something like this to him? Balaam is forced to
answer 'No'! At that very moment, the Lord opens Balaam's eyes
and he sees the angel with his drawn sword. He prostrates himself
to the ground. The angel of the Lord berates Balaam for beating
his donkey three times because it was he, the angel, not the
donkey, who was the cause of his misfortune. He came out to bar
his way, but Balaam had made straight for him. Had not the
donkey seen him these three times and turned aside, he would
have killed Balaam, but spared the donkey. Balaam tells the angel
that he has been remiss because he did not know he was standing
in the way. But he is willing to return home if that is what God
wishes. To this offer, the angel of the Lord instructs Balaam to
proceed on his way, but reminds him again that he can say only
what the angel tells him to say. The story concludes with the
report that Balaam continued on his way with Balak's representatives.

Nearly all commentators are agreed that this story represents
an addition to the primary story of Balaam and Balak as recorded
in chapters 22 thru 25 of the Book of Numbers.[3] There are
obvious discrepancies between this story and what has preceded.
In the first case, Balaam is portrayed here as travelling with his
two servants (v. 21), whereas in the previous verse and at the very

---

[3] For example, Martin Noth, *Numbers*, 178; John Sturdy, *Numbers*, 165;
Alexander Rofé, *The Book of Balaam*, 40-57; Jonathan D. Safren, "Balaam
and Abraham," 105; and Milgrom, *Numbers*, 469.

end of the story (v. 35) he is said to be travelling with the Moabite
ambassadors. Second, the terrain mentioned in this story, a fenced
path surrounded by open fields and narrow lanes suggests an area
of cultivated land, not a highway that would have been taken by
official emissaries.[4] Third, in the primary story, God has already
given permission to go to Balak (v. 20) with the same condition
that Balaam speak only what God tells him (v. 20). This permission and condition is repeated in our story (v. 35).

There is general agreement that this story represents a sharp
criticism of the non-Israelite prophet, Balaam. But, in addition,
the story contains all the elements that we outlined in the last
chapter as necessary for a satire. There is a clearly defined target
(Balaam); a preponderance of satiric elements such as fantastic
situations, irony, ridicule, parody; and many rhetorical techniques. For these reasons, we maintain that this story constitutes the
first example of anti-prophetic satire in the Hebrew Bible.

**Fantastic situations**

The first fantastic situation in the story consists of the appearance
of an angel of the Lord in invisible form. The presence of
invisible beings is, of course, a staple of folklore, and is the stuff
of legends. The second extraordinary event is the famous scene
when the donkey is portrayed as talking. As we have already
observed, a talking animal is a familiar device of satirists who
often make animals serve as symbolic extensions of human
beings.[5]

---

[4] Cf., "the king's highway" (דֶּרֶךְ הַמֶּלֶךְ) in Num. 21:22.
[5] P. 10 above.

**Irony**

As we noted in the previous chapter, the feature which is common
to all forms of irony is a contrast of appearance and reality.[6] An
ironist seems to be saying one thing but is really saying something
quite different. Our story exhibits a considerable number of situational ironies (which we introduce with the phrase "it is ironic
that...").

It is ironic that Balaam, who elsewhere boasts of his prow-
ess as a professional seer,[7] cannot see what is so obvious to a
donkey![8] The one who is euphemistically termed in one place,
שְׁתֻם הָעָיִן, literally "the one with closed eye" (Num. 24:3, 15),
which is an antiphrasis meaning the opposite "the open-eyed" or
"the perspicacious one,"[9] and in another place, "the all seeing
one" (Num. 24:5), cannot see till God opens his eyes (Num.
22:31).

It is ironic that the one who elsewhere boasts that he "obtains
knowlege from the Most High" (Num. 24:16) has to acknowledge
that he did not know (Num. 22:34).[10]

It is ironic that the seer who normally exercises great power
with his words, and of whom it is said earlier that "he whom you
bless is blessed indeed, and he whom you curse is cursed" (Num.
22:6), cannot control his own donkey with words, but has to use a
stick.[11] There is, of course, a constant irony on this theme running
throughout the entire Balaam pericope that the one who is hired to

---

[6] See p. 13 above.

[7] "Word of Balaam son of Beor, word of the man with open eyes, word of
him who hears God's speech, who beholds divine visions, prostrate with eyes
unveiled" (Num. 24:3-4).

[8] Rofé, *The Book of Balaam*, 50.

[9] See my "Some Antiphrastic Euphemisms for a Blind Person in Akkadian
and Other Semitic Languages," 310.

[10] Mid. *Tanhuma*, Balak 10.

[11] Ibid., 9.

curse can only bless!

It is ironic that the man of words is reduced to using brute force, whereas the brute (his donkey), teaches him with words. Balaam is thereby shown to be more of a brute than his donkey! The Midrash notes the irony in this situation. Here was this donkey, the most stupid of all beasts, and there was the wisest of all wise men. Yet as soon as she opened her mouth he could not stand his ground against her.[12] Wenham phrases it in similar terms: "This animal, proverbial for its dullness and obstinacy, is shown to have more spiritual insight than the super-prophet of Mesopotamia."[13] A further irony on this theme is in the fact that Balaam wishes he had a sword with which to kill his donkey. Yet, as Milgrom recently observed, that sword is actually "close at hand with the angel, whom he, the seer, cannot see."[14] The Midrash also comments on the irony of the situation that the one who has set out to destroy a whole nation with words needs a sword to kill his donkey: "If Baalam could not kill his donkey without a sword how was he going to be able to destroy a whole people with just words?"[15]

In the preceding chapter, we mentioned that "measure for measure" irony is a regular feature of biblical satire.[16] Here the ironic feature occurs in connection with the anger of God and the anger of Balaam. Just as God is angry (וַיִּחַר־אַף אֱלֹהִים) because Balaam went on his journey against his will (22:22), so Balaam is angry (וַיִּחַר־אַף) at his donkey. Because, by lying down, he goes against Balaam's wishes (22:27).[17] However, in both cases the recipient of the anger seems to be innocent. In the earlier part of

[12] *Num. Rab.* 20:14.

[13] Gordon J. Wenham, *Numbers*, 164.

[14] Milgrom, *Numbers*, 191.

[15] *Num. Rab.* 20:21.

[16] P. 16 above.

[17] Yair Zakovitch, *The Pattern of the Numerical Sequence Three-Four in the Bible*, 103.

the pericope Balaam was given permission by God to go on this journey (v. 20), and the donkey can hardly have had much choice in the matter since the angel of the Lord blocked her path (22:27).

## Ridicule

Balaam is ridiculed by the author in a number of ways. He is placed in undignified situations by having his foot squeezed against the fence and by the donkey falling down with him on its back. He is ridiculed by his impetuous rage because he gets angry with his donkey and repeatedly beats her even though she had just saved his life. He is ridiculed by not seeming to notice the fact that his donkey was talking, as though arguing with a talking donkey was a natural and ordinary phenomenon. He is ridiculed by the contrast shown between him and his donkey. In some respects, the donkey and he have changed places. Balaam, by unjustifiably beating the donkey has become brutish, he has become like a donkey! The donkey, on the other hand, has become like a seer! Not only can she, like a seer, see the angel, but like a wise sorcerer, she uses her intelligence to save both her life and that of her master. Moreover, like a master of words, she is able to respond to the one who has just beaten her in measured tones.

A final example of ridicule, hitherto unnoticed by all commentators, is the fact that Balaam is shown to be ignorant of the conventions of proper discourse. He speaks when he should not speak and answers a rhetorical question incorrectly. We recall that when the donkey was granted the gift of speech, or as the text says: "the Lord opened the donkey's mouth," she asks Balaam why he has beaten her these past three times. Balaam responds that it was because she had mocked him, and that if he had a sword he would have killed her. The donkey protests using two rhetorical questions: "Am I not your donkey that you have been

riding for years?" and "Have I been in the habit of doing something like this to you?" Balaam's answer to both questions is 'No'!
But, here lies the ridicule. In the first place, rhetorical questions
need no answer[18] and are never answered anywhere else in the
Hebrew Bible.[19] Thus, for example, we do not expect, and we do
not get, an answer to rhetorical questions posed by Amos such as
"Can horses gallop on a rock?" (6:12) or Jeremiah's "Is Israel a
bondman, is he a home-born slave?" (2:14), nor to any other
rhetorical question in the Bible. So Balaam, by answering his
donkey's rhetorical questions, is ridiculed as ignorant of the conventions of proper discourse.

Secondly, Balaam responded 'no' to his donkey's questions.
But his negative answer is only appropriate, even though it was
unnecessary, for the second rhetorical question: "Have I been in
the habit of doing something like this to you?" No! she had not
been in the habit of doing something like this. But the first rhetorical question was introduced with the form הֲלוֹא which requires a
positive answer:[20] "Am I not your donkey (that you have been

---

[18] P. Joüon & T. Muraoka, *A Grammar of Biblical Hebrew*, #161.

[19] "A rhetorical question poses a question which requires no answer since
either the speaker or the listener knows the answer" (W. G. E. Watson,
*Classical Hebrew Poetry: A Guide to Its Techniques*, 338).

[20] An affirmative answer is expected after הֲלֹא just as if, in a similar construction in English, we were to add the tag question "is that not so?" (Bruce
K. Waltke and M. O'Connor, *An Introduction to Biblical Hebrew Syntax*,
684, n. 48). Similarly, the Latin *nonne*, a double negative, is used in questions which suggest an affirmative answer. See further, H. Brongers, "Some
Remarks on the Biblical Particle *halo'*," 177-89; and Michael A. Brown,
"'Is It Not?' or 'Indeed!': HL in Northwest Semitic," 201-19. It is true that
הֲלֹא, since it always requires a positive answer, can have an exclamatory
sense and be translated by an assertion such as 'only', 'surely', 'certainly',
'behold', 'indeed', or "of course" (Joüon & Muraoka, *A Grammar of Biblical Hebrew*, #161c). Thus, the JPS, *Tanakh*, translates our passage as a positive exclamation: "Look, I am the ass that you have been riding all along
until this day!"

riding for years)?" Yes! She was his donkey that he had been
riding these many years. The structure of both these rhetorical
questions employed by the donkey is that of polar questions
(known in English as yes or no questions),[21] one introduced by
הֲלֹא and the other introduced by the regular interrogative הֲ.
Hence, we have two rhetorical questions, one requiring a 'yes'
answer and the other a 'no' answer. There are seventeen other
examples in the Hebrew Bible of double rhetorical questions of
this type requiring different answers.[22] But it is remarkable that all
the others go the other way. That is, the interrogative sentence
with הֲ comes first and then the הֲלֹא clause. The logic behind this
arrangement is that the הֲלֹא clause backs up the other הֲ interrogative clause with a statement of fact. Thus Miriam and Aaron complain: "Has (הֲרַק) the Lord spoken only through Moses?" expecting a negative answer 'No!' The Lord has not spoken only
through Moses. Their complaint is backed up by a הֲלֹא clause,
"He has surely (הֲלֹא) spoken through us as well!" (Num. 12:2).
Or Abner, in proposing a truce to Joab, asks rhetorically: "Shall
the sword devour forever (הֲלָנֶצַח)?" His plea is backed up by a
הֲלֹא clause: "Surely (הֲלֹא), you know how bitterly it is going to
end!" (2 Sam. 2:26). Similarly, the Ammonite officials say to the
new king Hanun: "Do you think David is really honoring (הַמְכַבֵּד)
your father just because he sent you men with condolences?" The
expected negative answer is reinforced by a הֲלוֹא clause: "Why
(הֲלֹא), David has sent his courtiers to you to explore and spy out
the city, and to overthrow it!" (2 Sam. 10:3). These two rhetorical
questions in our passage are thus contrary to the norm. Here the

---

[21] Polar questions differ from question word questions in that the entire
proposition is questioned rather than just one feature of it (Waltke &
O'Connor, *An Introduction to Biblical Hebrew Syntax*, #40.3.a).
[22] Num. 12:2; Deut. 32:6; 2 Sam. 2:26; 10:3; 2 Kgs. 4:28; Isa. 36:12; Jer.
3:1; 7:19; 22:15; 26:19; Mic. 2:7; Ezek. 17:10; 18:23, 29; Ps. 85:6-7;
Ezra 9:14; 1 Chr. 19:3.

הֲלֹא question precedes the הֲ interrogative. This fact, of course, adds to the satire. To sum up, we see that not only does Balaam unnecessarily respond to a rhetorical question, but he is placed in the ridiculous situation of answering 'No!' to two rhetorical questions, one of which requires a positive response. This, in our opinion, consitutes yet another way in which the narrator ridicules Balaam.

## Parody

As we noted in our preceding chapter, parody occurs when a character does not conform to expected modes of behavior, and when traditional texts are used in a distorted fashion.[23] In our story, Balaam is parodied because he does not conform to the expected behavior of a professional seer. In point of fact he miserably failed the test of his profession. When he encountered the angel of the Lord the qualities of divination for which he was famed failed him.[24] Balaam is parodied as a seer because instead of the seer being in control of events, the seer is depicted as a passive observer. He is shown to be completely unaware that anything was amiss and misinterpreted the entire situation. Balaam did not realize, as a professional seer should have, that his donkey's strange actions were the equivalent of a portent or sign.[25] Wenham correctly observed that "as a specialist in this sort of divination he ought to have realized that the deity had a message for him."[26]

Some scholars have indicated that Balaam is parodied here by being contrasted with stories involving other well-known biblical figures. Two stories have been proposed to suggest this contrast:

---

[23] P. 19 above.
[24] Rofé, *The Book of Balaam*, 51.
[25] René Largement, "Les oracles des Bile'am et la mantique Suméro-Akkadienne," 40-41; Milgrom, *Numbers*, 190.
[26] Wenham, *Numbers*, 164.

the "Call of Samuel," and the "Binding of Isaac." The "Call of
Samuel" story has been proposed because our story has the
unusual characteristic of revelation occurring according to a three-
four pattern.[27] The angel of the Lord appeared three times to
Balaam, but Balaam was not aware of it till the fourth time. A
similar numerical sequence of events occurs in the story of
Samuel's call (1 Sam. 3). Samuel, likewise, was called three
times, but on each occasion he did not recognize the identity of
the caller. Only on the fourth occasion was he receptive to hearing
the word of God. Our story is said to parody this incident. On
three occasions Balaam is not aware of what his donkey can
plainly see---that God is trying to communicate with him: only on
the fourth occasion, when God opens his eyes, does Baalam see
the angel of the Lord standing in front of him. Unlike Samuel,
however, on this fourth occasion Balaam is rebuked, but his
donkey is commended.

The second story proposed as the model on which Balaam is
parodied is the story of the binding of Isaac (Gen. 22).[28] The
thematic links between the two stories are that both stories relate
journeys on donkeys, undertaken by characters considered to be
'prophets', one (Abraham) in conformity with divine will, and the
other (Balaam) in opposition to the divine will.[29] In both narratives
an angel reveals himself at the climax of the plot, and reverses
God's original intention. Abraham is ordered not to sacrifice
Isaac, and Balaam is allowed to proceed on his way. There are
also linguistic links between the two stories. In both stories the
main characters get up in the morning and saddle their donkeys.

---

[27] Zakovitch, *The Pattern of the Numerical Sequence Three-Four in the
Bible*, IX, 107-9.
[28] Safren, "Balaam and Abraham," 105-13.
[29] As Safren notes, this inverse relationship was noted already by the Rabbis
in *b. Sanh.* 105b, *Gen. Rab.* 55.8, and *Num. Rab.* 20.12 ("Balaam and
Abraham," 106).

Abraham "got up early in the morning," "and saddled his donkey" (Gen. 22:3). Balaam, likewise, "arose up in the morning," and "saddled his she-donkey" (v. 21). While the phrases "getting up in the morning" and "saddling a donkey" are common in the Hebrew Bible, these are the only two texts where they both occur together.[30] The second linguistic link between the two passages is in the description of the assistants accompanying both Abraham and Balaam: they are both similarly described as "two servants." In Genesis it is said that Abraham "took with him two of his servants" (Gen. 22:3). In our story, it is related that Balaam had "two servants with him" (v. 22). On the basis of these thematic and linguistic links, the reader is able to draw the appropriate contrasts between Abraham and Balaam with the result being that Balaam is ridiculed and Abraham is venerated.

## Rhetorical features

Our story has been described as "a masterpiece of ancient Israelite narrative art."[31] The donkey holds center stage in the story since she is mentioned 14 times, whereas Balaam and the angel of the Lord are mentioned only 10 times each. The story is clearly demarcated by use of the literary device of inclusio: it starts with Balaam going with the "dignitaries of Moab" (שָׂרֵי מוֹאָב, v. 21), and ends with the same information using the parallel phrase "Balak's dignitaries" (שָׂרֵי בָלָק, v. 35).

The story revolves around a numerical motif: the number three. There is a three-fold repetition of events, as emphasized by three-fold use of the phrase "three times" (שָׁלֹשׁ רְגָלִים, vv. 28, 32, & 33). Three times the angel of the Lord stands in Balaam's way (vv. 22, 24, & 26); three times, it is recorded that the donkey sees the angel (using the identical phrase, וַתֵּרֶא הָאָתוֹן אֶת־מַלְאַךְ יְהוָה,

---

30 Safren, "Balaam and Abraham," 109.
31 Noth, Numbers, 178.

vv. 23, 25, & 27); three times the donkey attempts to turn aside
(twice she is successful and the third time she simply lies down);
three times Balaam beats the donkey (vv. 23, 25, & 27);[32] and,
whereas the donkey only responds twice to Balaam, she does so
with a triad of questions (one an interrogative, v. 28, and two
rhetorical, v. 30).

Some other noteworthy repetitions form a type of concentric
arrangement where phrases in the first part of the story parallel
phrases later on in the story. For example, the phrase "the angel
of the Lord" standing in the way as an adversary (לְשָׂטָן, v. 22)
parallels the phrase "It is I [the angel] who came out as an adversary" (לְשָׂטָן, in v. 32). Similarly, the phrase "the donkey saw the
angel of the Lord standing in the way with his sword drawn in his
hand" (v. 23) parallels concentrically the phrase "he saw the angel
of the Lord standing in the way with his sword drawn in his hand"
(v. 31).

Other rhetorical devices in our text include: (a) the use of the
"active-passive construction" of the same verb[33] in v. 25, where
the *niphal* of the verb לָחַץ "to press," "to squeeze" is used
reflexively (וַתִּלָּחֵץ "she pressed herself") together with the *qal* of
the same verb (וַתִּלְחַץ "she squeezed [Balaam's foot]"); (b) the
employment of a double-rhetorical question introduced by the
interrogative prefixes הֲלוֹא and הַ in v. 30, הֲלוֹא אָנֹכִי אֲתֹנְךָ "Am
I not your donkey?" and הַהַסְכֵּן הִסְכַּנְתִּי לַעֲשׂוֹת לְךָ כֹּה "have I been
in the habit of doing this to you?" As for the vocabulary
employed, one notices the use of the verb לְהִתְעַלֵּל when Balaam
complains to his donkey that she has made a mockery of him
(הִתְעַלַּלְתְּ, v. 29). This verb recurs in another satire, when the
Philistine priests quote scripture (in this case Exod. 10:2).[34] The

---

[32] Alter, *The Art of Biblical Narrative*, 106; Milgrom, *Numbers*, 190.

[33] On this rhetorical device in Biblical Hebrew, see Held, "The Action-Result
(Factitive-Passive) Sequence of Identical Verbs in Biblical Hebrew and
Ugaritic," 272-82.

[34] See pp. 21-22 above.

Philistines must not harden their hearts as Pharaoh and the Egyptians did when the Israelites were in Egypt. At that time the God of Israel "made a mockery of them" (הִתְעַלֵּל, 1 Sam. 6:6).

The three-fold motif, the concentric arrangements, and the other rhetorical devices clearly illustrate the artistic nature of this story. When they are added together with the other satiric elements outlined above we see that the story contains all the elements necessary for satire. The purpose of the satire is to belittle Balaam and expose him to ridicule. Through the satire, it is demonstrated that Balaam, supposedly the best of his profession, is not such an expert after all. He is no match when faced with real competition like the angel of the Lord. In terms of 'seeing', he is even bested by his donkey.[35]

This first anti-prophetic satire in our corpus was directed at a non-Israelite, the Aramaean seer, Balaam. The next three satires in our book will all be directed at Israelite prophets. The first one, which we will discuss in the next chapter, is against Elisha as recorded in the story of the boys and the bald prophet (2 Kgs. 2:23-25).

---

[35] Milgrom writes: "The lampooning of Balaam serves the purpose of downgrading his reputation. It aims to demonstrate that this heathen seer, who was intent on cursing Israel without God's consent, is in reality a fool, a caricature of a seer, one outwitted even by his dumb beast" (*Numbers*, 469).

# IV

## The Boys and The Bald Prophet

The extremely short story of the boys and the bald prophet is related in just three verses (2 Kgs. 2:23-25). It tells of a group of boys who jeer a prophet, most probably Elisha,[1] because he is bald. In response, the prophet curses the children with the result that two bears emerge from the woods and maul forty-two of them. The story reads as follows:

> From there he went up to Bethel. As he was going up the road, some little boys came out of the town and jeered at him, saying, "Go away, bald head! Go away, bald head!" He turned around and looked at them and cursed them in the name of the Lord. Thereupon, two she-bears came out of the woods and mangled forty-two of the children. He went on from there to Mount Carmel, and from there returned to Samaria.

Not surprisingly, this episode has distressed many observers over the years. That a prophet of God would curse a group of children just because they had jeered at him is startling enough. But the ensuing cruel punishment of a massive mauling, seemingly out of all proportion to the provocation, is thought to be incomprehensible. The story has been termed possibly the most embarrassing tale in the Bible.[2] How could a prophet of God act so venge-

---

[1] The story occurs immediately after that in which Elisha, mentioned by name, cures the bitter waters of Jericho (2:19-22).

fully in God's name? Indeed the story so troubled the great
modern Bible commentator Arnold Ehrlich that he wrote, "I, from
my youth to this very day whenever I read this passage, say:
'Thank God I was not created a prophet like Elisha.'"[3] Some
writers have declared the story to be completely immoral,[4] and
almost blasphemous.[5] According to John Gray, there is no serious
point in this incident, it is just a "puerile tale."[6] Similarly, Julius
A. Bewer maintained that the story has no particular purpose: it is
just a legend, one of the many told about spiritual heroes and
wonder workers.[7]

The standard interpretation of this story is that it is didactic
in intent. Some believe that it was told to teach children respect
for their elders. The story is thus a *Bubenmärchen*, literally, "a
boys' folktale," to frighten the young into respect for their
reverend elders.[8] Others believe that the message of the story is

---

[2] H. C. Brichto, *Toward a Grammar of Biblical Poetics*, 196.

[3] Arnold B. Ehrlich, *Mikrä ki-Pheschutö*, 2:334.

[4] "The story will not stand examination from any moral point of view"
(Norman H. Snaith, *II Kings, Exegesis*, 197); "at that moment he [Elisha]
was more like the wild beasts than like a little child" (William Lyon Phelps,
*Human Nature in the Bible*, 186).

[5] "The supposition that Elisha invoked the name of Yahweh to curse the
boys, with such terrible consequences, is derogatory to the great public figure, and borders on blasphemy" (John Gray, *I & II Kings*, 480).

[6] Ibid., 479-80.

[7] *The Literature of the Old Testament in Its Historical Development*, 55-56.
Elliott mentions an Irish story which he says parallels our story. There was a
saint by the name of Féchín (d. 664 C.E.) who was disturbed in his devo-
tions by the noise of children playing outside of his cell. He cursed them by
drowning, whereupon the children went into the lake and were drowned.
That is why, the lake is caled today *Loch Macraide*, "The Children's Lake"
(*The Power of Satire*, 290).

[8] James A. Montgomery, *A Critical and Exegetical Commentary on The
Books of Kings*, 355; and see my remarks in "Juvenile Delinquency in the
Bible and the Ancient Near East," 51, where I noted that contempt of parents
elsewhere in the Bible (such as Exod. 21:17 and Lev. 20;9) has to be interpreted in its widest sense as contempt of elders in general, which would then

not directed solely against children so much as to warn people in general to respect the prophets as holy men of God.[9] A man of god is a holy figure,[10] and as such must be treated with respect and veneration.[11] The point of the story is held to be that anyone who impugns the honor of the prophets should be punished.[12]

While not denying the validity of these interpretations, we believe, however, that another line of interpretation is possible: that this story represents a satire against the prophet Elisha. Our reasons for this suggestion are that the story has all the hallmarks of a good piece of satire and, although it is very terse, all the major characteristic features of satire appear in it. There is a clearly defined target (Elisha); a preponderance in the story of satiric elements such as fantastic events, grotesqueries, exaggerations, irony, ridicule, parody; and rhetorical techniques. The first set of satirical elements that we observe in the story are the

---

include such authority figures as prophets.

[9] For example, Snaith, *II Kings*, 197.

[10] Elisha is actually termed a "Holy Man of God" in another miracle story (2 Kgs. 4:9).

[11] According to Johannes Lindblom, this is an illustration that the prophets were sacrosanct. It was dangerous to offend them; their own persons were sacred and must not be insulted or injured (*Prophecy in Ancient Israel*, 62).

[12] S. L. Gordon, *The Book of Second Kings*, 10; and Bernard P. Robinson, "II Kings 2:23-25. Elisha and The She-Bears," 3. This line of interpretation has been very popular with more conservative observers among whom our story was thought to be a great source of spiritual value. For example, George Rawlinson, the same man of cuneiform fame, declared: "This was a tremendous homily of Divine justice to the whole population--a sermon that would thunder in the hearts of the fathers, the mothers, and the neighbors" (*II Kings*, 34). Likewise, Richard G. Messner saw almost apocalyptic significance in its message: "This was a judgment designed to wake the people up, lest a worse disaster befall them. These blasphemous youths were the direct ancestors of a generation which was swept into captivity because of its abominable sins in the sight of the Lord, notwithstanding the repeated admonitions of His prophets" ("Elisha and the Bears," 22).

unbelievable situations which consist of fantastic events, grotesqueries, and distortions.

## Fantastic situations

The first fantastic situation in this story is the fact that Elisha's curse becomes effective only when he *looks* at the boys.[13] Elisha's looking at the boys while cursing them is akin to the other types of magical action which Elisha performs with his other miracles. Once he throws salt out of a new dish to cure bad water (2 Kgs. 2:20); another time he throws flour into the bitter stew (2 Kgs. 4:41); and yet another time he throws a stick at the spot where the axe head had sunk (2 Kgs. 6:6). All these are magical acts well known from other cultures and periods.[14] In this case, our incident reflects the belief that a prophet could perform a miracle on someone only if he actually saw the individual. We recall another Elisha story when Elisha attempted to revive the dead child of the Shunamite woman. He first tried to revive the child by having his servant Gehazi placing his staff on the lad. But that had no effect. He could revive the lad only when he himself saw him (2 Kgs. 4:29ff). Similarly, Balaam had to see all of Israel in order to curse them (Num. 22:41; 23:13; 24:2, 20, 21).[15] Some Talmudic rabbis concurred with this assessment.[16] It was believed that even some

---

[13] For a recent review of the folklore of the evil eye, see Michel Meslin, "Eye," 5:238.

[14] See Alexander Rofé, *The Prophetical Stories*, 17.

[15] A number of other biblical events can probably be explained according to this belief. For example, that is why God comes down in the Tower of Babel story in Gen. 7:11, and that is why Dathan and Abiram had to come out of their tents in the Korah story in Num. 16:27. Moses had to see them or the miraculous punishment would have no effect, see Ehrlich, *Mikrä ki-Pheschutö*, 1: 271; idem, *Randglossen zur hebräischen Bibel*, 2:172-73; 7:282).

[16] For example, "Rab said: 'He actually looked upon them.'" (*b. Sota* 46b).

rabbis possessed this power and certain people could curse their enemies with just a look. "Rabban Simeon ben Gamaliel says: 'Wherever the Sages set their eyes there is either death or calamity',"[17] and it is related that "Rabbi Simeon ben Yohai cast his eyes upon a certain person and made him a heap of bones."[18]

The second fantastic situation is the sudden appearance of the two she-bears and the woods. Again the rabbis in the Talmud were in the forefront of recognizing the miraculous nature of this event. They looked upon the appearance of the bears and the woods either as one miracle, or as two miracles.[19] According to Rab, the advocate of the one miracle theory, the miracle lay in the fact that there were woods but there were no bears, the latter having been miraculously created for the occasion. This, the medieval Jewish exegete David Kimḥi (1160-1235) later explained, was necessary because "in those woods it was not usual to find wild animals."[20] According to Samuel, there were two miracles, the second one being the appearance of the woods which, like the bears, was originally not there. In response to those who question the need for woods at all when just bears would have been sufficient, the rabbis stated that it was required because without the woods the bears would have been frightened! To this, another medieval Jewish exegete, Rashi (Rabbi Solomon ben Isaac [1040-1105]), added that if there were no woods provided for them in which they could hide, they would not have dared attack the children![21] Arising out of the discussion of this passage in the Talmud, the two terms דֻּבִּים "she-bears" and יַעַר 'woods' used together have entered the later language as an idiom connoting an imaginary tale or a complete fabrication. Thus the

---

[17] Ibid.

[18] *B. Shab.* 34a.

[19] For more examples of this type of "miracle within a miracle," see Zakovitch, *The Concept of the Miracle in the Bible*, 53-55.

[20] In his commentary in *Miqra'ot Gedolot, ad loc.*

[21] See his commentary on *B. Sota* 47a.

48 From Balaam to Jonah

Hebrew phrase לֹא דֻבִּים וְלֹא יַעַר, which literally means "no she-bears and no woods," describes something completely imaginary. There were really no she-bears, nor was there really a woods, it is all made up![22]

## Grotesqueries

The grotesque elements in this story consist in the fact that the bears mangle forty-two of the children, and in the fact that these appear to have been very young, under-age, children. As far as the she-bears[23] are concerned, invoking them against the children seems exceptionally cruel and gruesome. Elsewhere in the Bible the bear, particularly the bereaved she-bear (דֹּב שַׁכּוּל), appears as a peculiarly fierce animal,[24] and is paired with the lion and the leopard. For example, in Hos. 13:7-8, "So I am become like a lion to them, like a leopard I lurk on the way; like a bear robbed of her young I attack them, and rip open the casing of their hearts; I will devour them there like a lion, the beasts of the field shall

---

[22] Abraham Eben-Shoshan, *Millon Chadash*, I:211.

[23] That the bears were female is shown by the feminine forms of the verb used (וַתִּבְקַעְנָה and וַתֵּצֶאנָה).

[24] E.g., in 2 Sam. 17:8 and in Prov. 17:12. The prevalence of the bear in ancient Palestine, and identification of the exact species (*ursus arctos syriacus*) has been pointed out by those intent on proving the veracity of the account. Thus to confirm the prevalence of wild beasts in the immediate neighborhood of cities, and particularly Bethel, J. Rawson Lumby recalls the stories of David who slew a lion and a bear as he was keeping his father's flock (1 Sam. 17:36), and that of the disobedient prophet who was torn by a lion near Bethel (1 Kgs. 13:24, see our next chapter) (*The First and Second Book of the Kings*, 21). Brichto argues that this picture of the murderous bears is "so out of keeping with the nature of these shy beasts as to be almost ludicrous." He maintains that bears keep to themselves and will normally run from humans (*Toward a Grammar of Biblical Poetics*, 197). But, as can be seen from the above references, all the portrayals of the she-bear in the Bible are of fierce and vicious animals.

mangle them (חַיַּת הַשָּׂדֶה תְּבַקְּעֵם).'' We observe in this Hosea passage the same verb בָּקַע 'mangle' (lit. 'cleave' or "rip open"), which occurs in our passage as וַתְּבַקַּעְנָה.

The second grotesquery in the story is the fact that the curse was directed against children who are described as very young, and hence scarcely accountable for their conduct.[25] Two terms are used in the story to describe the children: once they are described as נְעָרִים קְטַנִּים, and once as יְלָדִים.[26] Both terms נַעַר and יֶלֶד can denote children anywhere from an infant up.[27] However, the fact that נַעַר is here modified by the adjective קָטָן would seem to indicate that these children were indeed young. Nevertheless, there is a body of opinion that believes that the children here were not young at all, but young persons who were old enough to know what they were doing. This opinion is found both among the rabbis in the Talmud and among some modern commentators, both groups attempting thereby to justify Elisha and blame the children. Thus, the Talmud records the view of one rabbi that: They were youths but they behaved like little children.''[28] Among

---

[25] Phelps detected a certain universalism in our story, applicable to all ages and cultures: "These children are the same in all places and all times; they are the children of the streets, the newsboys, gamins, sharp-eyed waifs. The muckers of the city of Bethel were in nowise different from the muckers of Paris, London, or Chicago; they saluted Elisha in the same derisory fashion as they would any rather pompous pedestrian" (*Human Nature in the Bible*, 186).

[26] In the Targum and Peshitta both נְעָרִים and יְלָדִים are translated by the same word (יַנְקִין in the Targum, and טַלְיֵי in the Peshitta). The Septuagint uses παιδάρια μικρὰ "little children" for נְעָרִים קְטַנִּים and παῖδας 'children' for יְלָדִים.

[27] The term נַעַר is used of the infant Moses in Exod. 2:6, and of the newborn Ichabod in 1 Sam. 4:21. But נַעַר is also used to describe Isaac in his early twenties (Gen. 22:12), of Joseph as a lad (Gen. 37:2) and of warriors (1 Kgs. 20:14-15). יֶלֶד too has a similar range denoting a child or youth. Thus it is used to describe the infant Hebrews in Exod. 1:17-18 as well as Rehoboam's advisors in 1 Kgs. 12:8.

[28] *B. Sota* 46b.

the moderns, Messner declares, "these children were old enough to know what they were doing, and cannot be excused for their vicious behavior on the grounds that they were under-aged."[29] In his recent book *Toward a Grammar of Biblical Poetics*, Brichto states: "The mockers of Elisha were not young children, they were 'worthless oafs, hooligans, hoodlums'."[30] Adducing linguistic support for their point of view, some modern scholars have noted that the phrase נַעַר קָטֹן is said of Solomon in 1 Kgs. 3:7 upon his accession to the throne, and he was not literally a young child. Also David is called the קָטָן, youngest of Jesse's נְעָרִים (1 Sam. 16:11), yet he was not exactly a child. But, in the first case, Solomon may be simply using a conventional terminology of humility of prayer, or echoing a familiar ancient Near Eastern theme of a god having selected the king before he was born or when he was still very young.[31] Or more likely, Solomon is deliberately disparaging himself by saying that he has none of the expected qualities for kingship: he has not the usual fine physical qualities, he is not a warrior, etc., rather, he is akin to a young child. In the second place, David is being correctly described as the 'youngest' קָטָן of Jesse's sons, but the phrase נַעַר קָטָן is not used in that passage. So the terminology there has little bearing on our passage. Hence, there is no real linguistic barrier for an

---

[29] "Elisha and the Bears," 17. Similarly, Lumby, "they were well aware of the outrage and wickedness of their conduct" (*The First and Second Book of Kings* 20). Rawlinson, possibly on the basis of his own personal experiences in the Near East, characterizes the children of our story: "Such mischievous youths are among the chief nuisances of Oriental towns; they waylay the traveler, deride him, jeer him---are keen to remark any personal defect that he might have, and are merciless in flouting it; they dog his steps, shout out their rude remarks and sometimes proceed from abusive words to violent acts, as the throwing of sticks, or stones, or mud. On this occasion they only got as far as rude words" (*II Kings*, 23).

[30] P. 198.

[31] For references, see Gray, *I & II Kings*, 121, 125-26.

assumption that the נְעָרִים קְטַנִּים were young, underage, children. These were children who should *not* have been held responsible for their actions. Hence Elisha's cursing them with such a severe punishment must be considered grotesque and cruel.

## Distortions

The first exaggeration is that the punishment of the children is way out of proportion to the crime.[32] To avenge a personal insult one does not call up vicious animals to maul young children. One assumes that, given his miraculous powers as a prophet of God, Elisha might have been able to silence them in a less indelicate fashion. Previous commentators have had great difficulty explaining this part of the story. One view is that there is no logic here. We are dealing not with ethical categories of right and wrong, with retribution (sin and punishment), but rather with the categories of the sacred and the profane.[33] Like the sons of Aaron (Lev. 10:1-3) or Uzzah with the ark (2 Sam. 6:6-7), who acted with no intent of malice, these youths profaned the Holy Man of God, and their punishment is swift and terrible.[34] We would have here another example of Rudolf Otto's imponderable *mysterium tremendum*.[35]

But not everyone agrees that the punishment was unjust. There have been quite a number of ancient and modern commentators who, in an attempt to rationalize Elisha's actions, maintained that the children deserved the punishment they received. For example, the rabbis in the Talmud believed the punishment

---

[32] Elliott refers to this episode (not as a satirical element), but as an example of "one of the most dreadful of all curses in the disproportionate violence of its fulfillment" (*The Power of Satire*, 289).

[33] Rofé, *Prophetical Stories*, 15-16.

[34] Ibid., 16.

[35] See his *The Idea of The Holy*. Edward L. Greenstein has recently discussed these two episodes in his "Deconstruction and Biblical Narrative," 61-62.

was deserved for a variety of reasons. Firstly, because their parents were guilty of past transgressions.[36] Secondly, because of the fact that the children themselves were not pious individuals,[37] and thirdly it was thought there was no hope in the future for them.[38] Likewise some medieval and modern scholars have noted that the boys deserved the punishment because it was assumed they came from Bethel.[39] Bethel, it is believed, was the seat of Baal worship and headquarters of idolatry in Israel,[40] and the place where their fathers taught them to mock the prophets of God.[41] The boys deserved the punishment because they were reflecting the teaching of their Baal-worshipping parents who encouraged their mockery.[42] The punishment they received affected the parents in a way which nothing else could have done.[43]

---

[36] "Samuel said: He saw that their mothers had all become conceived with them on the Day of Atonement [when cohabitation is forbidden]" (*b. Sota* 46b-47a).

[37] "Rabbi Isaac, the smith, said: He saw that their hair was plaited as with Amorites [that is, they aped heathen manners]. Rabbi Yohanan said: He saw that there was no sap of the commandments in them. But the objection is raised, perhaps there would have been such in their descendants! [so why should they have perished on that account?]" (*b. Sota* 47a).

[38] "Rabbi Eleazar said: Neither in them nor in their descendants unto the end of all generations [was there a sap of the commandments]" (*b. Sotah*, 47a).

[39] But the boys did not come from Bethel, they came from Jericho, see below.

[40] Messner, "Elisha and the Bears," 21; and C. F. Keil and F. Delitzsch, *The Books of the Kings*, 300.

[41] The medieval Jewish exegete Isaac Abravanel (1437-1508) commented that in Bethel, the site of Jeroboam's calf, people had little respect for God's prophets (*Commentary on the Former Prophets, ad loc*).

[42] "Their home education and all the associations of the place would have given them a contempt for the true servants of God. The fault of what they did lay as much in their surroundings as in themselves" (Messner, "Elisha and the Bears," 19).

[43] Lumby, *The First and Second Book of the Kings*, 20-21. Similarly, William Jenks remarked, "Had he cut them off by a fever no one would have

The second exaggeration in our story is in the number of children, said to be forty-two, which were mangled by the two she-bears. We note that the same number appears elsewhere in the book of Kings, when Jehu slays forty-two brothers of Ahaziah, king of Judah (2 Kgs. 10:14). It also occurs, in another satirical story, that of Jephthah and the Ephraimites (Judg. 12:1-9).[44] Here an extraordinarily high number of Ephraimites, some forty-two thousand, are said to have been killed by the Gileadites (Judg. 12:6). So the number forty-two may be just a convention,[45] an unreal number, an exaggerated detail in the narrative.[46] But there are those who believe that the number forty-two is a real one and, by avoiding the round number forty, the narrator is giving a precise number and adding realism to the story.[47] However, it should be borne in mind that if forty-two children were caught by the bears, a fairly sizable number of others must have escaped,[48]

---

objected too strenuously to it; but, it would not have been suitable, in any adequate measure, to make the same useful impression on the minds of the survivors, or to inculcate the same important instruction to other ages and nations, as this solemn sentence and immediate execution were" (*Comprehensive Commentary*, 296).

[44] See my recent treatment of this text in "Ridiculing the Ephraimites: The Shibboleth Incident (Judges 12:6)," 95-105.

[45] Gray, *I and II Kings*, 480. In the Talmud, Rabbi Hanina explains the number forty-two as occasioned by the forty-two sacrifices which Balak, king of Moab, made [Num. 23:1, 14, 29]: "On account of the forty-two sacrifices which Balak, king of Moab, offered, were forty-two children cut off from Israel" (*b. Sota* 47a).

[46] Robinson aptly cites Gilbert and Sullivan, themselves masters of the art of satire, "it [the number forty-two] is no more than, in Pooh-Bah's words, 'corroborative detail intended to give artistic verisimilitude to an otherwise bald! and unconvincing narrative'" ("II Kings 2:23-25," 2).

[47] Montgomery, *The Books of Kings*, 356; Messner, "Elisha and the Bears," 21.

[48] Brichto notes the incongruity of the entire scene (*Toward a Grammar of Biblical Poetics*, 197).

bringing the total number of the youthful mob to a hundred or
several hundred depending on one's estimate of how many children could escape for each one caught![49] So, whether the number
forty-two is considered real or not, the narrator has embellished
his story with a fine stroke of distortion.

## Irony

We recall our definition of situational irony as, "a condition of
affairs or events of a character opposite to what was, or might naturally be, expected."[50] Our story contains three examples of such
situational irony. The first example of situational irony is the fact
that our short story does not fit the pattern of the other five short
stories (from two to seven verses) about Elisha. The other five all
recount miraculous acts.[51] In these stories Elisha performs
miracles to help people. He provides food, saves a family from
the shame of slavery, and floats a sunken axe head which had
been borrowed by a poor man. Here we have a prophet of God
seemingly out of character with what we know of him in the other
stories. Elsewhere he is depicted as a wonder worker, a life-giver,
and a life-restorer; here he is portrayed as a life-taker. In the other
stories, he is helpful and compassionate even with Israel's enemies
(2 Kgs. 6:22). Here he is vindictive and vengeful. The cursing of
the children by Elisha is in sharp contrast to his other wondrous
acts, which are all of a beneficial and positive nature.[52] So we

---

[49] According to Messner, two children would have escaped for every one that
was hurt, which would make the crowd who followed Elisha number at least
one hundred ("Elisha and the Bears," 21).

[50] See p. 14 above.

[51] The healing of the spring (2 Kgs. 2:19-22); the widow's continuous pour-
ing of the oil (2 Kgs. 4:1-7); the curing of the stew (2 Kgs. 4:38-41); the
multiplication of the loaves and grain (2 Kgs. 4:42-44); and the floating of
the axe head (2 Kgs. 6:1-7).

[52] Gehazi's punishment (2 Kgs. 5:27) is the only other wondrous act which is
not positive, but there the punishment which takes the form of "a measure

have the irony of the prophet who elsewhere helps people in life-threatening situations, but here is responsible for destroying life.

The second example of irony in the story is that "the name of the Lord," which ought to be employed in a positive or blessing context, is used as a curse ("He cursed them in the name of the Lord"). An example of the use of "the name of the Lord" in a positive context is David's blessing of the people when the ark is brought to Jerusalem. Here it is said that David blessed the people "in the name of the Lord."[53] There is no other instance in the Hebrew Bible when someone curses by the Lord's name,[54] and only one other case when a non-Israelite curses by his god.[55]

The third example of situational irony in our story arises from the fact that the boys came from Jericho. One of the general assumptions made by most commentators is that the boys of our story came not from Jericho, but from Bethel. However, the text says only that they came out of "the town" without specifying which town. One of the difficulties in assuming that the boys came from Bethel is the fact that after the boys taunted Elisha, the text says "he turned around and looked at them."[56] But Elisha was travelling towards Bethel. How could he have turned around and looked at the boys if they came from Bethel? The obvious solution is that the boys did not come from Bethel, but from the same town that Elisha had just left, namely Jericho. It was at Jericho that

---

for measure" irony (the transference of the leprosy from Naaman to him) is a justified exception.

[53] 1 Chr. 16:2. The parallel account in 2 Sam. 6:18 has "in the name of the Lord of Hosts."

[54] Yair Zakovitch, "Get up Baldy! Get up Baldy!" 11.

[55] That is when the Philistine giant Goliath cursed David before their fight, "the Philistine cursed David by his gods" (1 Sam. 17:43).

[56] Each of the four other usages of וַיִּפֶן, "he turned," plus the preposition אַחֲרֵי, (Josh. 8:20 [the people of Ai]; 20:40 [the Benjaminites]; 2 Sam. 2:20 [Abner and Amassa]); (2 Sam. 2:20 [Saul and the Amalekite]) clearly implies a "turning around" to face someone or something.

Elisha had performed his life-saving wonder for the town by
purifying the polluted water (2 Kgs. 2:19-22).[57] Zakovitch has
noted two more striking ironies which arise from our story.[58] The
first is that it is ironic that boys from Jericho should jeer the person who had saved their town. Second, Elisha who had saved the
town from water which caused "death and bereavement" is now
the cause of death and bereavement for some of the town's children.

## Ridicule

As we have remarked in chapter two,[59] by using ridicule an author
is able to portray a target unkindly with the intent of making fun
of it. The author can make unkind observations about a target's
personal characteristics, which is precisely what the children in
this story do. The fact that the children jeered the prophet is clear
from the verb used to introduce the taunt. The form וַיִּתְקַלְּסוּ
comes from a root קָלַס, which in its *Hithpael* form means "to
jeer." In its two other *Hithpael* occurrences (Ezek. 22:5; Hab.
1:10), the verb has similar meanings. Ezek. 22:5 reads: "both the
near and far shall scorn you (יִתְקַלְּסוּ־בָךְ)." In the Habakkuk verse
which reads וְהוּא בַּמְּלָכִים יִתְקַלָּס וְרֹזְנִים מִשְׂחָק לוֹ "kings they hold
in derision, and princes are a joke to them," the verb יִתְקַלָּס is

---

[57] This point was seen already by the Rabbis. They remarked: "What they
said to him was 'Go up, thou who hast made this place bald for us'!" Rashi
explains that Elisha had sweetened the waters in that place [Jericho], and so
had caused loss to the people of the vicinity who had profited by selling
drinkable water (*b. Sota* 46b). Hence the ill-feeling against him. The boys
are termed קְטַנִּים, 'little', because they were "little of faith," which Rashi
explains was because they thought that since they were no longer needed to
bring water, there was no other means by which to earn a livelihood (Rashi
on *b. Sota* 46b).

[58] Zakovitch, "Get up Baldy! Get up Baldy!" 17.

[59] P. 18 above.

parallel to the noun מִשְׂחָק "object of laughter," "a joke."[60] In order to magnify the culpability of the children toward the prophet, and thereby in some respects justify Elisha's reaction, the Lucian version of the LXX adds וַיִּסְקְלוּהוּ "and stoned him" after וַיִּתְקַלְּסוּ "they jeered him."[61]

When we analyze the literary structure of this short story (see below), we shall demonstrate that it displays a clear concentric symmetry with the taunt of the children as its major emphasis. But what precisely was the taunt? The children said "Go away, bald head! Go away, bald head!" (עֲלֵה קֵרֵחַ עֲלֵה קֵרֵחַ). Was the taunt in one of the words, either עֲלֵה "go away!" or קֵרֵחַ "bald head!" or in both of them? If it was in the word קֵרֵחַ "bald head" then what did the children mean? Was Elisha really bald? and was calling someone "bald head" really considered insulting?[62] As far as the first question is concerned, we cannot answer with certainty. If this incident occurred at the beginning of his ministry (which is where it is placed in the text), then Elisha would have been only a young man at the time.[63] If he was bald, it

---

[60] The noun form קֶלֶס 'mockery' occurs parallel with the nouns חֶרְפָּה 'derision' and לַעַג 'mockery' in Pss. 44:14 and 79:4.

[61] Since this form comes from a root סָקַל, whereas the form וַיִּתְקַלְּסוּ comes from a root קָלַס, it is possible we are dealing with a scribal error involving metathesis. M. Cogan and H. Tadmor suggest that this Lucianic reading represents "an embellishment which sought to explain the prophet's violent outburst against the children" (*II Kings*, 38). Others think that the Lucianic version may have been influenced by the story of Shimei ben Gera in 2 Sam. 16:5-7, who also threw stones (וַיְסַקֵּל) as he cursed David. See Zakovitch, "Get up Baldy! Get up Baldy!" 10, n. 7.

[62] So, for example, according to J. Sidlow Baxter, "used as a word of insult, it [bald head] has in it, to the easterner, a spite, a slime, a venom, and an implication of despicableness which make it the lowest of insults" (*Mark These Men*, 66). Similarly, Messner, "to call someone a 'bald head' was an epithet of utter contempt" and "a most vulgar and cutting of insults" ("Elisha and the Bears," 18).

[63] Elisha's ministry lasted some sixty years. Since he died circa 797 B.C.E., he must have been a young man at the time of Elijah's assumption (856

must have been with premature baldness. But it is more likely that the children were making fun of the fact that Elisha was just a bit thin on top.[64]

Some believe that the baldness refers to a ritual tonsure, a shaving of the head or crown of the head, which characterized, like the mark on the prophet in 1 Kgs. 20:41, his prophetic office.[65] But there is little to support the assumption of a ritual tonsure for prophets. The only other evidence we have with regard to the other prophets concerning their hair or lack of it, is with Elijah who most definitely did not have a tonsure, since his shaggy locks was a clear measure of identification.[66]

As far as the second question is concerned, whether calling someone "bald head" was considered insulting, this is the only supporting text we have. It is true that removal of hair is used as

---

B.C.E.).

[64] So David Kimḥi (1160-1235) in his commentary (in *Miqra'ot Gedolot, ad loc*). Of course, the objection has been raised that it is unlikely that, because of the heat, Elisha would have traveled without a head covering, hence his head would not have been visible to the children (so J. Robinson, *The Second Book of Kings*, 28). Gray believes that the boys were children of other prophets, and they knew Elisha from before, so that even though he had his head covered, they knew that he was 'bald' (*I & II Kings*, 480).

[65] So Robinson, "II Kings 2:23-25," and Gray, (*I & II Kings*, 480). Because of this assumed tonsure, Brichto, translates: "Move on, scarface!" (*Toward a Grammar of Biblical Poetics*, 198). Lindblom believes that the taunting of the children was directed not so much at Elisha personally but at the office of prophet which he represented. The offense of the children would then be regarded as blasphemy in that mocking God's prophet was equivalent to mocking God himself (*Prophecy in Ancient Israel*, 68).

[66] Cogan and Tadmor note that "lengthy hair, rather than close shaving of the head, was an accepted feature of asceticism as is reflected in the Nazirite law in Num 6:5; cf. Jud 13:5. Moreover the ritual cutting of hair is prohibited in Lev 19:27, 21:5" (*II Kings*, 38). In Zech. 13:4, there is a reference to prophets no longer wearing their "hairy mantle" (אַדֶּרֶת שֵׂעָר), but the allusion here is to a characteristic garment (perhaps in imitation of Elijah), not to the hair itself.

one of the threatened punishments for the ladies of Jerusalem (Isa. 3:17, 24), and there are certain restrictions in the Talmud concerning bald headed people, e.g., they are prohibited from being priests.[67] But there is no evidence in any ancient Near Eastern society that baldness was regarded as a mark of shame,[68] or that calling someone "bald head" was regarded as an insult at all.[69] However, if it was insulting, and Elisha seems to have taken it that way, it is possible to posit a variety of symbolic interpretations for the insult. For example, if hairiness represents vigor, baldness represents indolence; if hairiness represents youth, baldness represents old age,[70] or impotence, etc.

But there are two parts to the boys' taunt. As well as calling him baldhead, they say: "go up!" "go up!" Where was the taunt in these words? Despite the fact that Elisha was travelling uphill from Jericho, which lies some 1300 feet below the level of the Mediterranean Sea, to Bethel, which is situated about 2000 feet above, it is unlikely that the boys were referring to a literal "going up." The boys were taunting him to move on, to get out of the way, to "beat it."[71] The effect of the taunt may be seen in the JPS translation, "Go away, bald head! Go away, bald head!"[72] or more colloquially, "beat it baldy! beat it baldy!"[73]

---

[67] *M. Bek.* 7:2.

[68] Brichto, *Toward a Grammar of Biblical Poetics*, 197.

[69] Gaster, however, gives examples from classical sources (in Juvenal and Aristophanes) that a bald man was "an object not only of fun but also of opprobrium" (*Myth, Legend, and Custom in The Old Testament*, 517).

[70] Christopher R. Hallpike, "Hair," 6:154.

[71] That a taunt is contained in the word עֲלֵה is hinted at from the Septuagint, since there the second קֵרֵחַ is omitted, hence there is a stress on the verb עֲלֵה.

[72] *Tanakh*, 567. According to Brichto, the children are telling Elisha "to keep going, not to enter their city" (*Toward a Grammar of Biblical Poetics*, 197). But their city was Jericho, not Bethel! See pp. 55-56 above.

[73] Zakovitch believes that the emphasis on this verb is to indicate that the physical act of "going up" was difficult for Elisha. Hence the boys were ridiculing Elisha because he literally had difficulty in walking ("Get up

## Parody

One of the characteristics of parody is that it attacks its target by
contrasting it in a distorted manner with another known person.[74]
If we have parody in the boy's taunt, it is very likely that the boys
are alluding to Elisha's mentor, Elijah, and they are comparing
Elisha unfavorably with him. In the first parody, the boys contrast
Elisha's lack of hair with Elijah's long hair. They make fun of
Elisha by comparing him unfavorably to Elijah who was known to
have long shaggy locks, since he is called "a hairy man" (אִישׁ בַּעַל
שֵׂעָר, 2 Kgs. 1:8). Using the term 'bald head', the boys would be
referring sarcastically to Elijah's shaggy locks.[75] An alternate possibility is that the children were not referring to any contrast
between Elijah and Elisha but a similarity. They both had long
hair. This was the mark of the prophet. In this reading, the term
קֵרֵחַ then will be used antiphrastically, to indicate the opposite of
its real meaning. The children call him 'bald' when he really is
'hairy'. Thus it is akin to our calling a fat man 'thinny'; a fool a
"wise man" or a poor man 'Rockefeller'. We recall that in the
satire of Balaam and his donkey, Balaam called himself "closed
eye" (שְׁתֻם עָיִן), when he really meant "all seeing," 'omnis-
cient'.[76] Hence the children ridicule Elisha calling him "bald
head" knowing well that he is not "thin on top," but very hairy.

---

Baldy! Get up Baldy!" 9-10). But there is no indication that Elisha had difficulty in walking in this story. Nor is there in any of the others of the Elisha
cycle.

[74] See page 19 above.

[75] See the traditional commentaries of Meṣudat David (Yeḥiel Hillel
Altschuler, 18th century) and the Malbim (Meir Loeb ben Yeḥiel Michal
1809-1879) in *Miqra'ot Gedolot, ad loc*, and the moderns Ehrlich, *Mikrä ki-
Pheschutö*, 334; Lumby, *The First and Second Book of the Kings*, 20; and
Zakovitch, "Get up Baldy! Get up Baldy!" 20.

[76] See p. 32 above.

A second parody in the story is that the boys contrast Elisha's prophetic abilities with Elijah who was swept up to heaven. The same verb, which the boys use (עָלָה), is the very one used in describing Elijah's translation to heaven.[77] The effect of the taunt would be then that Elisha should "go up" to heaven just like his master, Elijah. The 19th century Jewish commentator Malbim[78] seems to have caught the correct satirical sense when he commented: "they mocked him: 'go up to heaven you baldy just like your hairy master went up'." The boys then taunt Elisha that he should "go up," as his master is alleged to have done, i.e., he should emulate Elijah's act.

## Rhetorical features

Our story is replete with fine rhetorical features including a concentric symmetry, key words, word play, alliteration, and assonance. In our discussion above about the taunt, we noted that a structural analysis of the story demonstrates that the taunt is in fact the place where the principal emphasis of the story lies. Here we shall show that the story displays a clear concentric symmetry. It is curious that the only other short story which similarly displays such a concentric symmetry is yet another satire, that against the Mesopotamians in the story of the Tower of Babel in Genesis 11.[79] The concentric symmetry may be observed in the diagram on the opposite page.

---

[77] The pertinent verses read, "When the Lord was about to take Elijah up (בְּהַעֲלוֹת) to heaven in a whirlwind" (2 Kgs. 2:1), and "Elijah went up (וַיַּעַל) to heaven in a whirlwind" (2 Kgs. 2:11).

[78] Meir Loeb ben Jehiel (1809-1879), *ad loc.*

[79] The concentric arrangement and literary details have all been highlighted by Jan P. Fokkelman, *Narrative Art in Genesis*, 11-45.

A  וַיַּעַל מִשָּׁם בֵּית־אֵל   [וְהוּא עֹלֶה בַדֶּרֶךְ]

B  וּנְעָרִים קְטַנִּים

C  יָצְאוּ מִן־הָעִיר

D  וַיִּתְקַלְּסוּ־בוֹ וַיֹּאמְרוּ לוֹ

E  עֲלֵה קֵרֵחַ

E′  עֲלֵה קֵרֵחַ

[וַיִּפֶן אַחֲרָיו]
D′  וַיִּרְאֵם וַיְקַלְלֵם בְּשֵׁם יְהוָה

C′  וַתֵּצֶאנָה שְׁתַּיִם דֻּבִּים מִן־הַיַּעַר

B′  וַתְּבַקַּעְנָה מֵהֶם אַרְבָּעִים וּשְׁנֵי יְלָדִים

A′  וַיֵּלֶךְ מִשָּׁם אֶל־הַר הַכַּרְמֶל   [וּמִשָּׁם שָׁב שֹׁמְרוֹן]

In terms of basic ideas, the symmetry may be outlined succinctly as follows:

    A//A′  He went up//He went
    B//B′  Young children// 42 children
    C//C′  [Children] came out// Bears came out
    D//D′  What the children did //What Elijah did
    E//E′  The taunt//The taunt

In line A, the phrase וַיַּעַל מִשָּׁם בֵּית־אֵל "from there he went up to Bethel" is paralleled by line A′ וַיֵּלֶךְ מִשָּׁם אֶל־הַר הַכַּרְמֶל "he went on from there to Mount Carmel." In both lines there is: (a) a verb of motion---וַיַּעַל "he went up" in line A, and וַיֵּלֶךְ "he went" in line A′; (b) an adverbial phrase---מִשָּׁם "from there" in line A paralleled by another מִשָּׁם "from there" in line A′; (c) and a place name---בֵּית־אֵל 'Bethel' in line A paralleling הַר הַכַּרְמֶל "Mount Carmel" in line A′.

In line B, the word for children נְעָרִים is synonymously paralleled in line B′ with another word for children יְלָדִים. The first noun is modified by the adjective קְטַנִּים 'little', while the second one is modified by the numeral אַרְבָּעִים וּשְׁנֵי "forty-two."

In line C and line C′ the same verb יָצָא, "to go out" occurs with the preposition מִן 'from'. In the first case, it is said of the children coming out of the town יָצְאוּ מִן־הָעִיר and, in the second case, of the bears coming out of the woods וַתֵּצֶאנָה שְׁתַּיִם דֻּבִּים מִן־הַיַּעַר. We note the word play on the forms הָעִיר "the town" and הַיַּעַר "the woods." In a purely consonantal text, these words would apppear as העיר and היער, the different forms possible being explained as a metathesis of the letters ע and י.

In lines D and D′, the symmetry is one of the uses of parallel verbal forms. There is a correspondence between the boys jeering the prophet and the prophet cursing the boys. In the first case (D), the children 'jeer' (וַיִּתְקַלְּסוּ־בוֹ) at the prophet and 'speak' to him וַיֹּאמְרוּ לוֹ. In the second case (D′), the prophet responds by 'looking' at the children וַיִּרְאֵם, and 'cursing' them וַיְקַלְלֵם.

Finally, lines E and line E′ contain the symmetrical parallelism of the two words of the taunt עֲלֵה קֵרֵחַ, "Go away, bald head!" // עֲלֵה קֵרֵחַ "Go away, bald head!" These words constitute the centerpiece of the concentric arrangement, and formally indicate where the focus of the story lies.

In addition to the concentric arrangement, there are other literary features including repetition of key words, word play, alliteration, and assonance. The key-word going through this passage is the verb עָלָה "to go up," occurring four times in v. 23, וַיַּעַל "he went up" and עֹלֶה "going up," and twice in the taunt in

v. 23, עֲלֵה "go away!" עֲלֵה "go away!" There is a threefold repetition of the adverbial phrase מִשָּׁם "from there" in v. 23, and twice in v. 25. The repetition of the consonants שׁ and מ as in מִשָּׁם forms an assonance in the forms בְּשֵׁם "in the name of" in v. 24, and in the city name שֹׁמְרוֹן 'Samaria' in v. 25. We have already observed the word play of עִיר 'town' in v. 23 with יַעַר 'woods' in v. 24 involving the metathesis of the letters ע and י. There is alliteration in the phrases עֲלֵה קֵרֵחַ עֲלֵה קֵרֵחַ, which we could capture in translation if we render them colloquially as "Beat it baldy! Beat it baldy!" There is alliteration in the combinations of the words נְעָרִים קְטַנִּים in line 23, in וַיִּרְאֵם וַיְקַלְלֵם and שְׁתַּיִם דֻּבִּים in line 24, and in the concentric parallel verbs (by means of the consonant ל) in וַיַּעַל of line 23 and וַיֵּלֶךְ of line 25 (A//A'). Finally there is the prevalence of the infrequent letter ק occurring in six words of this short passage: in קְטַנִּים, וַיִּתְקַלְּסוּ, קֵרֵחַ, and קֵרֵחַ (line 23), וַיְקַלְלֵם and וַתְּבַקַּעְנָה (line 24), a feature which adds to the overall assonance of the passage.

These literary characteristics, the concentric arrangement, the repetition of key words, word play, alliteration, and assonance all point to a highly stylized artistic work which befits a satiric interpretation. When added to the other satirical features that we have pointed out above, namely that the story contains major characteristics of satire, such as fantastic situations, grotesqueries, exaggerations, irony, parody, and ridicule, we see that this story too contains all the elements necessary for satire. A satirical reading of the story enables us to posit an alternate interpretation to the standard one, that the story is a warning to people to respect the prophets or their elders. In this reading, the concern of the narrator would be entirely in the other direction, to satirize the behavior of the prophet,[80] and not the behavior of the children. The satire then would represent a criticism of the abuse of

---

[80] This view would be in accord with the Talmudic one expressed in *b. Sanh.* 107b which comments negatively on Elisha's conduct for which, it was believed, he was eventually punished.

prophetic power by a prophet who invoked an atrociously severe curse for a seemingly mild offense.

In our "Afterward" in chapter eight, we shall discuss what this satire has in common with the other satires of our corpus and offer some suggestions as to when and why this satire may have been written and how it got into the canon. We now turn to an analysis of the third of our anti-prophetic satires, the story of the lying prophet from Bethel. This satire differs from the two satires we have just reviewed in that it is much longer and it targets not one prophet, but two. Because this story is probably the most unfamiliar one in our corpus, and because parts of the text need explanation, it is necessary, before commencing our literary analysis, to present a synopsis of the story.

# V

## The Lying Prophet

1 Kings 13 relates one of the most extraordinary stories in the
Hebrew Bible. Jeroboam, the first king of the new northern state
of Israel, is standing atop his recently constructed altar[1] at Bethel
about to offer sacrifice, when an unnamed Judean "man of God"[2]
appears. This "man of God" addresses an oracle, not to
Jeroboam, but to the altar: "altar! altar!"[3] The oracle forecasts the
birth of a future king of Judah,[4] Josiah of the House of David.

---

[1] Jeroboam must have been standing at the top of the altar's steps because it
was recorded three times in the last two verses of chapter 12 (vv. 32 and 33)
that he had 'ascended' his new altar.

[2] The Judean prophet is always referred to by this designation (vv. 1, 4, 5,
6x2, 7, 8, 11, 12, 14x2, 21, 26, 29, 31), but never by נָבִיא, "a prophet."
Once, he is indirectly called a prophet, when the old man prophet declares,
"I am a prophet like you" (v. 18). On the other hand, the old man is always
called a נָבִיא, never an אִישׁ אֱלֹהִים.

[3] Nowhere else in the Bible is an inanimate object addressed in this fashion,
though this double form of address does occur with individuals (Gen. 22:11;
46:2; Exod. 3:4; 1 Sam. 3:10). Cyrus Gordon noted that this double form of
address to inanimate objects also occurs in the Epic of Gilgamesh (tablet 11,
line 21), when Ea addresses Utnapishtim's hut: "reed wall! reed wall! wall!
wall!" (kikkiš kikkiš igār igār) (Introduction to Old Testament Times, 37, n.
30).

[4] The participle form נוֹלָד used here (v. 2), and in 1 Chr. 22:9 (announcing
Solomon's birth), is for an annunciation. For a real birth announcement
("has been born"), the verb is placed in the qal passive, see Simon B.
Parker, "The Birth Announcement," 149.

This Josiah will eliminate worship at the Bethel altar by burning human bones on it which will have the effect of permanently polluting it,[5] rendering such a place unusable ever again for worship. To validate his oracle, the "man of God" announces a sign about something that is going to happen right now:[6] the altar will crack, and the fat-soaked ashes on top of it will spill to the ground.[7]

When Jeroboam hears the man of God's words of condemnation against the altar, his initial reaction is to stretch forth his hand over the altar and order the arrest of the man of God. But as he stretches hishand out, it becomes paralyzed and he cannot move it. At that very moment the sign, which the man of God predicted, occurs: the altar cracks, and the fat-soaked ashes spill to the ground. The king appeals to the man of God to pray for the restoration of his hand. The man of God does so, and the paralysis disappears. This immediate demonstration of the man of God's power serves to underscore the legitimacy of his commission.[8] Jeroboam's response is unexpected: he invites the man of God home to dine with him, and promises him a gift. However, the man of God refuses saying that even if the king were to offer him half his kingdom he would not accept. For, he explains, he was

---

[5] The first part of the oracle literally speaks of sacrificing the priests of the high places. But, as Menachem Haran has correctly noted, the reference here (and in 2 Kgs. 23:20), is not to human sacrifice, rather to the burning of the priests' bones after they are dead (*Temples and Temple Service in Ancient Israel*, 138-39, n. 8). The bones were taken from graves in the vicinity where the priests were buried. The ashes penetrated into the ruins making the defilement irreversible.

[6] The text of v. 3 reads as though the sign is not going to take place until Josiah's day, "and he will give (וְנָתַן) in that day (a sign)," but the Peshitta version has the verb in the past tense.

[7] A sign which would invalidate the sacrifice since normally (Lev. 1:16; 4:12), the fat-soaked ashes had to be carefully disposed of (Gray, *I & II Kings*, 326).

[8] A. Graeme Auld, *I & II Kings*, 90.

bidden by God to observe three prohibitions in Bethel: first, not to eat; secondly, not to drink; and thirdly, not to return in the way he came. With that, the man of God leaves, going home on foot by a different route than the one he had used to come to Bethel.

Meanwhile, another prophet, an old man who lived in Bethel, learns from his sons[9] what had transpired at the sanctuary. He wants to meet the man of God, and asks his sons to saddle his donkey and show him[10] which way the man of God had gone when he left Bethel. The sons saddle the donkey for their father, and the old prophet rides off to meet his Judean colleague. He finds him resting under a terebinth tree[11] and, after ascertaining that he is indeed the man of God who had come from Judah, the old prophet, just like Jeroboam had done earlier in the day, invites the man of God home to dine with him. Once again, as he did with King Jeroboam, the man of God repeats the prohibitions which God had commanded him before going to Bethel: not to eat, nor drink there, nor to return by the way he came. The old prophet then informs his Judean counterpart that he, too, is a prophet, and that he had just received a divine oracle through an angel, permitting the man of God to go home with him to eat and drink. This, of course, is a blatant untruth, and the narrator highlights the deception by inserting an observation that the old prophet is indeed lying to the Judean. Nevertheless, to the reader's great surprise, the man of God accepts the old prophet's invitation, and returns to Bethel with him.

They eat and drink but, while they are sitting at the table, the

---

[9] In v. 11 there is an incongruity about the number of the old prophet's sons, but from the ensuing narrative, however, there seems little doubt that the prophet had more than one son (see vv. 12, 13, 27, 31). These 'sons' may, of course, be disciples of the prophet rather than his biological sons.

[10] In v. 12 the text has a *qal* form "(his sons) saw," but the context requires a *hiphil*, "(his sons) showed" (וַיַּרְאֻו), a reading which is found in the Septuagint and the Targum

[11] Elsewhere in the Bible (in the story of Gideon), another messenger of God, the angel of the Lord (מַלְאַךְ יְהוָה) sits under a terebinth (Judg. 6:11).

old prophet receives a genuine divine oracle which he immediately
relates to the Judean man of God. The message of the oracle is
that because the man of God has disobeyed God's word and eaten
and drunk in Bethel, he will die a premature death and will not be
buried in his ancestral grave. At this point, the man of God fin-
ishes his meal and prepares to go home to Judah on one of the old
man's donkeys.[12] But on his way a lion meets him, and kills
him.[13] Unexpectedly, it does not consume any part of his body.
Even more surprising is the fact that the lion does not touch the
donkey on which the man of God was riding, but remains standing, vigil-like, over both the corpse and the donkey. The action of
the lion thus prevents passers-by from being able to identify the
corpse. When news of what happens reaches Bethel, the old
prophet comprehends at once the tremendous significance of the
event. The victim, he declares, is the man of God who was
punished for breaking God's word and who had met his death by a
lion precisely in the way it was foretold. The old man then
prepares to go to witness the extraordinary scenes for himself, and
once more orders his sons to saddle his donkey for him.

When he reaches the spot, he observes what he had been told
about the man of God's body being cast aside on the road, and
that the lion had not consumed the body, nor had it touched the
donkey on which the man of God had been riding. The old

---

[12] This verse is usually taken to indicate that the old prophet saddled a
donkey for the man of God as a mark of respect (e.g., David Kimḥi (1160-
1235) in *Miqra'ot Gedolot, ad loc*; Uriel Simon, "1 Kings 13: A Prophetic
Sign--Denial and Persistence," 94-95, n. 35). However, we believe that the
ambiguous phrase, וַיַּחֲבָשׁ־לוֹ הַחֲמוֹר לַנָּבִיא אֲשֶׁר הֱשִׁיבוֹ, in v. 23 should be
rendered, "he (the man of God) saddled for himself the donkey belonging to
the prophet who brought him back [= the old man, as in vv. 20 & 26]."
For the usage of the preposition ל as a marker of the genitive case and
indicating possession, see, for example, 2 Sam. 19:27, and *GKC*, #129b;
Waltke & O'Connor, *An Introduction to Biblical Hebrew Syntax*, #11.2.10d.
[13] Another example of a lion killing a disobedient prophet is in 1 Kgs. 20:36.

prophet then has the man of God's body placed on the same donkey on which the man of God had ridden, and escorts him back to Bethel. In Bethel he conducts mourning rites for him, laments him with all the rites due a fellow prophet, and buries him in a tomb of his own.[14] So convinced is the old prophet that everything which the man of God prophesied would eventually come to pass that he instructs his sons that, when he dies, his body should be placed in the same grave as the man of God. The sequel of the story occurs some 300 years later and is reported in 2 Kgs. 23:15-18, when the very same Josiah mentioned by the man of God to Jeroboam does destroy the altar at Bethel and does order the bones from nearby graves to be burnt on it. This, the text says, was in direct fulfillment of the prophecy which the man of God had foretold. However, by Josiah's time the grave of the man of God had become a local monument and had a special marker on it. When Josiah inquired about the marker, he was told the story of the man of God, and how he had prophesied in Jeroboam's time about what Josiah would do to the altar at Bethel. Josiah then orders the man of God's grave to remain untouched. So, since the remains of the old Bethel prophet were buried alongside the man of God, they, too, were saved from desecration, illustrating the prescience of the old prophet some three hundred years previously.

This long and involved story has been the subject of a considerable amount of interest among scholars. Some have attempted to reconstruct hypothetical "pre-Deuteronomistic forms" or alleged original stories behind the present narrative. But none of these is very satisfactory, and there is no widespread agreement on the boundaries of these earlier forms.[15] Some believe that the

---

[14] Not in the prophet's tomb (so Burke O. Long, *1 Kings With An Introduction To Historical Literature*, 148, and Simon, "1 Kings 13," 96), otherwise there would be no need for the old man to give the specific directions to his sons to bury him with the man of God.

[15] See, for example, Ernst Würthwein, "Die Erzählung vom Gottesmann aus

intent of the story is etiological, to explain why there was a venerated grave site of a prophet in the vicinity of the illegitimate Bethel sanctuary.[16] This was the tomb of the Judean man of God who was buried here, far from his ancestral grave, because he disobeyed God's word by eating with the Bethel prophet.[17]

Two principal themes have been noticed in the story. One is that the story is concerned with competing revelations. Two prophets claim to have received revelation on a certain matter, and one revelation is contrary to the other one. Which revelation is the true one? In this case, the narrator informs us that the second revelation is the false one (v. 18). The lesson for prophets is that revelations of others--even prophets--may be untrustworthy, and it is not prudent to rely on them.[18] The second theme is that of obedience and disobedience.[19] The emphasis of the story is on God's commandment (vv. 9 & 17) and the breach thereof (vv. 21, 22, & 26). The Judean man of God was given a commission by God and did not carry it out, hence he was punished.[20]

---

Juda in Bethel," 181-89; Walter Gross, "Lying Prophet and Disobedient Man of God in 1 Kings 13: Role Analysis as an Instrument of Theological Interpretation of an OT Narrative Text," 100-6; and Thomas B. Dozeman, "The Way of the Man of God from Judah: True and False Prophecy in the Pre-D Legend of 1 Kings 13," 380-83.

[16] Like a *wali* among the Arabs, a tomb of one regarded as a notable saint (Montgomery, *The Books of Kings*, 261; Gray, *I & II Kings*, 323).

[17] Montgomery, *The Books of Kings*, 261; B. Uffenheimer, *Ancient Prophecy in Israel*, 170; Ernst Würthwein, *Das Erste Buch der Könige*, 171.

[18] Lindblom, *Prophecy in Ancient Israel*, 63-64; Uffenheimer, *Ancient Prophecy in Israel*, 170; Robert R. Wilson, *Prophecy and Society in Ancient Israel*, 191; Dozeman, "The Way of the Man of God," 379-93.

[19] Werner E. Lemke, "The Way of Obedience: 1 Kings 13 and the Structure of the Deuteronomistic History," 301-26; Gross, "Lying Prophet and Disobedient Man of God in 1 Kings 13," 97-135; Simon J. De Vries, *1 Kings*, 169, 173-74; D. W. Van Winkle, "1 Kings XIII: True and False Prophecy," 36-42.

[20] Uriel Simon believes that the point of the story is to show that nothing avails against the word of the Lord, that is, against the oracle regarding

We would like to suggest another possible interpretation, that this story is a satire representing a sardonic comment on the curious ways and petty concerns of some prophets. We note that the necessary characteristic features of satire predominate. It has a number of fantastic situations, a considerable amount of ironies, many examples of ridicule and parody, and a variety of fine rhetorical features. Furthermore, it has a target, or to be more precise targets, the man of God and the prophet of Bethel.

**Fantastic situations**

The first fantastic situation in this story is the absurdity of the oracle of destruction. The oracle consists of the announcement to Jeroboam, the king of Israel, of the birth of a future king of Judah, Josiah of the House of David. This Josiah will eliminate worship at the Bethel altar by burning human bones on it. The absurdity arises because Josiah will not appear on the historical scene till the seventh century, some three hundred later than the time of Jeroboam whose dates are 924-903 B.C.E.[21] This being an example of a prophecy *post eventuum* or *vaticinium ex eventu*,[22] the author must have lived either during, or after, the time of Josiah (639-609 B.C.E.).[23] Nevertheless, he chose to set his story

---

Bethel. He who impairs it will be forced to strengthen it, just as he who betrays his mission will be forced to bolster it even at the cost of his own life (Simon, "1 Kings 13," 112).

[21] Another anachronism occurs in v. 32 which has the old prophet confirming the authenticity of the Judean's prophecy against "all the cult places in the towns of Samaria." But not only would the city of Samaria not exist for another fifty years when Omri will found it (1 Kgs. 16:24), but Samaria as a region would not be known until after 734 (see Gray, *I & II Kings*, 321).

[22] Lindblom, *Prophecy in Ancient Israel*, 49.

[23] While the *terminus a quo* for the story is the reign of Josiah (639-609 B.C.E), the *terminus ad quem* is the date of the final revision of the book of Kings by the Deuteronomistic school (during the Babylonian exile in the 6th century B.C.E.). See Norman K. Gottwald, *The Hebrew Bible*, 139.

in the time of Jeroboam some 300 years earlier than Josiah. The
prophecy is on its face absurd. It is a "Back to the Future"
unreality. It could have no meaning for its hearers since they
could in no way be expected to know the name of a king or of
events promised to occur 300 years in the future. For the author's
later audience, however, the effect of this 300 years delay
between the announcement of the destruction of the altar and its
eventual fulfillment in 300 years must have been considered ironically humorous. For, from the hindsight of time, the audience
would realize that the announcement would have the opposite of
its intended effect. The prophecy to the effect that the altar would
not be desecrated until 300 years later leads to the absurdity that
the sanctuary would last at least three hundred years.[24] Far from
having to worry about suffering any dire consequences for their
unlawful sanctuary, Jeroboam's contemporaries could be confi-
dent that their sanctuary would be secure in their lifetimes and in
their children's lifetimes.

The second fantastic event is the paralysis of Jeroboam's
hand when he stretches it out to arrest the man of God.[25] The
restoration of the hand to its normal condition[26] constitutes the

---

[24] For examples of oracles to be fulfilled way in the future, see Bickerman,
*Four Strange Books of the Bible*, 31. The Pythia declared that Gyges, who
had murdered his king, would reign in Lydia, but that divine punishment
would fall on Gyges' fifth descendant. This descendant was Croesus, doomed
thus long before his birth (Herodotus I:13). The raving mouth of the Sibyl
uttered words which foreordained events a thousand years ahead, according
to Heraclitus (5th century B.C.E.).

[25] For the motif in folklore of a hand withering for impiety, see Gaster,
*Myth, Legend, and Custom in The Old Testament*, 497.

[26] In his appeal for restoration, Jeroboam requests that the man of God
entreat "the Lord, your God" (v. 6). This appears to be a stock means of
address to prophets, particularly in times of distress. For example, the people
request that Samuel intercede for them, "with the Lord *your God*," that they
may not die (1 Sam. 12:19). Saul, when he appeals to Samuel (1 Sam.
15:15, 21, 30), and Hezekiah, when he implores Isaiah (2 Kgs. 19:4), both
use the phrase, "the Lord, your God." Also Obadiah, the functionary in the

second fantastic event. The performance of a fantastic event and its reverse is well known in other biblical stories, the most notable being that of Moses announcing the occurrence, and then the removal of plagues. These are, in effect, double miracles.[27] The third fantastic event is the fulfillment of the sign, announced by the man of God that the altar would break apart and the fat-soaked ashes would be spilled. The altar does indeed break apart and its fat-soaked ashes are spilled to the ground (v. 5).

The fourth fantastic event in our story is the fact that the lion who has just killed the wayward man of God does not eat his carcass and, more surprisingly, does not so much as touch the donkey on which the man of God had been riding. Rather the lion is found standing by its side as the old prophet approaches. The text makes a special note of these extraordinary events by observing: "The lion had not eaten the corpse nor had it mauled the ass" (v. 28). The behavior of the lion in not eating the corpse,[28] and especially in not touching the donkey constitutes a remarkable and unbelievable event.[29] This type of animal behavior is comparable to the behavior of animals in our other anti-prophetic stories: to the donkey of Balaam, to the she-bears in the tale of boys and the

---

palace of Ahab, who was a confirmed Yahwist ("Obadiah revered the Lord greatly" [1 Kgs. 18:3]), addresses Elijah similarly, "as the Lord *your God* lives" (1 Kgs. 18:10).

[27] For more examples, see Zakovitch, *The Concept of the Miracle in the Bible*, 46-48.

[28] It might be thought that since lions only eat to satisfy their appetites the lion was simply not hungry, and the only extraordinary event was his not killing of the donkey. But lions only kill when they wish to eat. The lion killed the man of God so presumably he had originally intended to eat him.

[29] Lindblom waxes a little poetic when he points to this incident as an illustration that even the wild beasts respected the prophets! (*Prophecy in Ancient Israel*, 62).

bald prophet, and to the great fish that swallows Jonah. All are
illustrations of the contrast between the faithful behavior of
animals as contrasted with man's rejection of God's directives.[30]

## Irony

Our story exhibits a considerable number of situational ironies
(which we introduce with the phrase "it is ironic that...").[31] many
of which have been noticed by other commentators particularly by
Uriel Simon in his seminal study on this story.[32] The most notable
ironies are the fact that it is ironic that the hand that stretches forth
to arrest the man of God is itself arrested and paralyzed.  This
incident also illustrates the familiar folkloristic motif of being
unable to harm the super hero represented here in the person of
the man of God.[33]

It is ironic that the one who was the original bearer of the
word of God occasioned an oracle of God to be directed against
him.[34] The man of God was originally protected by God against
the king's power, but he is now destroyed by Him.

It is ironic that the old prophet from Bethel, who deceives the
man of God, is not only the very one to announce the punishment
of God to him, but later declares the man of God to be "his
brother."

It is ironic that the man of God's oracle is confirmed by his
death,[35] because it demonstrates that the one who has the power to

---

[30] See Uffenheimer, *Ancient Prophecy in Israel*, 170; Alexander Rofé,
"Classes in the Prophetical Stories: Didactic Legenda and Parable," 158.

[31] See p. 14 above.

[32] In his "1 Kings 13," 81-117.

[33] According to Lindblom, this is an illustration that the prophets were
sacrosanct. It was dangerous to offend them; their own persons were sacred
and must not be insulted or injured (*Prophecy in Ancient Israel*, 62).

[34] Simon, "1 Kings 13," 93.

[35] He who transgressed the word of the Lord became its confirmation
(Simon, "1 Kings 13," 109). According to Gross the threat to the altar had

punish also has the power to destroy the sanctuary at Bethel. Just as God's threatened punishment against the prophet came true, so will his threatened punishment against the sanctuary come to pass. Ironically, it was a "no win" situation for the man of God. If he died, that meant that he had indeed received genuine revelation, and his original message was true. He was indeed a true prophet, but one who had gone astray. If he did *not* die, it would not only mean that the revelation received in the old man's house in Bethel was false, but that his original message also was false.

It is ironic that whereas the man of God who is told not to eat or drink[36] subsequently does eat and drink, but that the lion who had no such restrictions, abstains from eating the carcass of the man of God.[37]

Finally, it is ironic that the bones of the man of God protect the grave of the man who had brought about his death.[38]

We believe that yet another irony helps elucidate a section of the story which has up till now been cloaked in controversy. The problem occurs in the meaning of the third prohibition enjoined on the man of God. The prohibitions are mentioned three times in the text. The first two occur in refusing invitations. The first invitation is when Jeroboam invites the man of God home to dine with him and the man of God refuses saying that even if the king were to offer him half his kingdom he would not accept. For, he

---

already been carried out (v. 5), and requires no confirmation. The death of the man of God was a punishment from God for disobedience only ("Lying Prophet and Disobedient Man of God in 1 Kings 13," 128, n. 9).

[36] Emphasis on the ban on food and drink being in force in all of Bethel is achieved by a triple mention of בַּמָּקוֹם הַזֶּה "in this place" (vv. 8, 16, & 22) plus the additional place reference to 'there' in v. 17.

[37] According to Simon, the lion's abstention from eating serves to emphasize retrospectively the transgression of the man of God by eating in Bethel ("1 Kings 13," 96, n. 37).

[38] Ibid., 81.

explains, he was bidden by God to observe three prohibitions in Bethel: one, not to eat; two, not to drink; and three, not to return in the way he came. The second invitation occurs when the old prophet from Bethel invites the man of God home to dinner. Once again the man of God refuses and repeats the three prohibitions which God had commanded him before going to Bethel: not to eat, nor drink there, nor to return by the way he came.

The injunction not to eat and not to drink is quite clear,[39] but what does the third part of the prohibition "not to return by the way he came" mean? This injunction has usually been taken to mean going home to Judah by a different route,[40] particularly in light of v. 10: "So he left by another road and did not go back by the road on which he had come to Bethel."[41] The problem with

---

[39] There is no evidence that the prohibitions enjoining the man of God not to eat or drink in Bethel was because Bethel was considered unclean, its inhabitants unclean, and their food unclean. According to A. Šanda, the man of God by appearing suddenly ("and behold", v. 1), and disappearing suddenly (not lingering to eat, drink and going back by a different unexpected route), creates the best possible effect ("shock value") for his message (*Die Bücher der Könige*, 355). Rofé believes that the man of God acts like an angel. Just as heavenly angels of popular legends do not eat or drink, and disappear suddenly, so the man of God was prohibited to eat, drink and return to Bethel ("Classes in the Prophetical Stories," 159-60).

[40] Simon, one of the strongest advocates of this point of view, argues that the prohibition of the return is an important element in the prophecy. Just as the prohibition of eating and drinking stressed the depth of the Lord's abhorrence of Bethel, so did the prohibition of returning by the same route *concretize the absoluteness and irrevocability of the verdict*. According to Simon, "If the harbinger cannot be sent back on his footsteps, neither can his utterance," and the "retracing of one's footsteps [may] be regarded as voiding the mission and abandoning the goal." Simon illustrates his contention with examples about people retracing footsteps, and that this is regarded in biblical thought as a failure of mission ("1 Kings 13," 88-91). But we are not dealing here with a retracing of footsteps. The Judean prophet is not forbidden to go back to his point of origin, i.e., home to Judah. He is forbidden only from going back to Bethel!

[41] According to Arnold B. Ehrlich, this verse is an explanatory phrase

this interpretation is, as Ehrlich pointed out years ago,[42] that if the prohibition really means going back to Judah by a different route, there would be no point in mentioning this as a possible breach of the divine commandment to the king (v. 9). Also there would certainly have been no point in mentioning it to the old prophet (v. 17), since at this stage in the story he was indeed taking a different route. On the other hand, if the prohibition means not to return to Bethel,[43] the man of God's accepting both the king and the old prophet's invitations to go to their homes within Bethel would indeed transgress the command not to go back to Bethel. But, if the third part of the prohibition is indeed not to return to Bethel, how then can v. 10, "So he left by another road and did not go back by the road on which he had come to Bethel," which seems to imply a different route, be explained? The problem appears to have a geographical solution. Over eighty years ago, Šanda observed that Bethel lies on the main north-south highway,[44] and that the sanctuary of Bethel was located outside of the city proper probably on a hill to the east or south-east of the city of Bethel.[45] Thus the route of the man of God would have brought him from the south passing through Bethel, then going eastward to the sanctuary. If the man of God "left by another road and did not go back by the road on which he had come to Bethel" (v. 10), this would mean the man of God, upon leaving the sanctuary, started homeward avoiding the main route he came from via Bethel,

---

inserted by a later editor who wished to explain what the ambiguous "nor shall you return by the way which you came" really meant (*Randglossen zur Hebräischen Bibel*, 3: 248).

[42] Ehrlich, *Mikrä ki-Pheschutö*, 2: 298.

[43] A. Hartoum, *The Book of Kings*, 62.

[44] On this major longitudinal road, see Yohanan Aharoni, *The Land of the Bible: A Historical Geography*, 57.

[45] *Die Bücher der Könige*, 353. See Nadav Na'aman ("Beth-Aven, Bethel and Early Israelite Sanctuaries," 13-21), who locates the sanctuary about three quarters of a mile to the south-east of Bethel, modern Beitin.

thereby fulfilling the original prohibition "not to return by the way he came." That he must have gone on a different route other than the main route back is supported by the fact that the old prophet had to inquire from his sons which route the man of God had taken.

Two more details in the story support the supposition that the original prohibition was not to return to Bethel. Firstly, there is the fact that the old prophet pretends that he had received an oracle from God with "new instructions" for the man of God. The new instructions as reported by the old prophet are "bring him back with you to your house and let him eat and drink" (v. 18). Indeed, from this time on the old prophet is now termed "the one who brought him back" (vv. 20, 23, 26).[46] If these were the "new instructions," the old instructions, and the original prohibition, must have included not going back to Bethel. Secondly, an ironic reading of our story supports the supposition that the original prohibition was not to return to Bethel. For if the original prohibition was not to go back to Bethel then it produces the following irony. The Judean man of God was prohibited to return to Bethel. Since he violated the command, as his measure for measure punishment, he (that is, his dead body) will not be permitted to go home (to his family grave),[47] but would actually be buried in Bethel.[48] This interpretation may be illustrated clearly by an analysis of the literary structure of the three speeches where the prohibitions occur. The speeches form a stereotyped pattern as can be seen from the chart on the adjoining page.

---

[46] In v. 26 the epithet is expanded to "the one who brought him back from the way."

[47] Ehrlich, *Randglossen*, 3:299.

[48] Yehuda Keel, *Book of Kings*, 292.

## THE THREE SPEECHES

| TO JEROBOAM (vv. 8-9) | TO THE PROPHET (vv. 16-17) | ORACLE OF THE PROPHET (v. 22) |
|---|---|---|
| **A** I will not go with you, [to Bethel] | I may not return with you and enter your home; [to Bethel] | You returned; [to Bethel] |
| **B** Nor will I eat bread or drink water in this place. | And I may not eat bread or drink water in this place; | You ate bread and drunk water in the place |
| **X** For so I was commanded by the word of the Lord: | For the order I received by the word of the Lord was: | of which He said to you, |
| **B'** "You shall eat no bread and drink no water, | "You shall not bread or drink water there; | "Do not eat bread or drink water [there]." |
| **A'** Nor shall you return by the way you came." | Nor shall you return by the way you came." | Your corpse shall not come into your ancestors' grave. |

The pattern forms a chiastic structure **A-B-X-B'-A'**, where **A** represents a return to Bethel, **B** eating and drinking in Bethel, **X** the divine command, **B'** the prohibition against eating and drinking, and **A'** the prohibition from returning "by the way you came."[49] Since **A'** corresponds with **A**, which represents a return to Bethel, then **A'**, likewise, must indicate a return to Bethel. It will be observed that in the third speech, which is the oracle of the old prophet, the section **A'** departs from the regular formula. It

---

[49] Dozeman also noticed this stereotyped pattern, but defines the chiastic structure slightly differently. He divides the "eating and drinking" clause (our B) into two, the "eating" (B) and the "drinking" (C) ("The Way of the Man of God from Judah," 385-86). Unfortunately, this leads to an incomplete chiastic structure A, B, C, D, B',C',A' whereas our division leads to a complete one (A, B, X, B', A').

does not, like its counterparts in the first two speeches, literally repeat the third prohibition ("not to return by the way you came" [= "not to return to Bethel"]). Rather, it outlines the punishment that will come to the Judean man of God: "Your corpse shall not come into your ancestors' grave." Since the man of God was buried in Bethel, here there is a poetic justice about the punishment. The original prohibition was not to go back to Bethel. Since the Judean man of God violated the command, as his measure for measure punishment, he would not be permitted to go home, but would actually be buried in Bethel. We have here yet another, and a final, irony. The man of God who was prohibited to return to Bethel alive does return as a result of his punishment, albeit dead.

## Ridicule

In our story all three of the main characters, namely the king, the man of God, and the prophet of Bethel are the subject of ridicule. It is no surprise that a Judean author such as the Deuteronomist would ridicule Jeroboam who was considered to be responsible for the great religious apostasy in Northern Israel. Our story is actually wedged between two parts of a framework commenting negatively on Jeroboam for his religious innovations.[50] In many respects the approach of the man of God and his oracle of denunciation just when Jeroboam is about to offer sacrifice are testimony to the fact that the author viewed both the king and his new altar as illegitimate. The fact that the man of God does not

---

[50] The preceding verses 26-33 of chapter 12 describe how Jeroboam established the two new sanctuaries at Bethel and Dan, how he made the golden calves, how he changed the calendar, and how he appointed new priests who were not Levites. Chapter 13 starts with the word וְהִנֵּה, "now behold," which always starts a new scene, never a new narrative (see Simon, "1 Kings 13," 99), thus continuing the action of the last verses of chapter 12. The last two verses of chapter 13 state that the incident with the Judean prophet had no effect on Jeroboam. He "did not turn back from his evil way, but kept on appointing priests for the shrine from the ranks of the people."

even address the king, but rather the altar, an inanimate object, constitutes a slight to the royal presence.[51] Jeroboam is ridiculed by being portrayed in an almost slapstick manner. He is lampooned by seeming to ignore the collapse of the altar, the very altar on top of whose steps he was standing at the time.[52] In this scene the king's only reaction is to ask for the healing of his hand. And when that was brought about, he exhibits a completely unexpected *volte face*. Abruptly changing his order to arrest the man of God, he extends an invitation to him to come home with him for dinner. The complete disregard by the king of the tumult around him, with cracking and crumbling masonry on all sides, seems to be absolutely incomprehensible and results in a rather incongruous scene.

The first time the man of God is ridiculed is when he is lied to by the prophet of Bethel. Here is a man who speaks God's word and intercedes with Him on behalf of the king yet who is also easily fooled by the false utterance of the old prophet. We note that the lie is outrageous and unexpected. It has remarkable shock value. The reader is shocked by the fact that a prophet would lie,[53] and shocked also by the fact that the man of God was deceived by the lie. The second time the man of God is ridiculed is in the manner of his punishment. This includes not only an unnatural death, being killed by the lion, but also the disgrace that he will not be buried, as was customary, in his family tomb.[54]

---

[51] Jerome T. Walsh believes this insult also implies that Yahweh too is spurning Jeroboam because of his role in the sacrifice ("The Contexts of 1 Kings xiii," 358).

[52] Only Robert Cohn seems to have noticed this detail, "the immediate demolition of the altar does not make strict logical sense" ("Literary Technique in the Jeroboam Narrative," 32, n. 36).

[53] The motif of the deception of prophets is found elsewhere in the Hebrew Bible, but only with God as the deceiver. See 1 Kgs. 22:23, "So the Lord has put a lying spirit in the mouth of all these prophets of yours," and Ezek. 14:9, "And if a prophet is seduced and does speak a word [to such a man] it was I the Lord who seduced that prophet."

[54] Not "to be gathered to one's ancestors" or "to be buried in the grave of

That the Judean will die an unnatural death is seen from the use in the oracle of the word נְבֵלָה 'corpse', a term which is used no less than ten times in the story.[55] The term נְבֵלָה indicates unnatural and violent death[56] and is often associated with טְרֵפָה which means "torn by beasts,"[57] the very means of the man of God's death. It is primarily used in contexts which illustrate that a corpse does not have a normal burial. So, for example, the word often appears in Jeremiah's threats of punishment that, as an illustration of the coming debacle of the people, their corpses (נְבֵלָה) will not have a proper burial: they will be left unburied, like dung or refuse to be eaten by the birds and the wild animals.[58] All of this serves to indicate the great dishonor that will accrue to them after death.

The third indication of ridicule against the man of God is that his corpse cannot be retrieved for burial. Because of the presence

---

one's family" generally signified a violent and unnatural death, and the opposite situation meant a peaceful (i.e., natural) death. Sometimes death oracles do not materialize. Jeremiah threatened Jehoiakim with a violent death (22:18-19; 36:30), yet Jehoiakim ended up having a normal burial ("he slept with his fathers," 2 Kgs. 24:6). The opposite occurred with Josiah. He had been promised a 'peaceful' death by the prophetess Huldah (2 Kgs. 22:20), but he actually died violently at the hand of Pharaoh Necho (2 Kgs. 23:29). Of course, the phrase could simply be interpreted literally. The Judean prophet will not be buried at home, but will be buried among strangers (cf. Gen. 47:30 and 50:25). No matter how the prophet died, his body would not be brought back to Judah. Thus the Judean man of God is told that not only will he die an unnatural death (being torn by a lion), but his remains will not be sent back to Judah for burial.

[55] In vv. 22, 24, 25x2, 28x3, 29, & 30.

[56] In three cases the term is used to refer to the bodies of executed individuals. The rule stated in Deuteronomy that the corpse of an executed man should be buried at nightfall is put into effect by Joshua after the execution of the king of Ai. Jer. 26:23 records the execution of the prophet Uriah whose corpse was cast into a common grave.

[57] In Lev. 7:24; 17:15; 11:18.

[58] The same threat was made by Elijah against Jezebel. Her carcass will be cast out like dung on the ground. It will be unrecognizable and nobody will be able to identify her and say "this was Jezebel" (2 Kgs. 9:37).

of the lion standing beside his corpse, no one can retrieve his body for burial. His corpse is described three times as "lying on the road" (מֻשְׁלֶכֶת בַּדֶּרֶךְ). This phrase is elsewhere used for unburied corpses. Jeremiah warns that the people to whom the false prophets prophesy will be left lying (מֻשְׁלָכִים) unburied in the streets of Jerusalem (Jer. 14:16). Similarly, Jeremiah prophesies that Jehoiakim's corpse would not be buried, but would remain open to natural elements of heat and cold (Jer. 36:30).[59]

The old prophet is ridiculed by being openly portrayed as a liar. He tells the man of God that an angel had come to him and, in God's name, had instructed him to bring the man of God back home with him to eat and drink. This was a blatant untruth, as the narrator informs us in v. 18, כִּחֵשׁ לוֹ, "he lied to him." The prophet's lie will have the effect of unleashing a train of events, which will ultimately end with the man of God's dishonorable death. The old prophet is also ridiculed by being portrayed as having an inordinate concern about burial.[60] His greatest concern is for the disposition of his own remains for which he makes provision during his lifetime.[61] He is convinced that the prophecy of the man of God will eventually come to fruition.[62] When that

---

[59] Studies by Mordechai Cogan ("A Technical Term for Exposure," 133-35), and by Meir Malul ("Adoption of Foundlings in the Bible and Mesopotamian Documents: A Study of Some Legal Metaphors in Ezekiel 16:1-7," 97-126) have shown that casting of dead bodies in the street outside the city or in the fields has legal significance beyond that of merely maltreating the dead and dishonoring their remains. It indicates a state of ownerlessness. Not surprising then, after Uriah the prophet is executed, his carcass is cast (וַיַּשְׁלֵךְ) into a commoner's grave (Jer. 26:23).

[60] Ehrlich comments that it is the nature of old people to have a great concern for the disposition of their remains (*Randglossen*, 3: 248).

[61] Graves were often protected by curses (see *KAI* 1: nos. 13 and 14). By removing and burning bones, a person would have to believe that he was doing more harm to the dead than could be done to him by the protective curse (Francis Andersen and David Noel Freedman, *Amos*, 288).

[62] The fear of exhumation, prevalent all over the Near East, was especially acute in Israel (Eric M. Meyers, *Jewish Ossuaries: Reburial and Rebirth*, 15). This can be seen clearly in the curses in Deuteronomy and in the

happens, he fears exhumation of his bones which, as we recall, would occur in fulfillment of that part of the oracle which stated that, "human bones shall be burned upon [the altar]" (v. 2). The bones would be taken from graves in the vicinity of the sanctuary.[63] The old prophet asks that when the time for reinterment of his bones comes about, they should be placed in the tomb of the Judean man of God, reflecting a belief that even after death a certain power inhered in the bones of holy men.[64] The motivation for the old man's request, "that my bones may be preserved with his bones," is supplied by the Septuagint in v. 31b.[65] This motivation is also reflected in David Kimhi's comment on v. 22 that "were the oracle to be fulfilled and bones of people burnt on the altar, his bones would be saved because he is a man of God, and so his bones will save my bones!" The fulfillment of the old man's wish is recorded in 2 Kgs. 23:18, "so they left his bones undisturbed together with the bones of the prophet who came from Samaria." It would appear then that in wanting to be buried with the man of God, the old prophet acted for purely selfish reasons.[66]

---

prophets (e.g., Jer. 8:1ff and 25:33). Exhumation represents a desecration of the remains, and also a tremendous dishonor to the person's memory. In biblical thought, the bones of the dead, however incomplete they many be, represent the full significance of a man (see Meyers, *Ibid*, 13). In Amos (2:1), the Edomites are condemned for the heinous offense of burning the bones of the Moabite kings until they had completely disintegrated into lime.

[63] Haran, *Temples and Temple Service in Ancient Israel*, 138-39, n. 8.

[64] Yair Zakovitch has recently written about the incident of the revival of the dead man who touched the bones of Elisha ("'Elisha Died...He Came to Life and Stood Up' (2 Kgs. 13:20-21): A Short 'Short Story' in Exegetical Circles," 57* 58* 62*).

[65] ἵνα σωθῶσι τὰ ὀστᾶ μου μετὰ τῶν ὀστῶν αὐτοῦ.

[66] Simon, "1 Kings 13," 97. The standard interpretation is that the old man, by having himself buried with the man of God, gives public, permanent testimony to the truth of the oracle they have both proclaimed (Walsh, "The Contexts of 1 Kings xiii," 367 n. 24). But the old man does not spread the word of the Lord to the townsfolk. It is only to his sons, and in the context of his being buried, that the old man affirms the truth of the oracle in order to save his own bones.

## Parody

The first example of parody in our story is when the man of God delivers his oracle to Jeroboam, an oracle that we have pointed out above as being absurd.[67] We recall that in the oracle he announces to Jeroboam, the king of Israel, the birth of a future king of Judah, Josiah of the House of David. Burke Long believes that we have here a parody on the traditional biblical annunciation type scene. For, at first, the oracle, with the announcement of the birth of a son to the House of David, suggests hope and salvation. But then it develops into polemical sarcasm. Instead of hope, we hear of desecration and violation.[68] Josiah will eliminate worship at the altar and human bones will be burnt on it.

The next example of parody occurs in our story in the almost burlesque scene when the Bethel prophet announces God's oracle and subsequent punishment of the man of God. The oracle seems to be addressed to the wrong person. The old prophet, the one who had invited the man of God home, receives a divine message which condemns his guest to death as the result of a breach for which he was directly responsible.[69] We have here an incongruous scene. The old prophet who deliberately misleads the man of God by lying to him[70] now announces that as a result of his [the old

---

[67] See p. 73 above.

[68] *1 Kings With An Introduction to Historical Literature*, 147.

[69] Do we have here a variation of the type-scene which Carole Fontaine has dubbed a "banquet set-up"? ("The Deceptive Goddess In Ancient Near Eastern Myth: Inanna and Inarash," 96-98). Normally the deception occurs at the banquet where the hero is lured to his death: Yael and Sisera (Judges 4); Absalom and Amnon (2 Sam. 13); and Esther and Haman (Esth. 5:4-8; 7:1-10). Here the deception occurs before "the banquet," although the actual death pronouncement occurs at "the banquet."

[70] The motivation of the old prophet has been much debated. Here are a sample of the various opinions: (1) he (the old man) had good intentions: it was a "white lie" to press the foreigner to accept hospitality (H. Gressmann, *Die älteste Geschichtsschreibung und Prophetie Israels*, 248; and Rofé, "Classes in the Prophetical Stories," 162). Therefore, he did not merit punishment since lying *per se* is not always condemned in the Bible, see the cases

man's] deception, he [the Judean] will die a premature death. It is as though the wrong party is being punished and the instigator escapes unharmed. Furthermore, contrary to normal usage, the oracle seems to be addressed to the wrong person.[71] Normally, oracles go directly to the recipient. The recipient of the word of the Lord is always the one to whom God calls.

The standard phraseology introducing an oracle is either כֹּה אָמַר יהוה "thus said the Lord" or X וַיְהִי דְבַר יהוה אֶל "the word of the Lord came to X," followed by a verb for speech either לֵאמֹר 'saying' (Jer. 13:8-9; 24:4-5 etc.), וְאָמַרְתָּ 'tell!' (Isa. 38:4-5), אֱמֹר 'speak!' (Hag. 1:1-3; 2:20-21; 2 Chr. 11:2-3) or וְקָרָאתָ 'proclaim!' (Jer. 2:1-2). Here the first part of the standard oracle is addressed to the Bethel prophet (וַיְהִי דְבַר־יְהוָה "the word of the Lord came"), and the second part, the message, is addressed by the Bethel prophet to the man of God (וַיִּקְרָא אֶל־אִישׁ הָאֱלֹהִים "he proclaimed to the man of God"). Nowhere else is there such a bifurcation of phraseology.

In these last two examples, it is the breach of the literary norms or rhetorical rules that allow for the parody. It would not

---

of David at Nob (1 Sam. 21:1-9) of Elisha and the Aramaean army (2 Kgs. 6:19), etc.; (2) he was testing the man of God: he wanted to ascertain the genuineness of the man of God's commission to test the validity of the word of the Lord (Gray, *I & II Kings*, 322), or to discredit the word of the Lord by violating the sign that gave it authority (Simon, "1 Kings 13," 92); (3) he was interested in protecting the Bethel altar to which he was professionally attached (Martin A. Klopfenstein, "1. Könige 13," 646; Martin Noth, *Könige*, 1968), 300; and Alfred Jepsen, "Gottesmann und Prophet: Anmerkungen zum Kapital 1. Könige 13," 178; (4) he had purely selfish motifs: to gain esteem through contact with the wonder worker (Šanda, *Die Bücher der Könige*, 353), or to protect himself against the effects of the threat against Bethel (J. Robinson, *The First Book of Kings*, 161).

[71] Note the remarks of Robinson: "If he were a true prophet, then God would have communicated directly with him and not through an intermediary" (*The First Book of Kings*, 162).

be expected that an annunciation would develop into an oracle of destruction. Yet this one did. It would not be expected that an oracle be transmitted through an intermediary. Yet this one was.

## Rhetorical features

Our story is replete with fine rhetorical devices. There are key words, paronomasia, artful repetition of verbs, chiastic structures, etc. The most frequent key words which appear in the story are: שׁוּב "to return," (15x);[72] דֶּרֶךְ 'way', (12x);[73] מִזְבֵּחַ 'altar' (10x);[74] נְבֵלָה 'carcass' (10x);[75] אָכַל "to eat" and שָׁתָה "to drink" (8x);[76] בִּדְבַר יהוה "by the word of the Lord" (7x).[77] A good example of paronomasia in the story is the narrator's use of the key word דֶּרֶךְ. He does so by playing on the fact that Hebrew דֶּרֶךְ 'way' (like its Akkadian cognate *alaktu*)[78] has both literal and metaphorical meanings.[79] The word occurs twelve times in the narrative. In its literal sense it occurs ten times.[80] In v. 33, it is clearly metaphorical: "Even after this incident, Jeroboam did not turn back from his evil way (מִדַּרְכּוֹ הָרָעָה)." In v. 26, it may well

---

[72] Vv. 4, 6x2, 9, 10, 16, 17, 18, 19, 20, 22, 23, 26, & 29.

[73] Vv. 9, 10x2, 12x2, 17, 24x2, 25, 26, 28, & 33.

[74] Vv. 1, 2x3, 3, 4x2, 5x2, & 32.

[75] Vv. 22, 24, 25x2, 28x3, 29, & 30.

[76] Vv. 4, 8, 16, 17, 18, 19, & 22.

[77] Vv. 1, 2, 5, 9, 17, 18, & 32.

[78] See *CAD*, *A/1*, sub *alaktu*; and Moshe Held, "Two Philological Notes on Enuma Elish," 238.

[79] Lemke, "The Way of Obedience," 301-26.

[80] In vv. 9, 10 (twice), 12 (twice), 17, 24, 24, 25, & 28. We note that the second דֶּרֶךְ in v. 10 is feminine (as it is in v. 17), whereas the first one is masculine. Robert J. Ratner has observed that this factor does not produce any discernible semantic difference ("*Derek*: Morpho-Syntactical Considerations," 471-73). However, the fact that the second form is feminine fully accords with his rule that in a relative clause (after אֲשֶׁר) the noun דֶּרֶךְ occurs only in the feminine.

be that the narrator intended that the דֶּרֶךְ ("the prophet who had
brought him back from the דֶּרֶךְ") be deliberately ambiguous:[81]
playing on the various nuances of the meaning of שׁוּב in conjunc-
tion with דֶּרֶךְ. The man of God turned from his proper דֶּרֶךְ, and
he ended up being cast in the דֶּרֶךְ.[82]

   The artful repetition of verbs is achieved a number of times
by means of the rhetorical device of "command-action,"[83] where
the completion of an act is described in precisely the same form it
was announced or commanded. So the execution of the oracle is
described in the same words as it was announced, due allowance
being made for the change of tenses, e.g., נִקְרָע "will break
apart," וְנִשְׁפַּךְ "will be spilled," in the announcement (v. 3), and
נִקְרָע "broke apart," וַיִּשָּׁפֵךְ "was spilled" (v. 5), in the completion.
Other command-action sequences in the story are חַל, 'entreat!' (v.
6), and וַיְחַל "(he) entreated" (v. 6); וְתָשֹׁב "(may my hand) be
healed!" and וַתָּשָׁב "(his hand) was healed" (v. 6); לֹא תָשׁוּב "do
not go back!" (v. 9) and לֹא־שָׁב "he did not go back" (v. 10);
חֲבֹשׁוּ 'saddle!' and וַיַּחְבֹּשׁוּ "they saddled" (vv. 13 & 27).

   Another form of repetition is the use of the same sequence of
verbs. Thus, the old man goes out (וַיֵּלֶךְ) to meet (וַיִּמְצָאֵהוּ) the
Judean man of God (v. 14), who will in turn go out (וַיֵּלֶךְ) and be
met (וַיִּמְצָאֵהוּ) by a lion (v. 24). Later, the old man will once again
go out and find (וַיֵּלֶךְ וַיִּמְצָא) the corpse of the Judean (v. 28).[84]

   A fine example of chiastic structure is seen in the three
speeches which describe the prohibition enjoined on the man of
God. The first speech is that of the man of God to Jeroboam (v. 8-

[81] So Lemke, "The Way of Obedience," 311.

[82] In a similar vein, Van Winkle maintains that the author used the word
מִצְוָה in a double meaning, one to refer to the specific commandment of God
to the prophet not to eat and drink, and the other to allude to the Decalogue
or the entire Deuteronomic law ("1 Kings XIII," 40-41).

[83] On command-action in Hebrew and Ugaritic narrative, see T. L. Fenton,
"Command and Fulfillment in Ugaritic: tqtl: yqtl and qtl: qtl," 34-38.

[84] Note also the contrast of the action of the lion who mauled the prophet:
וַיִּשְׁבְּרֵהוּ "(the lion) mauled him" (v. 26), but did not maul the donkey; וְלֹא
שָׁבַר "(the lion) did not maul (the donkey)" (v. 28).

9), the second that of the man of God to the old prophet of Bethel (vv. 16-17), and the third is in the oracle of the old prophet announcing the punishment and the reason for it to the man of God (v. 21-22). In our discussion above on irony,[85] we have already observed that the speeches form a stereotyped pattern which results in a chiastic structure **A-B-X-B'-A'**. In fact, it is this very chiastic structure which enabled us to determine that the third prohibition enjoined on the man of God "not to return in the way you came," meant in fact not to return to Bethel. This chiastic structure together with the presence of key words, paronomasia, and artful repetition of verbs shows how the story is studded with fine rhetorical devices. When added to the other satirical characteristics dominating the story, namely the fantastic situations, the ironies, the ridicule and the parody, it seems that a good case can be made for our story being a satire.

A satirical reading of the story enables us to posit an alternate interpretation to the standard ones: that the story is etiological, that it has to do with competing revelations or with obedience and disobedience. A satirical reading indicates that the principal concern of the story is to satirize its targets, the man of God and the prophet of Bethel. They are satirized, like Elisha in our previous satire, because of their behavior: for foolishness, lying, and concern with petty values.

In our "Afterward" in chapter eight, we shall discuss what this satire has in common with the other satires of our corpus, and see if it is possible to identify the prophets who are the objects of this satire. We shall also discuss the possibility that one or both of these prophets may have been false prophets. For now we turn to an analysis of the fourth, and most well-known, of our antiprophetic satires, that of the Book of Jonah.

---

[85] See p. 81 above.

# VI

## The Book of Jonah

The familiar story of the reluctant prophet Jonah, who refuses to carry out God's mission and who is swallowed by a big fish, is perhaps most well known of all the stories in our corpus. But the book in which this story is embedded is curious for at least five reasons. First, there is the content of the book.[1] It is not a collection of oracles like the other prophetic books, but a narrative about an incident in the life of a prophet.[2] As such, it is similar to the stories told about prophets such as Elijah and Elisha which are found in the book of Kings.[3] The second curiosity has to do with the book's theme. At first sight it seems to be altogether remarkable that a Hebrew author would make the salvation of Nineveh a major theme of his book. Nineveh was the capital city of Assyria, and it was the Assyrians who were responsible for the destruction

---

[1] Phyllis L. Trible correctly observes that "the uniqueness of its narrative form among the Latter Prophets bespeaks the uniqueness of its contents" (*Studies in the Book of Jonah*, 126).

[2] We know from 2 Kgs. 8:4, where Elisha's servant is asked to regale the king with Elisha's exploits, that telling stories about the prophets was popular even during their lifetime.

[3] The book of Jonah starts with one of the same formulas which introduces biographical material about Elijah in the book of Kings. Compare the phrases "the word of the Lord came to Jonah, son of Amittai, saying" (1:1) with "the word of the Lord came to him, saying" (1 Kgs. 17:2, 8), and "the word of the Lord came to Elijah, the Tishbite, saying" (1 Kgs. 21:17).

of the northern state of Israel. Thus Nineveh was one of the most despised foreign cities. It is not surprising that the prophet Nahum devoted his entire book to a condemnation of that city. He portrayed Nineveh as the "symbol of cruelty *par excellence*,"[4] and both he and his fellow prophet Zephaniah prophesied the city's ultimate fall.[5] Apparently, the author of the book of Jonah "could not have chosen more unlikely and undeserving recipients of divine grace."[6]

The third curious feature about this book is that the book's message, or purpose, is not made explicit within the book. Indeed the book ends with a question which is not answered.[7] The reader then is forced to supply his or her own meaning to the story,[8] and there has been little unanimity as to what precisely that is.[9] Fourth, whatever the message of the book, Jonah is portrayed as having a point of view contrary to that of God. Indeed, the prophet appears to act as a foil so that God can impart the final lesson. But, in all other prophetic books, it is the prophet who expounds the message: God and His prophet are on the same wavelength, so to speak. Not so in the book of Jonah, where the prophet is characterized as being opposed to God. Throughout the story, Jonah is portrayed as a very negative model of prophetic behavior. A prophet ought to be obedient to God's will, Jonah is not;[10] a prophet ought to intercede with God in times of trouble,

---

[4] Trible, *Studies in the Book of Jonah*, 271. Thus, Nahum describes Nineveh as a "lion's den" (2:12) and "a city of crime, utterly treacherous, full of violence, where killing never stop" (3:1).

[5] Nah. 2:1-4; 3:1-19; Zeph. 2:13-15.

[6] Hyers, *And God Created Laughter*, 94.

[7] Jacob Licht, *Storytelling in the Bible*, 1978), 27. Another narrative which ends on a question is the story of the Rape of Dinah (Gen. 34:31).

[8] Thayer S. Warshaw, "The Book of Jonah," 202. Walter B. Crouch in fact believes that this lack of a closure to the book is a literary device used to involve the reader into constructing an ending ("To Question an End, to End a Question: Opening the Closure of the Book of Jonah," 101-12).

[9] See chapter 7 below.

Jonah does not; a prophet ought to plead with his audience to repent from their evil ways, Jonah does not; a prophet ought not to wish that his prophecy of destruction come true, but Jonah does; a prophet ought not be overly concerned about his personal comfort, but Jonah is; a prophet should not be portrayed in uncompromising or ridiculous situations, but Jonah is (on the ship, in the fish, outside Nineveh). Thus, throughout the story, Jonah is portrayed as a very negative model of prophetic behavior.[11]

It is our contention that this negative portrayal of the prophet is, in fact, the principal message of the book. What we have here is nothing less than a satire on the prophet. Our contention is corroborated by the fact that the book displays all the formal characteristic features of a satire. There is a clearly defined target; the techniques of satire predominate in the work: preponderance of absurd, fantastic, or distorted elements;[12] scores of ironies and incongruities, and many instances of ridicule and parody. Furthermore, the book abounds in various classic Hebrew rhetorical techniques, such as symmetry, repetition, chiasmus, key words, and paronomasia.

---

[10] "He tried to frustrate the prophetic word of God, and to limit both the scope and intention of God's word" (John C. Holbert, "'Deliverance Belongs to Yahweh!': Satire in the Book of Jonah," 75).

[11] Landes, "Jonah: A *masal*?," 148; Robin Payne, "The Prophet Jonah: Reluctant Messenger and Intercessor," 132; Robert J. Ratner, "Jonah: Toward the Re-education of the Prophets," 10, 17; idem, "Jonah, The Runaway Servant," 304. Thus it is impossible to agree with opinions such as those of Etan Levine who states that "nowhere in the Book is Jonah ever denigrated or depicted in negative terms" ("Jonah as a Philosophical Book," 241).

[12] "Even by themselves, the series of fantastic events should be hints of the author's satiric intentions" (M. Orth, "Genre in Jonah: The Effects of Parody in the Book of Jonah," 270).

**Jonah as the target**

The target of the satire is the prophet Jonah. He was evidently
chosen as the anti-hero[13] either because of his name[14] or because
he was modelled after a prophet of the same name who occurs
elsewhere in the Bible.[15] The prophet belies his name. Jonah's full
name is יוֹנָה בֶן־אֲמִתַּי "dove, son of faithfulness" or "dove, faithful
son," but Jonah proves to be unfaithful at the first opportunity.
Holbert is no doubt correct when he observes that by choosing
this name, "the author establishes the expectation in the mind of
the reader that God has gotten the right man for the job."[16] As for
the other prophet on whom he may have been modelled, in 2 Kgs.
14:23-29 we are told that a Jonah, son of Amittai from the town of
Gath-hepher,[17] prophesied during the reign of Jeroboam II of
Israel (786-746 B.C.E.). This Jonah had predicted the expansion
of Jeroboam's kingdom: "It was he [Jeroboam II] who restored
the territory of Israel from Lebo-hamath to the sea of the Arabah,
in accordance with the promise that the Lord, the God of Israel,
had made through His servant, the prophet Jonah, son of Amittai
from Gath-hepher" (2 Kgs. 14:25). Hence this Jonah was a
nationalistic prophet, and if our Jonah was modelled after him,
then, had he been true to type, he "would have leaped at the
opportunity to call down doom upon Nineveh."[18]

---

[13] Terence E. Fretheim, *The Message of Jonah*, 67; and John D. W. Watts,
*The Books of Joel, Obadiah, Jonah, Nahum, Habakkuk and Zephaniah*, 72.
[14] Holbert, "Satire in the Book of Jonah," 63.
[15] Bruce Vawter, *Job and Jonah*, 89.
[16] "Satire in the Book of Jonah," 63-64.
[17] Gath-hepher is located in the northern territory of Zebulun (Josh. 19:13).
[18] Vawter, *Job and Jonah*, 89.

**Fantastic situations**

The swallowing and vomiting out of Jonah by the great fish constitutes the principal fantasy in the book.[19] Those readers who see a miracle in this event believe that the fish was a special one which God appointed for His particular purpose.[20] If the event is considered a miracle, then it is not a matter of concern that a fish capable of swallowing and preserving a man for three days is not known "to ichthyology or to any branch of zoology."[21] Clearly in the category of fantastic are the sudden natural occurrences of the great wind and storm while Jonah is on board the ship en route to Tarshish (1:4) and of the fierce east wind which intensifies the heat on Jonah's head while he is sitting outside of Nineveh (4:8). Also in the realm of fantastic is the sea's instantaneous calming

---

[19] For folkloristic parallels, especially the story of Heracles and the sea-monster, see Trible, *Studies in the Book of Jonah*, 134-48; Gaster, *Myth, Legend, and Custom in The Old Testament*, 653-55; and I. A. Ben-Yosef, "Jonah and the Fish as a Folk Motif," 102-17.

[20] Carl Friedrich Keil, *The Twelve Minor Prophets*, 1: 382; Bewer, *The Literature of the Old Testament*, 404; G. L. Archer, Jr., *A Survey of Old Testament Introduction*, 302-3; and J. H. Steck, "The Meaning of the Book of Jonah," 23-24.

[21] Burrows, "The Literary Category of the Book of Jonah," 82. Nor does one have to contend with details of realia of the type Burrows mentions, e.g., "it not only had a mouth and a maw sufficiently capacious to accommodate a man; it evidently did not have, or was able to restrain, the normal flow of digestive juices and the muscular activity involved in digestion. Otherwise Jonah would hardly have survived the passage back to shore, even if some kind of ventilation had been provided." Some commentators, however, firmly believe that such a fact could happen, and cite testimony of sailors who have survived Jonah-like or Pinnochio-like ordeals. See, John Ambrose Wilson, "The Sign of the Prophet Jonah," 636; G. Ch. Aalders, *The Problem of the Book of Jonah*, 6; Archer, *A Survey of Old Testament*, 302-3, n. 8; Eliyakim Ben Menachem, *Commentary on the Book of Jonah*, 5, and n. 5; and Gaster, *Myth, Legend, and Custom in The Old Testament*, 653-55.

when Jonah is thrown overboard (1:15) and the timely appearance
of the great fish to pick up Jonah immediately when he hits the
water (2:1). Although all these are natural events, and could occur
at any time, the fact of their occurrence at *precisely the right time*
makes for the fantasy. In the book, all of these events are characterized as being the work of God and, in a traditional reading of
the book, serve to underscore the message that all creatures and
creation are under God's control.

To any reader familiar with Nineveh's role in Israelite history, the idea that the Assyrians might contemplate changing their
ways at the word of a Hebrew prophet and that they would engage
in a massive repentance could only be considered as fantastic.
Some commentators, again recognizing the unnaturalness of the
event, have also termed this situation a miracle.[22] Three more
events in the book depict things happening outside of their
expected nature. First of all, there is the attribution of thought to
an inanimate object, as when during the fierce storm it is related
that "the ship thought it was going to be broken up" (וְהָאֳנִיָּה חִשְּׁבָה
לְהִשָּׁבֵר, 1:4).[23] A ship being given the faculty of thought is the
stuff of folklore and fable.[24] It fits in well in a story which has a

---

[22] According to Bewer, the repentance of the Ninevites "was a more astounding miracle than the miracle of the fish" (*The Literature of the Old Testament*, 404),

[23] Note that the verb חִשְּׁבָה, with the ship as subject, cannot be translated,
"was in danger of," or "threatened to be [broken up]," see Brichto, *Toward
a Grammar of Biblical Poetics*, 266, n. 8.

[24] Another biblical example of ships portrayed as animate is in Isa. 23:1 &
14 where, in the oracle against Tyre, ships of Tarshish are bidden to howl
("howl, O ships of Tarshish"). "Tarshish-ships" were merchant ships
capable of making long voyages, as far as Tarshish. Solomon had a Tarshish
fleet (1 Kgs. 10:22), and Jehoshaphat constructed "Tarshish-ships" for his
trips to Ophir (1 Kgs. 22:49). Edward J. Kissane's analogy of the term "East
Indiaman" which was applied to ships trading with India or the East Indies is
particularly apt (*The Book of Isaiah*, 1:260). The Isaiah references, no doubt,
are addressed to the crews of these fine merchant ships. But one cannot help
remarking on the coincidence of the occurrence of Tarshish in Jonah. Was

big fish swallowing a man and cattle donning sackcloth.[25] Secondly, there is the sudden appearance of the קִיקָיוֹן plant which
grows overnight to provide a shade for Jonah (4:6). Lastly, there
is the activity of the worm which is able to destroy the same large
plant instantaneously (4:8).

Also in the area of fantasy is the reason given for Jonah's
flight. In 4:2, Jonah purports to answer one of the major questions
of the story: what was reason for his initial refusal to prophecy to
Nineveh? The reason is not indicated to the reader at the time of
his flight[26] but is referred to here in a kind of flashback. Jonah
says that the reason he fled was that he expected God would
relent: "O Lord! Isn't this just what I said (הֲלוֹא־זֶה דְבָרִי)[27] when I
was still in my own country? That is why I fled beforehand to
Tarshish. For I know that You are a compassionate and gracious
God, slow to anger, abounding kindness, renouncing punish-

---

Jonah, who was Tarshish-bound, also in a Tarshish-ship, i.e., in a great merchant vessel?

[25] Holbert, "Satire in the Book of Jonah," 65.

[26] All that we learn from the text is that God told Jonah to condemn Nineveh
(קְרָא עַל). The usage of the phrase קְרָא עַל indicates that Jonah was *not* to
warn them into repentance but just to announce their doom (as the man of
God did against the Bethel sanctuary in our previous story in 1 Kgs. 13, or
when Isaiah announces Hezekiah's doom in 2 Kgs. 20:1-6). All sorts of
reasons have been suggested for Jonah's flight, such as he fled because he
feared for his own personal safety (lately, Jack M. Sasson, *Jonah*, 87), or
because he was depressed (Abraham D. Cohen, "The Tragedy of Jonah,"
170), or because of psychological reasons such as he was running away from
himself as well as God (Shula Abramsky, "Jonah's Alienation and Return,"
374). All these reasons are purely speculative.

[27] This formulation is found one other time in the Hebrew Bible. The
Israelites in the wilderness claimed to have said, while they were in Egypt,
that they would have preferred remaining as slaves rather than leaving Egypt,
"Is this not the very thing we told you in Egypt, saying, 'Let us be, and we
will serve the Egyptians'" (הֲלֹא־זֶה הַדָּבָר אֲשֶׁר דִּבַּרְנוּ, Exod. 14:12). But there
is no record in the text of such a statement.

ment." That is, Jonah states that he knew in advance that God, because of His merciful qualities, would have compassion on the Ninevites.[28] But Jonah's reasoning requires that a number of fantastic assumptions be made: that Jonah, a prophet from a far-away land, would be accepted and given a hearing in Nineveh; that Jonah's god, the god of Israel, would be accorded greater prestige and prominence than Nineveh's own gods, so much so that the message of this foreign god would be heeded without Jonah having to give any sign or act to support his threat;[29] that Jonah's message would be taken, not in the direct assertive manner in which it was delivered: "in forty days Nineveh shall be overthrown!" but as a warning: "this will happen if Nineveh does not repent!"; that the repentance of the Ninevites would be universal and would have behind it the full support of the king of Nineveh; that God would then automatically forgive the Ninevites and desist from the punishment he had initially threatened. Every one of these assumptions would be considered ridiculous to an Israelite listener and would thus add to the overall comic effect.

---

[28] This is in accord with the traditional Jewish explanation which holds that Jonah, being a prophet, knew in advance that Nineveh would repent and be saved (see M. Zlotowitz, *Yonah/Jonah*, 133-34). Curiously, most modern scholars accept this assumption as well. See the standard commentaries and the more specialized studies of Warshaw, "The Book of Jonah," 191; Uriel Simon, "Structure and Meaning in the Book of Jonah," 313; idem, *Jonah: Introduction and Commentary*, 74-75; Rofé, *Prophetical Stories*, 164; and Fretheim, *The Message of Jonah*, 77. Typical are the remarks of S. D. Goitein "the sailors knew the secret of God's repenting character, the Ninevites knew it, so it is only natural that the prophet should have an even more definite knowledge of it" ("Some Observations on Jonah," 72). Of recent writers only Allan John Hauser ("Jonah: In Pursuit of the Dove," 21), and Brichto (*Toward a Grammar of Biblical Poetics*, 77), question this assumption.

[29] No document yet discovered tells of any mass conversion at Nineveh. Ishtar and other native deities were still worshipped at Nineveh down to the fall of the city in 612 B.C.E. (Burrows, "The Literary Category of the Book of Jonah," 83-84).

## Distortions

Distortions consist of exaggerations or understatements. As far as exaggerations are concerned, our book has more than its fair share. Everything is either very big or very small. For example, in order to achieve His purposes, God uses the greatest of creatures, a large fish, and the smallest of creatures, a worm.[30] As for big items, the word גָּדוֹל 'big' 'great' is a key word in the story which is used 14 times: Everything in the story is big: the city (1:2; 3:2; 3:3; 4:11), the wind (1:4), the storm (1:4, 12) the fear of the sailors (1:10, 16), the fish (2:1), Jonah's distress (4:1), Jonah's joy (4:6). Also, גָּדוֹל is twice used as a noun; the city's repentance is done by "great (גָּדוֹל) and small alike" (3:5); the fasting decree is declared by the king of Nineveh and his "grandees" (גְּדוֹל, 3:7). Finally, as a verb, the root גדל occurs in God's final speech when God points out that Jonah did not 'grow' (lit. "make great," גִדַּלְתּוֹ) the קִיקָיוֹן-plant (4:10).

The city of Nineveh is described as being remarkably big. Four times the epithet עִיר גְּדוֹלָה "big city" is applied to it.[31] Once it is called an עִיר־גְּדוֹלָה לֵאלֹהִים "an exceptionally big city" (3:3). The addition of לֵאלֹהִים to the epithet magnifies the city even more. It is literally, "a big city to the gods (or to God)." The force of לֵאלֹהִים may be a form of the superlative[32] "a divinely big

---

[30] D. F. Rauber, "Jonah--The Prophet as Schlemiel," 35.

[31] Vv. 1:2; 3:2; 3:3; 4:11. The same epithet is used in the genealogical list of Genesis 10:11-12 either to collectively describe the four cities Rehoboth-Ir, Calah, Resen, and Nineveh, or just to describe one of them. H. L. Ginsberg was of the opinion that any of these four cities "would have served the writer's purpose equally well" ("Introduction to Jonah," 116). It was chosen by a later (perhaps 6th century) author to be a suitable foil for Jonah because it was thought to be the largest of the Mesopotamian cities of its time (8th century), and it represents, exactly as it is portrayed, a type of a sinful city in the East.

[32] D. Winton Thomas, "A Consideration of Some Unusual Ways of Expressing the Superlative in Hebrew," 210-6.

city" as in our colloquial "a godalmighty big city"[33] or a
"godawfully big city."[34] In addition, as a sign of its enormity, it is
said that Nineveh's population consisted of 120,000 people "who
do not know their right hand from their left" (4:11). The meaning
of this phrase has been variously interpreted. Some believe it is an
idiom for lack of knowledge or moral perception,[35] in which case
it would be a derogatory reference to the total population of the
city,[36] while others think it signifies only the 'children',[37] in which
case the actual population would have been more than 120,000.[38]
Sasson[39] has recently advanced a highly original interpretation of
the phrase. Nineveh was so large in size, so teeming with life, that
the inhabitants literally did not know who was living on the right
and left of them, that is, they did not know who their neighbors
were. Support for Sasson's theory may be found in Akkadian,
where the expression "to the right and the left" (*kīma imitti u*

---

[33] John Day, "The Book of Jonah," 34.
[34] Vawter, *Job and Jonah*, 105.
[35] "The idea is that until a certain age moral ignorance is assumed. Little
children don't know the difference, just as they don't know the difference
between their right hand and their left hand. Therefore they are not morally
responsible" (David Noel Freedman, "Did God Play a Dirty Trick on Jonah
at the End?" 31). See also Douglas Stuart, *Hosea-Jonah*, 507; Desmond
Alexander, *Jonah*, 130; and David Daube, "Jonah: A Reminiscence," 37.
[36] R. E. Clements, "The Purpose of the Book of Jonah," 18.
[37] On the basis of texts such as Deuteronomy 1:39 (children not knowing
good and evil) and Isaiah 7:16, which foretells when Israel and Syria will be
destroyed by Assyria. Sooner than it will take an infant born to a young
woman today to reach an age of discrimination (to understand between right
and wrong), that is, in a matter of a few years, very soon. See Rashi and
Kimḥi, *Miqra'ot Gedolot, ad loc*; and Julius A. Bewer, *A Critical and
Exegetical Commentary on Jonah*, 64.
[38] The population numbers have been speculated at 300,000 (Sasson, *Jonah*,
311-12) and even twice that amount (Archer, *A Survey of Old Testament*,
299; and Bewer, *Commentary on Jonah*, 64).
[39] *Jonah*, 315.

*šumēli*) is used for "neighbors to the right and left."[40] In any event, the figure given of 120,000 seems to be another of the hyperbolic numerical expressions in the book, indicating "a teeming population."[41]

A further exaggeration is that Jonah is said to be in the belly of the great fish for "three days and three nights." Elsewhere in the Bible, the expression "three days" may by itself indicate either a long period of time,[42] or a shorter time span, that is, three specific days.[43] However, when the phrase "three nights" is added to the "three days," as it is here, then it always indicates a long period of time.[44] So Jonah was in the big fish a very long time.[45]

Finally, Jonah's brief oracle is a remarkable understatement. Its five Hebrew words, עוֹד אַרְבָּעִים יוֹם וְנִינְוֵה נֶהְפָּכֶת "in forty days Nineveh will be overthrown" constitute the briefest prophetic denunciation on record.[46] This short oracle also produced the

---

[40] See *CAD*, *I*, 123.

[41] Leslie C. Allen, *The Books of Joel, Obadiah, Jonah and Micah*, 234.

[42] E.g., Josh. 2:16 and 2 Chr. 20:25. Cf., English usage "for days."

[43] E.g., Gen. 40:13, "within three days [= within a little while], Pharaoh will pardon you"; and Gen. 40:19 ("will remove your head"); Joshua 1:11 ("within three days [= within a few days], we will cross over the Jordan"; In 1 Kgs. 12:5, Rehoboam tells the Northerners to come back "within three days" = after a few days. Other examples are in 2 Sam. 20:4; 2 Kgs. 20:8; Hos. 6:2; Ezra 8:32; & Neh. 2:11.

[44] As in 1 Sam. 30:12 and Esth. 4:16. See J. H. Bauer, "Drei Tage," 356.

[45] Watts comments that "since three days and three nights indicate a very long period of time, it heightens the picture of the great power of God who can save his disobedient messenger even **after** three days and three nights" (*The Books of Joel, Obadiah, Jonah*, 83). George M. Landes suggests that the phrase "three days and three nights" represents an ancient Near Eastern motif referring to the time it takes to reach the Nether World ("The 'Three Days and Three Night' Motif in Jonah 2:1," 449).

[46] Rauber, "Jonah--The Prophet as Schlemiel," 33. As a comparison, Micah's famous short oracle against Jerusalem (Mic. 3:12), recalled in Jer. 26:18, "Zion shall be plowed as a field, and Jerusalem shall become heaps of ruins, and the Temple Mount a shrine in the woods" has ten Hebrew words.

greatest response. For upon its delivery, there was a massive repentance of the great and small alike (3:5). Not only did the people fast and cover themselves with sackcloth, but they cried mightily to God (3:8). Never before had a prophet been so successful and produced so great and so immediate an effect.[47]

## Irony

As we have previously mentioned,[48] irony is perhaps the most sophisticated weapon at the disposal of a satirist, and it is found in abundance in the book of Jonah. It is not our intention to be comprehensive and list every irony that has been suggested. In our initial discussion on irony we stated that it is basically interpretative, depending on the stance of the reader, and so often exists only in "the eye of the beholder."[49] Therefore, other readers, with different interpretations, have adduced different examples of irony in the book.[50] Also, we do not discuss here those ironies which are also parodic, since they will be considered below in our section on parody. For convenience of reference, we discuss our examples according to the order of their occurrence in the text.

One of the clues that a work is ironic is the names or epithets given to its characters.[51] Jonah's name, יוֹנָה בֶן־אֲמִתַּי "dove, son of faithfulness," or "dove, faithful son," admits of much irony because, in the story, the prophet belies his name. Of the various traits of the dove described in the Bible,[52] two are ironic when

---

[47] Simon, "Structure and Meaning," 311. See also the comments of John A. Miles, "Jonah was the most successful, if not the only successful, prophet in history" ("Laughing at the Bible: Jonah as Parody," 177), and R. E. Murphy, "in spite of himself Jonah appears to be the most successful missionary of all time" ("The Book of Jonah," 482).

[48] P. 13 above.

[49] See p. 16 above.

[50] For example, the lists of ironies assembled by Good, (*Irony In The Old Testament*, 39-55), and by Fretheim, (*The Message of Jonah*, 53-54), differ considerably from our own.

[51] Booth, *A Rhetoric of Irony*, 53.

applied to Jonah. If one of the characteristics of a dove is to soar aloft, Jonah, ironically, goes in a downwards direction. He first goes down to Joppa (וַיֵּרֶד, 1:3). Then he goes down into the ship (וַיֵּרֶד, 1:3). Next he descends to the hold of the ship (יָרַד, 1:5), and sleeps.[53] In the fish, Jonah is swallowed into the lowest part of the fish's belly (2:2) and, in his prayer, he declares that he has descended (יָרַדְתִּי, 2:7) to the "base of the mountains," the bottom of the cosmos.[54] If one of the characteristics of a dove is fidelity (we recall Noah's dove who performs his duty in Gen. 8:8-12), Jonah proves to be unfaithful at the first opportunity. He was commanded by God to get up (קוּם, 1:2) and go (לֵךְ, 1:2) but instead gets up (וַיָּקָם, 1:3) and flees (לִבְרֹחַ, 1:3). Hence the second part of Jonah's name, בֶּן־אֲמִתַּי "faithful son" must be considered as ironic.[55]

Jonah's act of fleeing God's commission to Nineveh (1:2) is ironic because it creates "a condition opposite to what might natu-

---

[52] Such as passivity, expressed through mourning or plaintive cooing (Isa. 38:14; 59:11; Nah. 2:7; Hos. 11:11), foolishness (Hos. 7:11), loyalty to its mate, and beauty (Cant. 2:14; 5:2; 6:9). In Ps. 55:6, Jer. 48:28, and Ezek. 7:16, the dove connotes flight from a foe or danger. For further discussion, see André Lacocque and Pierre-Emmanuel Lacocque, *The Jonah Complex*, 6-7. Hauser believes that 'flight' and 'passivity' characterize Jonah. He sees the irony as one of Jonah being portrayed, at the beginning and middle of the story, as a dove ('passive' and then 'obedient'), but turning out, at the end of the story, to be the opposite ('wrathful') ("Jonah: In Pursuit of the Dove," 21-37.

[53] The verb used is וַיֵּרְדַם, perhaps a word play that reinforces the ירד motif (James S. Ackerman, "Satire and Symbolism in the Song of Jonah," 231).

[54] George M. Landes has pointed out that the motif of descent is continued in the psalm to describe Jonah's descent to the belly of Sheol ("The Kerygma of the Book of Jonah: The Contextual Interpretation of the Jonah Psalm," 25). Jonathan Magonet has shown that the psalm is constructed to indicate a 'geographical' exactitude indicating a consecutive descent from "streams and floods" and "breakers and wavers" down to "the base of the mountains" and the "bars of the earth" (*Form and Meaning*, 17, 40). See also, Holbert, "Satire in the Book of Jonah," 72.

[55] Good, *Irony In The Old Testament*, 42.

rally be expected"[56] (obedience). The terminology employed is also ironic. Jonah is said to flee *from* the Lord's presence (מִלִּפְנֵי יְהוָה).[57] But it was *to* this very presence (לְפָנַי, 1:2) that the wickedness of Nineveh had come in the first place. His attempt to go to Tarshish (1:3) of all places is also ironic. But not every reader may perceive it as such. Here a knowledge of the geography involved helps illuminate the irony. Nineveh, to where God commands Jonah to go preach, is located in Mesopotamia, *in the east*. Jonah, however, flees to Tarshish which, whether it is to be identified with Tartessus in Spain[58] or not, must have been located somewhere *in the west* since Jonah has to reach it by ship starting from the port of Joppa in the eastern Mediterranean. Had he fled northwards or southwards, then the irony would not be as effective; but the fact that Jonah fled in the polar opposite direction to Nineveh creates the irony. God commands Jonah to go east (the expected direction), but he goes to the west (not only the unexpected, but the opposite direction).

The occurrence of the great wind and the big storm (1:4), the first of the natural forces sent by God to do his bidding, may be seen to constitute a situational irony. The irony arises here

---

[56] See p. 14 above.

[57] Holbert, "Satire in the Book of Jonah," 64. The phrase מִלִּפְנֵי יְהוָה means literally "from the face of Yahweh" and is used solely in connection with prophets. A fleeing מִלִּפְנֵי יְהוָה means a rejection of the prophetic call just as standing לְפָנָיו "before His face" indicates prophetic receptivity as related with Elijah (1 Kgs. 17:1; 18:15), Elisha (2 Kgs. 3:14; 5:16), and Jeremiah (Jer. 15:19). Jonah, in fleeing "from the face of Yahweh" rejects his call (Trible, *Studies in the Book of Jonah*, 267; Cohen, "The Tragedy of Jonah," 170; and Ben Menachem, *Commentary on the Book of Jonah*, 5). For recent arguments against the notion that Yahweh's power was confined to Israel's borders, or that Jonah was fleeing from Yahweh's cultic presence (so Landes, "The Kerygma of the Book of Jonah," 19-20; and Fretheim, *The Message of Jonah*, 81), see Brichto, *Toward a Grammar of Biblical Poetics*, 68-69, 265-66, n. 6.

[58] For speculations on the location of Tarshish, see Sasson, *Jonah*, 79.

because, in contrast to the prophet's refusal to serve, these forces of nature perform their missions "like clockwork."[59] Magonet also notes the irony that God, as he does elsewhere, 'answers' Jonah in his own language. Just as Jonah fled by sea, so God responds by means of a storm at sea.[60]

The sailors' response to their predicament (1:5) ironically resembles the storm's origin. The storm was caused by Yahweh casting (הֵטִיל) a mighty wind at (אֶל) the sea;[61] In response, the sailors fling (וַיָּטִלוּ) the ship's cargo at (אֶל) the sea to lighten its load.[62] Later Jonah suggests that the sailors cast him (הֲטִילֻנִי) into (אֶל) the sea (1:12), and they oblige by casting (וַיְטִלֻהוּ) him into (אֶל) the sea (1:15). It is ironic that the non-Israelite sailors pray to their gods, yet the prophet of God, who ought to be praying and interceding with God, is sleeping![63] Jonah's sleep is described by the verb רָדַם (וַיֵּרָדַם). But elsewhere in the Bible this verb רָדַם is only used in connection with divinely sent or involuntary sleep.[64] Hence it is ironic that God, who sent the storm presumably to persuade Jonah to fulfill his prophetic assignment, now puts him into a deep sleep.

It is ironic that the one who suggests prayer to Jonah, a Hebrew prophet, is a non-Israelite (1:5).[65] As Trible has

---

[59] Brichto, *Toward a Grammar of Biblical Poetics*, 82.

[60] Magonet, *Form and Meaning*, 58.

[61] Holbert here uses a baseball analogy for good effect, "the preposition אֶל provides the vivid picture here of God on the 'mound of heaven' throwing a mighty wind at the sea which results, upon impact, in a 'great tempest'" ("Satire in the Book of Jonah," 79, n. 32).

[62] Ibid., 65. Ratner, acutely observes that the sailors do not rely upon prayers alone. By jettisoning whatever unnecessary ballast they can, they express "their mild cynicism about placing full trust in often deaf and capricious gods" ("Jonah, The Runaway Servant," 298).

[63] Shula Abramsky notes that since Jonah, as he himself acknowledges, was responsible for the storm, there would be no point in *his* praying to God ("About Casting Lots in Order to Catch a Sinner," 376).

[64] T. H. McAlpine, *Sleep, Divine and Human in the Old Testament*, 56-59.

[65] Murphy, "The Book of Jonah," 481.

observed, "the disobedient prophet, who has turned away from his
God, is here urged by the pagan captain to call upon his god."[66]
The captain uses the same language that God did. God said
קוּם...וּקְרָא 'up!'...'call!' (1:2), and the captain says קוּם קְרָא 'up!'
'call!' It is a non-Israelite who has to command Jonah to do his
duty, to be true to his calling.[67] It is also ironic that it is the non-
Israelite sailors who successfully utilize one of Israel's oracular
methods (1:7), considered to reflect divine sanction,[68] to identify
Jonah as the culprit.[69] But, despite the fact that casting of lots is a
well-known technique for apprehending wrongdoers, its use in the
story at this point is slightly *incongruous*. Why would the sailors
think that their vessel is the only vessel caught up in the gale, and
that the storm has been caused by one of their number?[70] The
incongruity was noted in the Midrash which recorded a tradition
that Jonah's ship was the only one that suffered the storm: "the
tempest was directed only against Jonah's ship. The crew could
see other ships to their right and left plying to and fro peacefully
through the tranquility of the sea."[71]

Irony has been noted in the fact that the sailors ask too many
questions of Jonah (1:8), and at the wrong time. In the midst of a
life-threatening storm they request what seems to be a short
autobiography of Jonah:[72] "Tell us, what is your business. Where
have you come from? What is your country, and of what people
are you?" (1:8).[73] It is ironic that the sailors ask Jonah, the very

---

66 *Studies in the Book of Jonah*, 254.
67 Holbert, "Satire in the Book of Jonah," 66.
68 Zlotowitz, *Yonah/Jonah*, 92.
69 For a comparison with the two other biblical cases (with Achan in Josh.
7:16-18; with Jonathan in 1 Sam. 14:42-43) where lots are used to detect
wrongdoers, see Abramsky, "About Casting Lots in Order to Catch a Sinner," 231-66.
70 Zlotowitz, *Jonah/Yonah*, 92; and Brichto, *Toward a Grammar of Biblical
Poetics*, 69.
71 See Zlotowitz, Ibid (citing *Pirqe R. El.*).
72 Good, *Irony In The Old Testament*, 44-45.
73 Brichto suggests that the normal order of questioning has been reversed for

person who is the cause of the storm, what the remedy might be for allaying the storm (1:11).[74] It is ironic that the remedy Jonah chooses to placate the storm, namely, human sacrifice of himself (1:12), is one which is completely alien to Israel's religious philosophy.[75] It is further ironic that Jonah, who acknowledges being the cause of the sailors' distress, does not offer to throw himself into the water to alleviate their torment, only that the sailors should do it. Good has noted the linguistic irony that Jonah's offer to be thrown into the sea (וַהֲטִילֻנִי אֶל־הַיָּם "hurl me at the sea") contains the same language used to describe how God brought the storm (הֵטִיל...אֶל־הַיָּם, 1:4).[76]

The sailors do everything in their power to save the ship. They jettison the cargo, propitiate their gods, and finally attempt to row the ship to shore (1:13). But here lies an incongruity. As noted by Sasson, steering a ship to shore in the midst of a storm is considered by seasoned sailors to be a foolish, even a suicidal enterprise. Ancient manuals on sea travel advise to the contrary that "a ship must at all costs not be driven to the coastline where it will surely wreck."[77] There is also the irony here in the efforts of the sailors' doing everything possible to save the Hebrew prophet,

---

effect. The correct order should have been: "Who are you (that is, what people are you?), where do you come from, and what brings you aboard our ship (= what is your business)." In the text, the business question is first, and this is the only question that Jonah answers: he is an עִבְרִי "an indentured servant" of a god (the Lord), that is his business (*Toward a Grammar of Biblical Poetics*, 70-71).

[74] Zlotowitz, *Yonah/Jonah*, 98; and Holbert, "Satire in the Book of Jonah," 68.

[75] Vawter, *Job and Jonah*, 93; "Jonah, like the cargo, is to be jettisoned" (Murphy, "The Book of Jonah," 481). Trible notes an ironic act of nobility on Jonah's part: "the prophet who is running away from a command to announce destruction to the Gentiles here offers to sacrifice his own life that the others in the boat might be saved from the storm" (*Studies in the Book of Jonah*, 79-80).

[76] *Irony In The Old Testament*, 45.

[77] *Jonah*, 142, & n. 20.

one whose irresponsibility has endangered them.[78] Furthermore, it is ironic that God's demand to proclaim (קְרָא, 1:2), which was denied by his prophet, is picked up by the non-Israelite sailors (וַיִּקְרְאוּ אֶל־יְהוָה "they cried out to the Lord" 1:14). They, rather than the prophet of God, make the statement that the Lord has brought this about through His will.[79]

The second chapter begins with the irony that Jonah, who wanted to die, does not. He is saved by God through the great fish. Then follows a long series of ironies in Jonah's prayer (2:2-10). This prayer is, in fact, a psalm made up of familiar verses which can be found elsewhere in the Psalter.[80] It is usually categorized as a psalm of thanksgiving,[81] or a psalm of praise.[82]

---

[78] According to Chayim D. Rabinowitz, the sailors' reluctance to throw Jonah overboard was based on a practical consideration. Having been informed that God's wrath resulted from Jonah's refusal to fulfill God's mission to Nineveh, the sailors reasoned that the Divine fury would only be increased--and turned against them--if they caused Jonah to drown, since, in effect, the mission would then definitely go unfulfilled (*The Haftarot Arranged According to the Books of the Prophets*, 2: 426). Somewhat similar is the observation of Landes, "the reason the sailors row to shore is they realize, contrary to Jonah's suggestion to throw him overboard, that what is demanded is, not Jonah's death, but that he be brought back home where he can obey his divine commission" ("The Kerygma of the Book of Jonah," 23, n. 63).

[79] Holbert, "Satire in the Book of Jonah," 69.

[80] A good comparison may be found in Magonet, *Form and Meaning*, 44-54. Most commentaries on the book illustrate the correspondences. See Sasson's *Jonah*, 168-201. It is still a matter of debate among scholars as to whether the psalm is original or not. For an up-to-date survey of the question, see Day, "The Book of Jonah," 40-42; and Athalya Brenner, "Jonah's Poem Out of and Within its Context," 183-92.

[81] According to A. Lacocque and P.-E. Lacocque, it has the same structure as a thanksgiving psalm, namely: (1) a short introduction expressing the intent of showing gratitude (v. 2); (2) exposition of the psalmist's experience (vv. 4-7a); (3) a prayer (vv. 3 & 8); (4) statement of deliverance (v. 7b); (5) a vow to offer thanksgiving sacrifices (v. 10) (*Jonah: A Psycho-Religious Approach to the Prophet*, 98). Because of the water imagery it is thought that the psalm was originally composed as a thanksgiving for deliverance from

But a psalm of thanksgiving would not only seem to be out of character for Jonah,[83] it would also be inappropriate before his rescue.[84] Jonah is portrayed as reciting the psalm while in the belly of the fish, hence *before* God commands his safe return to dry land. His condition then does not warrant a hymn of praise, since he is still presumably in a situation of personal distress and danger.[85] Hence Jonah's prayer, being a psalm of thanksgiving, instead of an expected psalm of lament, may be considered ironic.[86]

As has often been pointed out, there are a number of details in the psalm which do not correspond to Jonah's condition:[87] (1)

---

shipwreck, or from drowning (see Trible, *Studies in the Book of Jonah*, 77).

[82] Landes, "The Kerygma of the Book of Jonah," 4, 7.

[83] So much so that Vawter thinks that "truly, Jonah is being ridiculed here as before and in what follows" (*Job and Jonah*, 98).

[84] See Bickerman, *Four Strange Books of the Bible*, 12; Miles, "Laughing at the Bible," 173; and Arnold J. Band, "Swallowing Jonah: The Eclipse of Parody," 187. Nevertheless, a number of scholars, (e.g., Goitein, "Some Observations on Jonah," 69; Landes, "The Kerygma of the Book of Jonah," 13; and Adele Berlin, "A Rejoinder to John A. Miles Jr., With Some Observations on the Nature of Prophecy," 228), believe that the psalm is appropriate in context, because Jonah was indeed saved from the stormy sea. It is true that the fish does save Jonah from drowning, but from Jonah's point of view his swallowing by the fish "was surely a case of 'out of the frying pan into the fire'--he had no certainty that he was ever going to get out of the fish" (Day, "The Book of Jonah," 40).

[85] Different, however, are the views of Landes and Berlin. According to Landes, the fish is simply a beneficent device for returning Jonah back to shore so that he may reassume the commission he had previously abandoned ("The Kerygma of the Book of Jonah," 10-13). While Berlin believes that the fish is "a sort of holding station" until he consents to follow divine orders. Jonah "has been spared but he is God's prisoner" ("A Rejoinder to John A. Miles Jr.," 228).

[86] Good, *Irony In The Old Testament*, 54; and Magonet, *Form and Meaning*, 52-53.

[87] In her dissertation, Trible believed that the psalm is out of place in terms of style and vocabulary (there are not as many "late forms" in the psalm as in the narrative) and it damages the symmetry of the book (*Studies in the*

The Psalm describes one who has escaped drowning in the
water,[88] not one suffering incarceration in the belly of a fish;[89] (2)
Jonah states that it is the Lord who cast him into the depth of the
seas (2:4) but, in the previous chapter, it was the sailors who
threw him into the waters (1:15);[90] (3) In the psalm, Jonah describes his present separation from God as one who is "driven
away" from God's sight and yearning to gaze upon God's holy
temple (2:5). Not only does the reference to the temple seem to be
strange in this oceanic setting,[91] but we know from chapter one
that Jonah fled from God on his own volition (1:2). Jonah is here
doing a complete *volte face*, yearning for the very presence he has
just fled.[92] It is ironic that the psalm commences with Jonah stat-
ing that "I have called" (קָרָאתִי), utilizing the very verb קְרָא,
'proclaim', used by God to Jonah (1:2). But instead of proclaim-
ing God's message to others, Jonah has called to God only for
himself in his distress.[93] It is also ironic that the psalm concludes

---

*Book of Jonah*, 77-82). But in her latest book (1994) she is not so definitive
(*Rhetorical Criticism*), 160-62.

[88] There are some scholars (such as Goitein, "Some Observations on Jonah,"
69, and Berlin, "A Rejoinder to John A. Miles Jr.," 228), who believe that
escaping from drowning is the very circumstance which prompts Jonah's
psalm. But others, like Trible believe that "no time is allowed in the prose
narrative for him to experience the conditions of drowning so elaborately
depicted in the psalm" (*Studies in the Book of Jonah*, 78).

[89] "There is not a single reference in the Psalm to Jonah's abode in the belly
of the fish. It speaks of weeds which wrap around one's head at the bottom
of the sea but nothing of the conditions of life inside a fish" (Trible, *Studies
in the Book of Jonah*, 78).

[90] Trible, *Rhetorical Criticism*, 160. Landes believes that the incongruity can
be solved by assuming that the sailors were just human instruments executing
the divine will ("The Kerygma of the Book of Jonah," 24).

[91] Trible, *Studies in the Book of Jonah*, 79; and Brichto, *Toward a Grammar
of Biblical Poetics*, 73. According to Holbert, the temple is the symbol of
God's presence ("Satire in the Book of Jonah," 72).

[92] Landes, "The Kerygma of the Book of Jonah," 4.

[93] Holbert, "Satire in the Book of Jonah," 71.

with Jonah's promise to do what the non-Israelite sailors have
already done (1:16), to sacrifice to God (2:10). Just as the sailors
had vowed vows so Jonah, in turn, promises to *fulfill* (אֲשַׁלֵּמָה) his
vows (2:10).[94]

There are a number of ironies involving Jonah at Nineveh.
Jonah's pronouncement of destruction for Nineveh, "forty days
more and Nineveh shall be overthrown" (3:4) is an example, not
of verbal irony, since Jonah believes his words are true, but of
situational irony. The irony is occasioned after Nineveh's
delivery, for his words effect their opposite. They are received by
the Ninevites as a call to repentance, and lead to salvation for the
city.[95] If, as is most likely, the book is written after the fall of
Nineveh (post 612 B.C.E.),[96] then the book's readers would be
well aware that Nineveh was indeed overthrown,[97] and so we
would have a dramatic irony of the reader knowing more than
Jonah did.[98] The foreign city's immediate acceptance of God's
word (3:5) stands in ironic contrast with the prophet of God's
instantaneous rejection of His command at the beginning of the
story. Brichto notices the irony of the situation that the Ninevites
immediately accepted the word of God which came to them
indirectly, but Jonah disregarded the word of God which came to

---

[94] For a more complete discussion of ironies in the psalm, see Ackerman,
"Satire and Symbolism in the Song of Jonah," 222-24.

[95] Trible, *Studies in the Book of Jonah*, 255, 269.

[96] See chapter eight below. Nineveh need not be equated with the capital of
the Assyrian Empire which fell in the 6th century. For no author writing in
the 6th century or later could expect his readers to take very seriously a story
which speaks about Nineveh's salvation when the city was already lying in
ruins. But there are some commentators such as B. D. Eerdmans who believe
that "if the story shall have any sense Nineveh must exist" (*The Religion of
Israel*, 176).

[97] David F. Payne, "Jonah from the Perspective of its Audience," 7; Day,
"The Book of Jonah," 46.

[98] Orth, "Genre in Jonah," 270. Cf., Magonet "to the ironies of the book
itself is added the irony of history" (*Form and Meaning*, 111).

him directly.[99] Lastly, in this episode, it is ironic that it is the Ninevites, not the prophet of God from whom one would expect it, who suggest fasting and prayer (3:5).

The last chapter opens with an ironic situtation. Just at the moment when God turns aside from His anger, Jonah expresses his (4:1).[100] It is extremely ironic that Jonah, following such an unprecedented successful response to his message, is so upset that he prays for death.[101] The reason Jonah gives as to why he refused God's commission and fled is ironic because of the hubris implied in it. He says he fled because he knew God is merciful. The irony is that Jonah cites God's merciful qualities as an excuse for his own disobedient behavior![102] Jonah's statement is ironic because of its placement.[103] It is placed between Jonah's expression of displeasure and anger in verse one ("this displeased Jonah greatly, and he was grieved" 4:1) and his request to die in verse three ("take my life, for I would rather die than live"). There is clearly a disjunction between his feeling of anger, his wish to die, and his positive statement about God's mercy.[104] Jonah uses the credo about God's mercy to express his disagreement with God. Here lies the irony, for Jonah is placed in a position that to those who are unaware of the irony is almost blasphemous:[105] he reproaches

---

[99] Brichto, *Toward a Grammar of Biblical Poetics*, 75.

[100] Allen, *The Books of Joel, Obadiah, Jonah and Micah*, 227; and Fretheim, *The Message of Jonah*, 53, 122.

[101] Terrence E. Fretheim, "Jonah and Theodicy," 233; and Brichto, *Toward a Grammar of Biblical Poetics*, 77.

[102] See the remarks of Burrows, "Jonah uses the exalted conception of God's nature to explain a course of conduct quite inconsistent with it" ("The Literary Category of The Book of Jonah," 99), and Good, "Jonah speaks the pious and well-worn words, but he thoroughly disapproves of their being true" (*Irony In The Old Testament*, 50).

[103] For placement as an indicator of irony, see Muecke, *The Compass of Irony*, 77.

[104] As noted already by Cohen, "The Tragedy of Jonah," 171-72.

[105] For example, Cohen states that "for Jonah to express the formula in its full and classical form, and then disagree with it...would be tantamount to a moral blasphemy that no prophet could rightfully maintain, and that no Bibli-

God for acting in a compassionate manner.[106] The narrator has created an absurd situation whereby he has a Hebrew prophet being at odds with one of the fundamental principles of Hebrew theology: God's mercy. For Jonah, God is *too* merciful,[107] and his unhappiness over this situation is so grievous that he yearns for death.[108] Unlike a normal Israelite prophet, who does not want the fulfillment of his prophecy of doom, and would be pleased by a people's repentance, Jonah is displeased by the relenting of God.[109]

The curious picture of Jonah's sitting outside the city of Nineveh lends itself to a considerable number of ironies. It is ironic that, whereas in the beginning of the book Jonah fled God's commission and refused to go to Nineveh here, after delivering God's message, he refuses to leave (4:5).[110] It is ironic that, whereas the king of Nineveh had sat in ashes (in discomfort) inside the city hoping it would be spared, Jonah sits in the shade (in comfort) outside the city, hoping it will be destroyed.[111] The

---

cal author could possibly ascribe to a Hebrew prophet" (Ibid., 165). Similarly, M. Pelli remarks, "it is inconceivable that the author would be insensitive to the unique situation he created, or that he would utilize it to portray a stupid prophet" (M. Pelli, "The Literary Art of Jonah," 22).

[106] Fretheim, trying to minimize the fact that Jonah's prayer "might appear somewhat abrasive in our eyes," states (presumably without tongue in cheek!) that "such honesty is typical of Israelite piety" (*The Message of Jonah*, 32). He further reduces the impact of Jonah's statement by comparing Jonah to Tevye in *Fiddler on the Roof*, "He tells it to God just as it is. He lets God know exactly what he is thinking."

[107] Magonet, *Form and Meaning*, 52; Ackerman comments that, according to Jonah, "God is too full of *ḥesed* and compassion. Jonah perceives this as inappropriate in a world which, according to covenant tradition, is to be ruled on the principle of justice" ("Satire and Symbolism in The Song of Jonah," 225).

[108] Robert C. Dentan, "The Literary Affinities of Exodus xxxiv 6f," 39.

[109] Lacocque and Lacocque, *The Jonah Complex*, 30.

[110] Simon, "Structure and Meaning in the Book of Jonah," 301.

[111] Magonet, *Form and Meaning*, 20, 96.

problem with Jonah's going out from the city at this point of the narrative "until he should see what happened to the city" (4:5) is that Nineveh's fate has already been decided. The Ninevites have repented and God has decided not to destroy the city. It is this very decision against which Jonah reacts with his outburst against God and his wish to die. Since Jonah already knows what has happened to the city there is no need for him to exit it "until he should see what happened to the city." As Trible has noted, "there is nothing in the remainder of the story (4:6-11) to suggest anything further is happening in the city."[112] So the description of Jonah exiting the city and waiting for something to happen to it is quite incongruous.[113]

In verse five it is stated that Jonah made for himself a booth (סֻכָּה) and sat under its shade. However, in verse six it is related that the Lord provided a plant (קִיקָיוֹן) "to provide shade for his head and save him from his discomfort." Jonah's booth disappears from the narrative and, in the following verses, we are told that Jonah has only this plant to rely on for shade. It is the appearance of this plant which is the cause of much joy to Jonah and, correspondingly, its sudden destruction causes Jonah so much distress that he longs for death. It is the destruction of this plant that forms the centerpiece of God's symbolic lesson to Jonah at the end of the book. Since it is not part of the ensuing story, the setting up of Jonah's booth seems to be yet another incongruity in the book.[114]

---

[112] Trible, *Studies in the Book of Jonah*, 92.

[113] It is usually suggested that there was an error in the transmission of the text and that this verse should belong after Jonah delivers the oracle to Nineveh (3:4). See N. Lohfink, "Jona ging zur Stadt hinaus (Jona 4,5)," 200; and Alfred Jepsen, "Anmerkungen zum Buche Jona," 297. Trible has collected the arguments made by those who attempt to defend the text such as the one that Jonah hopes that the city will yet be destroyed because he does not think the repentance of the Ninevites is genuine, or because he thinks that Yahweh will again change his mind and destroy the city (*Studies in the Book of Jonah*, 97-99).

[114] Magonet proposes an interesting solution. Jonah and God respond to each other "measure for measure." Jonah's response to God's question in 4:4 is

The plant itself provides the basis for the following ironies. It is ironic that Jonah rejoices over his own deliverance (the plant providing a gift of shade), whereas he apparently expressed great distress over Nineveh's deliverance.[115] When the plant perishes, Jonah wants to die (4:8). Jonah first wanted to die because of what he perceived as God's apparent lack of justice (4:2), it is ironic that he now wants to die because of what he perceives as God's apparent lack of mercy (4:8).[116] There is great sarcasm in God's second question to Jonah (4:9).[117] In the first question, which Jonah did not answer, "are you that deeply grieved?" (4:4), God inquired about Jonah's feelings with regard to the salvation of Nineveh. In the second question he asks about Jonah's feelings towards the plant, "are you that deeply grieved about the plant?" The addition of the object "about the plant" is quite sarcastic for the implication is: "surely you can not be as deeply grieved over a mere plant as you were over a city!" Jonah's answer serves to highlight the sarcasm in God's question. He is willing to die because of the plant! "Yes, so deeply that I want to die," a response which exhibits an unbelievable lack of proportion. Jonah is willing to die for a mere plant!

God's final speech (4:10-11) elaborates on his previous ironic question. It is also phrased rhetorically,[118] and ironically notes that

---

not a reply in words, but in deeds: he makes a סֻכָּה, indicating "a general concern for his comfort." God, in turn, replies by a deed by providing the קִיקָיוֹן plant. Symbolically God is saying: You are more concerned with your comfort than the destruction of a city full of people--very well, let us see what the implications of our concern are. Jonah then goes on to experience both the comfort which makes him rejoice, and the pain of destruction when the gourd withers (*Form and Meaning*, 58).

[115] Fretheim, "Jonah and Theodicy," 233.

[116] Gabriël H. Cohn, *Das Buch Jona*, 87-88; and N. Aviezer, "The Book of Jonah: An Ethical Confrontation between God and Prophet," 14.

[117] Ehrlich, *Randglossen zur Hebräischen Bibel*, 270; Magonet, *Form and Meaning*, 33; and Simon, "Structure and Meaning in the Book of Job," 315; idem *Jonah* 84.

[118] For a rhetorical question being a characteristic of irony, see Muecke, *The Compass of Irony*, 69. A rhetorical question may be used ironically since,

Jonah had compassion for a plant, with which he had no ties (he did not work for it and did not grow it), but not for Nineveh with its large population of tens of thousands of people. Even the cattle, introduced anticlimatically, are worth more than the plant.[119] Hence the narrator's point: the vegetable world can in no way be equated with the animal world. The speech is set in the form of an *a fortiori* argument that is, one making an analogy between a minor premise and a major one. Jonah pitied (חָסְתָּ),[120] the plant which he *did not* cultivate; should God then not pity (אָחוּס) the thousands of people and animals in the city of Nineveh [which He *did* cultivate]. Since Jonah pitied the plant, which he had neither created nor nourished, and which came and went instantly, then certainly God should pity Nineveh [because he has in fact created them]. The speech produces the following incongruities.

There is a disjunction between the point of the lesson concerning the Ninevites as related here and what is related concerning the Ninevites in the previous chapter. If, here, God relents because of his pity, there, it is said that God relents only after the Ninevites repented.[121] The argument assumes a congruence between Jonah and the plant on one side, and God and Nineveh on

---

while it can have only one answer, its form, the form of a question, implies the possibility of more than one.

[119] Warshaw, "The Book of Jonah," 199. John H. Walton's recent objection (1992) that "neither we nor Jonah need to be informed that people are more important than plants" ("The Object Lesson of Jonah 4:5-7 and the Purpose of the Book of Jonah," 48), misses the point of the irony.

[120] The verb חוס is used in the Hebrew Bible to indicate sovereignty. Superiors, like God, may or may not be moved to חוס toward those who are within their jurisdiction. Fretheim thus correctly points out that Jonah had no right to exercise חוס regarding the plant because he had no sovereignty over it (he did not create it) ("Jonah and Theodicy," 236).

[121] Fretheim, Ibid., 231; and Orth, "Genre in Jonah," 271.

the other. Nineveh is to God what the plant has become to Jonah. But Jonah's relation to the plant is different from God's relation to Nineveh. Jonah's relationship to the plant was as recipient of its shade, whereas God's relationship to Nineveh is as Creator to the created. Hence the analogy is incongruous.[122] According to the narrative, Jonah did not pity the plant, though he greatly regretted its loss. In many respects, by wishing to die because of the loss of the plant, Jonah pities only himself.[123] Jonah was upset because he lost the shade of his plant. For the analogy to work properly, then God presumably would have to be equally upset over something that the Ninevites provide which he might lose.[124] In this interpretation, God spares Nineveh not because of their repentance, nor because of His love or mercy but, like Jonah, for selfish reasons.[125]

## Ridicule

Jonah, the prophet of God, is ridiculed when he is portrayed as sleeping during an emergency on board ship. During this life threatening storm,[126] while the crew is jettisoning the cargo and calling on their gods for help, Jonah sleeps. In the Septuagint version the ridicule is intensified because there it is stated that not only was Jonah sleeping, but that he was also snoring (καὶ

---

[122] J. Tsmudi, "Jonah's Gourd," 45-46. According to Simon, the argument is emotional not logical ("Structure and Meaning," 316; idem, *Jonah*, 81).

[123] Bickerman, *Four Strange Books of the Bible*, 14; and Burrows, "The Literary Category of The Book of Jonah," 99.

[124] Orth suggests that perhaps the loss might be in the area of prayer and sacrifice ("Genre in Jonah," 271).

[125] In a recent article (1992) attempting to show that the purpose of the book is to illustrate divine caprice, Alan Cooper suggests that God's final question be taken, not as a question, but as a declarative assertion: "as for me, I do not care about Nineveh" ("In Praise of Divine Caprice: The Significance of the Book of Jonah," 158).

[126] "While the ship heaves, crashes, and shudders in the hurricane's grip" (Brichto, *Toward a Grammar of Biblical Poetics*, 69).

ἔρρεγχεν). If it was the snoring which attracted the captain's
attention, it would have to be have been so loud to have been
heard in the howling storm. Jonah is further ridiculed when he is
portrayed as being ignominiously thrown off the boat (1:15), when
he is depicted as being swallowed down by the big fish (2:1), and
in being deposited in the fish's lower regions (2:1).[127] Jonah is
also ridiculed in the manner in which he exits the fish: literally by
being vomited out (2:11).[128] A number of commentators have
noticed the comic effect of the fact that the fish throws up
immediately after Jonah has proclaimed "Deliverance is the
Lord's" at the end of his prayer (2:10). They remark that this
action represents God's response to Jonah's incongruous statements.[129] For example, Ackerman asks: "What does YHWH think
of Jonah and his song?" and answers his own question: "The great
fish is commanded to vomit!"[130] In the final scenes of the book,
Jonah is ridiculed by responding to events in a ridiculously
extreme fashion, once at the salvation of Nineveh and again at the
destruction of the plant. In his response, everything is for him
either life or death.[131] His only proposed solution on the boat is

---

[127] "His humiliation is also emphasized since he has to be transported inside
the belly of a fish" (Good, *Irony In The Old Testament*, 46).

[128] Many commentators have noted the humor in this description. Magonet
writes that "there is also a suggestion of malicious humour in this picture of
the prophet being disgorged in so undignified a fashion, and certainly more
than a hint of scorn and disgust if one examines the usage of the root קיא"
(*Form and Meaning*, 52). James S. Ackerman rightly observes that "if the
narrative had wanted to achieve any effect other than satire, there are many
other Hebrew words for 'bringing forth' our hero onto dry land" ("Jonah,"
238).

[129] Magonet, *Form and Meaning*, 53. According to Holbert, this episode is
"the book's hallmark claim and its sharpest satiric thrust" ("Satire in the
Book of Jonah," 74). Fretheim sardonically remarks, "the fish can't put up
with this character Jonah. He is relieved of his stomach troubles only when
he gets rid of Jonah. Three days of undigested Jonah!" (*The Message of
Jonah*, 96).

[130] Ackerman, "Satire and Symbolism in The Song of Jonah," 225.

[131] Hyers describes Jonah's actions as being "like an accelerated manic-

death; his reaction to the events of Nineveh is death; his reaction to the loss of his shade is death. The wish to die is part of Jonah's exaggerated character portrayal. He is thus ridiculed by sharp changes of mood. When he is unhappy he wants to die; when he is happy, when given the plant, he is overjoyed. Jonah is ridiculed by being exposed to the elements--the fierce heat and the strong wind. He is ridiculed when his concern for the קִיקָיוֹן plant[132] is exposed as mere self-centered irritability over his discomfort at being deprived of its shade.[133]

The Ninevites are also ridiculed in our story. The king of Nineveh,[134] who is not named,[135] not only endorses the fasting and

---

depressive" (*And God Created Laughter*, 106).

[132] The very name of the קִיקָיוֹן plant, about which Jonah is so concerned, may be another example of ridicule in the story. Do we have here a word play with וַיָּקֵא 'to vomit' (2:11)? Is the קִיקָיוֹן "a vomit tree"? (Baruch Halpern and Richard Elliott Friedman, "Composition and Paronomasia in the Book of Jonah," 85-86). For the various interpretations suggested for the identification of this plant, see Bernard P. Robinson, "Jonah's Qiqayon Plant," 390-403.

[133] Warshaw, "The Book of Jonah," 199. Brichto suggests another time in the story when Jonah is indirectly ridiculed. When the sailors ask him questions, they ask concerning his profession and origin, but not his name. Brichto translates verse 8 as "Mr. On-Whose-Account-This-Misfortune-Has-Come-Upon-Us" which is equal to calling Jonah "Mr. No-Name" (*Toward a Grammar of Biblical Poetics*, 69, and 266, n. 9).

[134] Assyrian kings were not called after their capital cities. We know from Assyrian annals and from the Bible itself (2 Kgs. 15:19; Isa. 7:17; etc.) they were called "king of Assyria." But two biblical kings in the 9th century, Ahab, king of Israel (869-850), and his son, Ahaziah (850-849), were named after their capital cities. Both are termed "king of Samaria" (1 Kgs. 21:1; 2 Kgs. 1:3). It should also be noted that in the time of Jeroboam II (786-746) when the story is set, Nimrud/Calah, not Nineveh, was the capital of Assyria. Nineveh became the capital of Assyria only with the rise of Sennacherib (704-682).

[135] The fact that the king is not named may indicate that that a later Hebrew author did not know the name of the Assyrian king. During the reign of Jeroboam II, 786-746, the Assyrian kings were Adad-Nirari III (810-783), Shalmaneser IV (782-772), and Ashur-dan III (771-746).

wearing of sackcloth proclaimed by the people, but also extends it
to the animals "the beasts, the flock, and the herd" (3:7). They,
too, are not only to be deprived of food and drink, but they are to
'don' sackcloth. So the Ninevites are ridiculed by having their
cattle fast and wear sackcloth (3:7-8). We are asked to imagine
cows, goats, sheep, and donkeys not only pretending they are
'fasting', but also strolling around in sackcloth.[136] There are some
scholars who believe that what is meant here is that it was the
owners of the animals who clothed their animals with mourning
apparel and denied them food. Examples from folklore, classical
and modern mourning customs are adduced for this custom.[137] But
even if animals participate in funeral processions, it is debatable
whether mourning is akin to repentance.[138] Also, the Hebrew form
used in the text וְיִתְכַּסּוּ is a *Hithpael* conjugation. It requires a
translation, not by a simple passive "they shall be covered," but
by a reflexive "they shall cover themselves."[139] Nonetheless,
whether the animals clothed themselves or were clothed by their
owners, both scenarios depict the Ninevites acting in a ridiculous
manner.

## Parody

As we have noted before, parody differs from ridicule in that
whereas the latter attacks a target's person, parody attacks the
target by contrasting it in a distorted manner with traditional texts,
known individuals or expected norms of behavior.[140] Jonah is
parodied because he uses traditional texts in a distorted fashion.[141]

---

[136] Vawter, *Job and Jonah*, 106-7.

[137] See Gaster, *Myth, Legend, and Custom in The Old Testament*, 655-56;
and Day, "The Book of Jonah," 34.

[138] Miles, "Laughing at the Bible," 176, n. 10.

[139] Brichto, *Toward a Grammar of Biblical Poetics*, 268, n. 17.

[140] See p. 19 above.

[141] Magonet notes that all of Jonah's recitals of traditional texts are ironic
(*Form and Meaning*, 52).

The first example is in 1:9 when he expresses the traditional Israelite view of the Lord's omnipresence[142] by acknowledging that he is a devotee (יָרֵא) of the Lord "the God of Heaven, who made both sea and land." But Jonah's words belie his actions, and the contrast between his statement and his current situation is ironic.[143] For it is he who has fled "from the Lord's presence" (מִלִּפְנֵי יְהוָה, 1:3). The contradiction between Jonah's words and deeds has often been noticed. If he truly considered himself a devotee of the Lord, then why did he refuse his commission to prophesy?[144] If he truly believed God to be lord of the sea, then surely he could not have hoped to escape across the sea from the Lord.[145] The second example is in his prayer (2:3-10). We have already remarked that Jonah's prayer is odd because a psalm of thanksgiving would not only seem to be out of character for Jonah, but would also appear to be inappropriate before his rescue. Jonah's condition does not warrant a hymn of praise, since presumably he is still in a situation of personal distress and danger.[146] But this very incongruity of reciting a psalm of thanksgiving in such circumstances amounts to "one of the story's most audacious parodies."[147] For not only does Jonah utilize familiar verses, which can be found elsewhere in the Psalter, but he uses these verses literally to describe his situation. That is, he uses phrases which were meant to be used metaphorically in a literal sense.[148] For example, elsewhere in the Hebrew Bible the

---

[142] See Amos 9:2-6; Ps. 139:7-8, etc.

[143] Trible, *Studies in the Book of Jonah*, 253-54; idem, *Rhetorical Criticism*, 141. Fretheim offers a contrary view, "there is no reason to consider it insincere or something learned by rote and repeated without conviction" (*The Message of Jonah*, 31).

[144] Ratner, "Jonah, The Runaway Servant," 299.

[145] E. G. Kraeling, *Daniel - Malachi*, 198; Good, *Irony In The Old Testament*, 43, 45; and Landes, ("The Kerygma of the Book of Jonah," 19).

[146] See pp. 111-12 above.

[147] J. Mather, "The Comic Art of the Book of Jonah," 284.

[148] Lacocque and Lacocque, *The Jonah Complex*, 25; Miles, "Laughing at the Bible," 174; Mather, "The Comic Art," 284; Daube, "Jonah: A

motif of descending into Sheol, or being cast into the depths of the seas, is used metaphorically to describe either human suffering or feelings of isolation or weakness.[149] Here, the motif is used in a setting where it can be interpreted literally.[150] The poet has Jonah descend into the depths, into the heart of the sea, where flood-waters, waves and weeds engulf him.[151] Instead of being taken as a metaphor to describe Jonah's sorry condition, this motif lends itself to be taken as a literal description of Jonah's condition. An English analogy would be that when we use the metaphoric saying "to go from the frying pan into the fire," we do not mean it literally.[152] But here it as though the poet actually puts Jonah in a frying pan!

A number of parodies may be observed in Jonah's prophecy (3:4). Since the time of the medieval Jewish commentator Rashi (1040-1105),[153] it has been thought that there is a paronomasia in

---

Reminiscence," 41; and Brenner, "Jonah's Poem Out of and Within its Context," 189. Band has observed that this "realization" of cliched imagery is a comic technique practiced from Aristophanes to Thomas Pynchon ("Swallowing Jonah," 187). Kernan, gives some examples from Swift's *Mechanical Operation*, where the spirit, often compared figuratively to a light, becomes an actual "Mechanick Light," which can be conveyed out of the body or spent by perspiration. Or where 'Enthusiasm' becomes a literal *grain* placed in every person (*The Plot of Satire*, 63-64).

[149] See, for example, in Pss. 69, 88, and 130, and for more details, Miles, "Laughing at the Bible," 174, and Ackerman, "Satire And Symbolism in The Song of Jonah," 225.

[150] Brichto appropriately remarks that its literal appositeness "would be most incongruous in the mouth of a person whose plight it actually described. A drowning man does not recite psalms, describe the ocean's canyon, or complain that he has been wreathed in a turban of seaweed" (*Toward a Grammar of Biblical Poetics*, 73).

[151] The psalm "unleashes a veritable flood of water imagery" (Miles, "Laughing at the Bible," 174).

[152] Ackerman gives the illustration of the metaphor "Rock of Ages" being taken literally for a real rock! ("Satire and Symbolism," 226-27).

[153] "Nineveh's transformation fulfills Jonah's prophecy," see his commentary in *Miqra'ot Gedolot, ad loc.*

the word נֶהְפָּכֶת 'overthrown'[154] in Jonah's pronouncement of destruction for Nineveh.[155] Jonah did not fully understand his own prediction.[156] He thought נֶהְפָּכֶת 'overthrown' meant that Nineveh would be physically 'overthrown' whereas the ensuing story shows that Nineveh was spiritually 'overthrown', that is, it underwent a change of heart by repenting.[157] Bickerman gives an example of a similar paronomasia associated with oracles. The Delphic oracle told Croesus that if he attacked the Persians he would destroy a mighty empire. When he was defeated and then complained to the oracle, he was told that had he been wise he would have inquired whether it was the Persian empire or his own that was meant; he therefore had only himself to blame.[158] The time frame mentioned in Jonah's pronouncement is also parodic.

---

[154] D. J. Wiseman points out that the same paronomasia is present in the Akkadian cognate *abāku*. It, too, can mean "to overthrow" both in the physical and behavioral sense, so an Assyrian hearer would also interpret Jonah's prophecy (*adi arbāt ūmē āl Ninūa innabak*) in a similar ambivalent way ("Jonah's Nineveh," 49).

[155] Good, *Irony In The Old Testament*, 48-49; Halpern and Friedman, "Composition and Paronomasia in the Book of Jonah," 87; and R. J. Lubeck, "Prophetic Sabotage: A Look at Jonah 3:2-4," 44-45.

[156] "Jonah, at least, is such a mantic bumpkin as to be oblivious to the second meaning of the words spoken to him" (Halpern and Friedman, "Composition and Paronomasia in the Book of Jonah," 89).

[157] In his recent commentary (1990), Sasson makes this paronomasia the centerpiece of his interpretation of the book (*Jonah*, 346). Because he never grasps the double-edged meaning behind the message he communicates, Jonah perceives God's change of mind as a breach of proper etiquette between God and prophet. He feels misused. Jonah regards the phrase as predicting doom only, and when the Ninevites do repent he is upset because he was not given the opportunity (like Isaiah to Hezekiah in 2 Kgs. 20:1-6) to announce salvation to the Ninevites. Jonah's complaint with God, then, is not about the saving of Nineveh, nor about God's mercy, but about his treatment as a prophet.

[158] Herodotus, Book 1, 52, 91. See Bickerman, *Four Strange Books of the Bible*, 111.

He forecasts Nineveh's destruction "within forty days." However, the use of forty days in the Bible favors the interpretation of a long time.[159] Elsewhere, "forty days" does not mean literally "thirty-nine plus one," but it is symbolic for a long period of time, like our "for months." Thus, the flood waters are said to have lasted forty days and nights,[160] and Moses was on the mountain communing with God for "forty days."[161] However, Jonah proclaims Nineveh's destruction will occur "in forty days," which ostensibly would mean in a very long time in the future.[162] Jonah means, of course, in a little while. Jonah is forecasting the imminent destruction of the city, within a short period of time, which is why the Ninevites reacted with such alacrity. Perhaps with this consideration in mind, the translators of the Septuagint (Codex Vaticanus) and the Old Latin read "three days" instead of "forty days."[163] In any event, the use of the number 'forty' is contrary to what one would expect in such a prophecy, and adds to the parodic effect of the prophecy.

Jonah's recital of the credo (4:2) is parodic because of the allusions it conveys. As as been widely noted, his statement is part of a traditional Hebrew credo which occurs, with minor variations,[164] in hymns of praise (Pss. 103:8; 145:8), in a psalm of

[159] Contra Fretheim, *The Message of Jonah*, 108, 110.

[160] Gen. 7:4, 12, 17; 8:6.

[161] Exod. 24:18; 34:28; Deut. 9:9,11, 18, 25;10:10. Other examples: the embalming of Jacob took forty days (Gen. 50:3); the spies returned at the end of forty days (Num. 13:25); after eating divinely provided food, Elijah was able to travel for forty days to the mountain of God at Horeb (1 Kgs. 19:8); Goliath taunted the Israelites for forty days (1 Sam. 17:16); and Ezekiel had to lie for forty days on his right side (Ezek. 4:6).

[162] In our previous satire, the man of God prophesied the destruction of the Bethel sanctuary to take place also a very long time in the future, see pp. 73-74 above.

[163] It is thought that the Septuagint translator was influenced by the "three days" in the previous verse (Cohn, *Das Buch Jona*, 17).

[164] See the charts in G. Vanoni, *Das Buch Jona. Liter- und formkritische Untersuchung*, 139; and in Sasson, *Jonah*, 280.

lamentation (Ps. 86:15), in Nehemiah's prayer (Neh. 9:17), and most famously pronounced with slight modifications by God Himself.[165] The parody may be based on the fact that Jonah utters the coda with an intent opposed to its use elsewhere. Elsewhere it is used to exalt God for being merciful and indulgent of evil, here Jonah uses it to criticize God for being merciful and indulgent of evil.[166] The parody may also have more specific allusions, in particular, with the book of Joel. For it has long been noted that it is only in Joel (2:13) that the phrase "renouncing punishment" (וְנִחָם עַל־הָרָעָה) is to be found as part of the credo. This phrase is highly significant in the book of Jonah for it is to this very characteristic of God that the Ninevites appeal: "Who knows but that God may turn and relent" (וְנִחַם, 3:9). It is this very characteristic which the narrator mentions as being God's reaction to the repentance of the Ninevites: "God renounced (וַיִּנָּחֶם) the punishment (עַל־הָרָעָה) He had planned to bring upon them, and did not carry it out" (3:10).[167] In providing such a precise parallel with the book of Joel, and having already placed another citation from the book of Joel in the mouth of the King of Nineveh (3:9 = Joel 2:14), it is possible that the author is alerting the reader to a background for Jonah similar to that in Joel. The irony then would lie

---

[165] In Exod. 34:6-7, the two attributes 'gracious' and 'compassionate' are reversed.

[166] Aviezer, "The Book of Jonah," 15.

[167] Magonet thinks that "the coincidence of two such phrases, so clearly interrelated in each case, in such similar context (a last opportunity for repentance before destruction comes) without some sort of mutual interrelationship is unlikely" (*Form and Meaning*, 77). Thomas B. Dozeman suggested that Jonah 3:1-4:11 represents a satirical inner-biblical interpretation of Joel 2:1-17 ("Inner-Biblical Interpretation of Yahweh's Gracious and Compassionate Character," 213). There is little consensus on which book is prior. Some scholars, (e.g., Rudolph [1970], Allen [1976], and Wolff [1986]) hold that Jonah is dependent on Joel, while others (e.g., Cohn [1969], and Magonet [1976] hold the reverse (for references, see Dozeman, "Inner Biblical Interpretation," 208, n. 5, and 216, n. 23).

in the comparison of the situation in Nineveh with that in the book of Joel. In Joel, the thought is that the peoples' repentance can prompt a divine reaction leading to divine compassion. There the people are advised to: "Rend your hearts, rather than your garments, and turn back to the Lord your God" (2:3). God is implored: "Oh, spare your people, Lord!" (2:17), and responds: "[Then the Lord] had compassion upon His people" (2:18). The irony would be that whereas the credo is used in Joel to exalt God for his merciful qualities for relenting at His people's repentance, Jonah uses it to express his disagreement with God for relenting at the repentance of the Ninevites.[168]

A second form of parody is when non-Israelites quote Hebrew scripture or appear to be aware of Hebrew theological concepts. The comic effect is created because these references come from the last place the reader would expect (non-Israelites).[169] It is ironic that when the sailors pray to God they use language which strongly echoes sections of the Hebrew Psalter. They say: "for You, O Lord, by Your will, have brought this about" (כִּי־אַתָּה יְהוָה כַּאֲשֶׁר חָפַצְתָּ עָשִׂיתָ, 1:14). One thinks of Ps. 115:3, "when our God is in heaven and all that He wills He accomplishes" (וֵאלֹהֵינוּ בַשָּׁמָיִם כֹּל אֲשֶׁר־חָפֵץ עָשָׂה), or Ps. 135:6, "whatever the Lord desires He does in heaven and earth, in the sea and all the depths" (כֹּל אֲשֶׁר־חָפֵץ יְהוָה עָשָׂה בַּשָּׁמַיִם וּבָאָרֶץ בַּיַּמִּים וְכָל־תְּהוֹמוֹת). It is also ironic that the non-Israelite sailors are familiar with the Israelite concept of "blood guilt" because they ask to be absolved for "killing an innocent person" (דָּם נָקִיא, 1:14).[170] The language which describes the Ninevites' reaction to

---

[168] Of course, if as some believe, (see Magonet, *Form and Meaning*, 77-79), Jonah precedes Joel, then this irony will not have been the intent of the original author and would only have been appreciated by later readers.

[169] Ibid., 70, 72.

[170] Hans Walter Wolff points out the ironic undertone if the words of the sailors be seen in the light of Jer. 26:15: "There a true prophet warns a wicked people (Jerusalem!) against shedding his innocent blood. Here good non-Israelites, who are face to face with a prophet who is not good at all, pray that they should not acquire guilt through his death" (*Obadiah and*

Jonah's message also evokes traditional Israelite material. The Ninevites are said to have "believed God" (וַיַּאֲמִינוּ אַנְשֵׁי נִינְוֵה בֵּאלֹהִים, 3:5). This is highly reminiscent of the Israelites reaction at the Red Sea, "They had faith in the Lord" (וַיַּאֲמִינוּ בַּיהוָה, Exod. 14:31).[171]

The unnamed king of Nineveh also employs traditional Israelite language. First of all, he states, "let everyone turn back from his evil ways" (וְיָשֻׁבוּ אִישׁ מִדַּרְכּוֹ הָרָעָה, 3:8), a phrase which occurs a number of times in Jeremiah who, of course, is speaking of Israel.[172] Next he says "who knows but that God may turn and relent?" (מִי־יוֹדֵעַ יָשׁוּב וְנִחַם, 3:9), a phrase which is elsewhere found only in the book of Joel (2:14).[173] With this statement, however, the king shows himself to be *au courant* with Israelite theology: about the possibility of repentance, and about God's mercy.[174] He, like Jeremiah,[175] knows there is no guarantee of God's relenting and that there is no mechanical relationship between repentance and God's compassion.[176] Finally, the king says, "He may turn back from His wrath, so that we do not

---

*Jonah*, 120). Magonet discusses the question whether the source of this "blood guilt" theme is Deut. 21:8 or Jer. 26:15 (*Form and Meaning*, 72-73).

[171] Magonet, Ibid., 70.

[172] Jer. 18:11; 23:14, 22; 25:5; 26:3; 35:15; 36:3, 7. See Magonet, Ibid., 71. According to A. Feuillet, Jeremiah was the principle source of the entire book of Jonah ("Les sources du livre de Jonas," 169-76).

[173] On the difficulties of being able to determine the primacy of this text, see Magonet, *Form and Meaning*, 77-79. For our purposes, it suffices that a foreign king quotes a sacred Hebrew text regardless of that text's original source.

[174] Good, *Irony In The Old Testament*, 50; and Murphy, "The Book of Jonah," 482.

[175] In 26:3 and 36:7, where the adverb אוּלַי 'perhaps' is used.

[176] Fretheim, *The Message of Jonah*, 112-13. In his later article, Fretheim observes that, "it is thus ironic that it is non-Israelites and the Ninevites who give voice to the theme of God's sovereignty; they are the ones who have such extraordinary insight into the sovereign freedom of God" ("Jonah and Theodicy," 231-32).

perish" (וְלֹא נֹאבֵד אַפּוֹ מֵחֲרוֹן וְשָׁב, 3:9). The latter is highly reminiscent of Moses' plea to God in Exod. 32:12, "turn from your blazing anger, and renounce the plan to punish Your people" (שׁוּב מֵחֲרוֹן אַפֶּךָ וְהִנָּחֵם עַל־הָרָעָה לְעַמֶּךָ). Indeed these are the only two passages which combine the elements of God "turning from his fierce anger" and "repenting of evil."[177] The phrase "God renounced the punishment He had planned to bring upon them, and did not carry it out" (וַיִּנָּחֶם הָאֱלֹהִים עַל־הָרָעָה אֲשֶׁר־דִּבֶּר לַעֲשׂוֹת־לָהֶם וְלֹא עָשָׂה, 3:10) parallels almost word for word the phrase used of God's forgiveness of the Israelites after the Golden Calf episode: "The Lord renounced the punishment He had planned to bring upon His people" (וַיִּנָּחֶם יְהוָה עַל־הָרָעָה אֲשֶׁר דִּבֶּר לַעֲשׂוֹת לְעַמּוֹ, Exod. 32:14).[178] The occurrence of the phrase in Jonah may be taken as parodic because in this text we have the repentance of God, which is normally applied to Israel, now being unexpectedly applied to non-Israelites.

Another of the characteristics of parody is that it attacks its target by contrasting him in a distorted manner with other well-known figures.[179] Many commentators have noticed in Jonah's pronouncement of destruction for Nineveh, "forty days more and Nineveh shall be overthrown," allusions to and parallels with Abraham with Sodom and Gomorrah in Genesis 18.[180] For the only other cities said to be 'overthrown' in the Bible, Sodom and Gomorrah, were also condemned for immorality. Like Nineveh, whose wickedness (רָעָתָם) had come before God (1:2),[181] Sodom

---

[177] The idea of God turning from his fierce anger (שׁוּב + חֲרוֹן אַפּוֹ) occurs twice in the Book of Jeremiah (4:8; 30:24) and חֲרוֹן אַפּוֹ without שׁוּב is found in 4:26; 12:13; 25:37, 38; 49:37; 51:45.

[178] The phrase also occurs with slight variations five times in Jeremiah (18:8; 26: 3, 13, 19; 42:10) again with reference to God renouncing punishment on Israel. See Magonet, *Form and Meaning*, 71.

[179] See p. 19 above.

[180] See, for example, the comments of Magonet, "no one familiar with the Bible can read about Nineveh and the word *nehpaket* without at once thinking of the overthrow of Sodom and Gomorrah" (*Form and Meaning*, 65).

[181] It is interesting to note that Nineveh is not condemned for any action

and Gomorrah's 'outrage' (זְעָקָה) and 'sin' (חַטָּאת) had become so grave that the time for their destruction had come (Gen. 18:20).[182] When it did occur, they were overthrown (הָפַךְ, Gen. 19:25), and their destruction was subsequently referred to as the "overthrow of Sodom and Gomorrah" (כְּמַהְפֵּכַת סְדֹם וַעֲמֹרָה).[183] The linguistic allusion would add to the contrast of Jonah with Abraham. Abraham, as any 'proper' prophet should do,[184] intercedes for Sodom, yet Jonah, the "anti-prophet" does not.[185]

There are so many ironic parallels[186] between the episode of Elijah when he fled for his life from Jezebel (1 Kgs. 19) and parts

---

committed against Israel but only for moral sins: דַּרְכּוֹ הָרָעָה "immoral way of life" and הֶחָמָס 'injustice' (3:8) (Ginsberg, "Introduction to Jonah," 115-16). See also Yehezkel Kaufmann who notes the fact that the book of Jonah, the narrative framework of Job, and Abraham's plea for Sodom, all stories which deal with moral problems of sin and evil, are placed in non-Israelite settings (*The Religion of Israel*, 283).

[182] These terms for the transgressions by the Ninevites רָעָה (1:2; 3:8) and חָמָס (3:8) are the same as those employed in Gen. 6:5, 11, 13 for the generation that was responsible for God's decision to bring the Flood upon the earth. See H. M. Orlinsky "Nationalism-Universalism and Internationalism in Ancient Israel," 109.

[183] Deut. 29:22; Isa. 13:19; Jer. 49:18; 50:40; Amos 4:11. Cf. Jer. 20:16 ("Let that man become like the cities which the Lord overthrew without relenting [כֶּעָרִים אֲשֶׁר־הָפַךְ יְהוָה וְלֹא נִחָם]) where the cities are not named, but it is generally agreed that the cities of the plain are implied here. See R. P. Carroll, *Jeremiah*, 402.

[184] As Moses, Samuel, Jeremiah, Amos, Ezekiel etc. do. On prophetic intercession in general, see Y. Muffs, *Love & Joy*, 9-48.

[185] See now (1993) Yair Zakovitch, "Through the Looking Glass: Reflections/Inversions of Genesis Stories in the Bible," 148.

[186] Other (non-ironic) parallels between the two stories include both prophets being upset and seeking solitude (Elijah in Beersheba [1 Kgs. 19:3], and Jonah outside of Nineveh [4:5]), and both prophets waiting (Elijah goes into a cave and waits [1 Kgs. 19:9], Jonah sits at the east of the city under a booth and waits [4:5]). In both narratives, God instructs the prophet by means of nature (wind, earthquake, and fire in 1 Kgs. 19:11-12), winds, storms, seas, fish, plants, and worms in Jonah's case.

of the story of Jonah that a good case can be made that Jonah's actions are but a parody of Elijah's.[187] Consider the following parodic elements which highlight and magnify the difference between the two prophets.[188] Both prophets sit under the shade of a plant, Jonah under his קִיקָיוֹן, and Elijah under a "broom tree" (רֹתֶם, 1 Kgs. 19:4). Both prophets lie down and sleep, Elijah sleeps under his broom tree (וַיִּשְׁכַּב וַיִּישָׁן, 1 Kgs. 19:5), and Jonah sleeps on the ship (וַיִּשְׁכַּב וַיֵּרָדַם, 1:5). Both prophets request to die in similar language. Elijah says, "Please, Lord, take my life" (עַתָּה יְהוָה קַח נַפְשִׁי, 1 Kgs. 19:4) as does Jonah, "Please, Lord, take my life" (וְעַתָּה יְהוָה קַח־נָא אֶת־נַפְשִׁי, 4:3). At another point the language is slightly different, but the structure is the same: both use the same expression "for it is better for me to...than...." (כִּי טוֹב...מִן). Elijah says, "for I am no better than my fathers" (כִּי־לֹא־טוֹב אָנֹכִי מֵאֲבֹתָי, 1 Kgs. 19:4), while Jonah says: "for I would rather die than live" (מֵחַיַּי כִּי טוֹב מוֹתִי, 4:3).[189] But Jonah's complaints are not credible, and are parodic. Elijah complains because of his apparent failure,[190] but Jonah's complaint comes after an incredible prophetic success![191] In both narratives there is

---

[187] The following scholars have made such a case: Feuillet (1947), "Le sources du livre de Jonas," 168-69; J. Schildenberger (1962), "Der Sinn des Buches Jona," 95; Good (1965), *Irony In The Old Testament*, 51; Miles (1975), "Laughing at the Bible," 180; Magonet (1976), *Form and Meaning*, 102; H. Witzenrath (1978), *Das Buch Jona*, 81; Vanoni (1978), *Das Buch Jona*, 151; and Lacocque and Lacocque (1990), *Jonah*, 140, 147-48, 150.

[188] Magonet, *Form and Meaning*, 102.

[189] The language here is reminiscent of the Israelites in Exod. 14:12, "for it would have been better for us to serve the Egyptians than that we should die in the wilderness" (כִּי טוֹב לָנוּ עֲבֹד אֶת־מִצְרַיִם מִמֻּתֵנוּ בַּמִּדְבָּר). See Magonet, Ibid., 75. It is interesting to note that after Jonah's complaint "for I would rather die than live" (כִּי טוֹב מוֹתִי מֵחַיָּי, 4:8), the Peshitta inserts "because I am no better than my ancestors," a direct quote from the Elijah story in 1 Kgs. 19:4. Later Jewish tradition also made a connection between Elijah and Jonah by making Jonah the son of the widow of Sarepta whom Elijah revived (*b. Sukkah* 80:5; *Pirqe. R. El.*, 33).

[190] As does Moses (Num. 11:10-15) and Jer. (20:7-8).

[191] Trible, *Studies in the Book of Jonah*, 268; Miles, "Laughing at the

a repeated question and answer dialogue between God and his prophet (1 Kgs. 19:9-14 & Jonah 4:4-11). God's question to Elijah, "What are you doing here, Elijah?" is parodied by the captain of the ship, "What are you doing here sleeping" (1:6).[192]

A third form of parody occurs when it can be shown that a target does not conform to expected forms of behavior.[193] Our book contains a number of parodies having to do with behavior expected in connection with the institution of prophecy.[194] It is assumed that the reader is acquainted with the formulae and styles of prophetic literature in which these expected behavioral patterns occur,[195] and that these be so standardized as to be immediately recognizable.[196] From the three other biblical accounts of prophetic calls (Moses, Isaiah, and Jeremiah),[197] it seems that the prophetic scenario calls for reluctance.[198] Moses claims to be inarticulate (Exod. 4:10), Isaiah to be unworthy (Isa. 6:5), and Jeremiah to be too young (Jer. 1:6). But in these cases, when the prophet protests his call, there is also an anguished recital of the prophet's unworthiness. By running away, Jonah is depicted as reluctant to accept the divine commission. Yet the narrator gives

---

Bible," 177, 180; Magonet, *Form and Meaning*, 102; Fretheim, *The Message of Jonah*, 121; Lacocque and Lacocque, *The Jonah Complex*, 25; Shlomo Bacher, "The Book of Jonah--The Author vs. His Hero," 39; and Band, "Swallowing Jonah," 187.

[192] Magonet, *Form and Meaning*, 102.

[193] See p. 19 above.

[194] Miles listed five of these *topoi*: the call to prophecy; behavior of the sailors; the psalm of thanksgiving; the rejection of the prophet by the king; Jonah's wish to die ("Laughing at the Bible," 170-80). These five are discussed by Band, "Swallowing Jonah," 185-88, and by Orth, "Genre in Jonah," 263-70.

[195] Rauber, "Jonah--The Prophet as Schlemiel," 32.

[196] Miles, "Laughing at the Bible," 170.

[197] Though not a prophet, Gideon is another example of a leader expressing a reluctance to take on a divine commission (Judg. 6:15).

[198] Miles, "Laughing at the Bible," 171.

the impression that Jonah remained silent. Later Jonah will claim that at his call, he was in fact not silent, but did engage in some dialogue with God (4:2). However, the reader has no way of knowing that at the beginning of the book. To the reader who is expecting some response from Jonah, his silence has parodic impact.[199] This method of parodying Jonah is utilized two more times by the narrator. First when Jonah is depicted as being sound asleep at the time God sends the fierce storm. For if the storm is meant to be a demonstrative sign to Jonah, his reaction, by sleeping, is one of silence. Second, when the captain suggests that Jonah pray to his god for help from the storm (1:6). Jonah remains mute. Not only is the silence parodic of a spokesman of God,[200] but also, as God's messenger and representative, Jonah would be expected to endorse prayer.

According to what we know about biblical prophecy, when a prophet is called by God, he must prophesy. Once called, the prophet has no other choice. Amos, possibly with his own case in mind,[201] observed: "A lion has roared, who can but fear? My Lord God has spoken, who can but prophesy?" (Amos 3:8). All the prophets lived under divine constraint. They had to go where they were commanded, do what they were ordered, and say what they were bidden to say. God threatened Ezekiel with death for disobedience. Jonah is the only prophet who flees from a divine commission. He refuses to prophesy, not out of perceptions of unfitness but because, as we later discover, he disagrees with the

---

[199] Miles has offered the amusing analogy that Jonah's silence has the parodic impact of silence of a modern bridegroom who, after the officiant's question "do you take this woman to be your lawfully wedded wife?" remains mute (Ibid., 172).

[200] Payne, "The Prophet Jonah," 132.

[201] Amos protests to Amaziah that he was not a professional prophet. He only became one after receiving God's call: "I am no prophet, nor a prophet's son; but I am a herdsman, and a dresser of sycamore trees, and the Lord took me from following the flock, and the Lord said to me, 'Go , prophesy to my people Israel'" (Amos 7:14-15).

message![202] In the light of what we know of all other prophets, Jonah's behavior is extraordinary and would "strike an ancient Israelite audience as discordant, incongruous, and absurd."[203] A Hebrew prophet who refused to prophesy, regardless of the message, would be regarded in ancient Israel as an oxymoron.[204]

Jonah's message consists of only five Hebrew words: עוֹד אַרְבָּעִים יוֹם וְנִינְוֵה נֶהְפָּכֶת, "forty days more and Nineveh shall be overthrown" (3:4). It constitutes the shortest oracle in the entire prophetic literature. Because of its brevity, it may well be intended to be a parody of other prophetic oracles which are known for their length.[205] On the other hand, since all the other parodies target Jonah, it is more likely that Jonah once again is being subjected to further criticism. We have the comic situation described by Fretheim as "little effort, poor skills, a terrible sermon---and total success."[206] Despite the sparse message, Jonah meets with a stunning triumph.

Normally a prophet's message is ignored. Kings do not usually listen to him. Consider, for example, the negative experi-

---

[202] Ben Menachem, *Commentary on the Book of Jonah*, 5.

[203] Brichto, *Toward a Grammar of Biblical Poetics*, 68.

[204] Band terms it "downright impossible" ("Swallowing Jonah," 183). See also Trible, *Studies in the Book of Jonah*, 266, 268. Miles believes that the detail of Jonah paying for his passage to Tarshish adds to the parody: "By presenting a prophet who actually buys out of his vocation, the author drains the last trace of numinosity from this most numinous *genre* [the prophetic genre] in the Bible. Moses could hardly have been more mundane than Jonah had he thrown water on the burning bush or pawned the miraculous staff to escape confrontation with Pharaoh" ("Laughing at the Bible," 172).

[205] But Goitein believes that these words are akin to Micah's short oracle concerning the destruction of the Temple and Jerusalem (Mic. 3:12; Jer. 26:18), and that "the simple announcement that so large and flourishing a city as Nineveh or so holy a place as the Temple of Jerusalem may be destroyed must have been considered so astonishing as to be much more effective in every sense than any sermon" ("Some Observations on Jonah," 70).

[206] Fretheim, *The Message of Jonah*, 108-9.

ences of Moses with Pharaoh, Isaiah with Manasseh, and
Jeremiah with Jehoiakim and Zedekiah.[207] But Jonah, who is a
foreign prophet, representing a foreign god, gets immediate
acceptance in a foreign city, first from the people and then from
the very king of Nineveh no less! Not only is his message taken
seriously and acted upon, but all the Ninevites earnestly seek
God's ear and reform their ways. The reaction of the king of
Nineveh and his people is, in fact, the very opposite of the reaction of Jehoiakim who was unmoved by the fast of the populace
(Jer. 36:9), does not heed the call of Jeremiah that the people
"turn back from their evil ways" (וְיָשֻׁבוּ אִישׁ מִדַּרְכּוֹ הָרָעָה, 36:7),
actually burnt Jeremiah's scroll of prophesy (36:20-26), and
ordered his arrest (36:26).[208] Jehoiakim's action leads to the
threatened destruction of the entire population ("human and beast"
אָדָם וּבְהֵמָה, 36:29).[209] The Ninevites, on the other hand, listen to
the Hebrew prophet and proclaim a fast. For his part, the king of
Nineveh responds by endorsing repentance, engaging in
repentance ritual, and requesting that the entire population,
"human and beast" (הָאָדָם וְהַבְּהֵמָה) turn back from their evil ways
(וְיָשֻׁבוּ אִישׁ מִדַּרְכּוֹ הָרָעָה, 3:8). The resulting irony is that Nineveh
is spared, but Jerusalem soon falls.[210]

All these events would delight the heart of any Israelite
prophet and be a cause for great rejoicing. That Jonah is upset by
the astounding success of his mission adds to the parody. For only
in a parody could a prophet attain such a mind-boggling success[211]

---

[207] "In all these incidents, the word of the prophet is lengthy and impas-
sioned, he himself is completely ignored or angrily rejected, and the fated
punishment comes to pass" (Miles, "Laughing at the Bible," 175).
[208] Magonet, *Form and Meaning*, 76-77, 93; and Murphy, "The Book of
Jonah," 482.
[209] The phrase "human and beast" is a standard formula in Jeremiah to indicate the whole of a given society. See 7:20; 21:6; 27:5; 31:27; 32:43;
33:10; 36:29.
[210] Ackerman, "Satire and Symbolism in The Song of Jonah," 237.
[211] Band, "Swallowing Jonah," 187. Good remarks on this scene: "The
author intends the overwhelming success of the reluctant prophet to surprise

or, for that matter, any success at all.[212] And only in a parody would a prophet regard the 'conversion' of his audience as a sign of his failure.[213] Jonah is parodied for his sense of values. In being willing literally to die because of the destruction of a plant, Jonah is characterized as being selfish and interested solely in his personal comfort. The prophet, who by right ought to be God's agent, is shown to be insensitive to the plight of the Ninevites, his fellow creatures, and blind "to the whole meaning of the prophetic enterprise, to reconcile creation with its Creator."[214]

## Rhetorical features

Satirical writings not only have the inner characteristics of satire, they also have outer characteristics, that is, they are well written. In a Hebrew context, this means attention to various rhetorical techniques, such as symmetry, repetition, chiasmus, paronomasia, etc. The book of Jonah exhibits many of these stylistic niceties, many of which have been detailed by previous writers,[215] and are now documented in the book's most recent commentaries.[216] It is our intention here to give only a brief survey of these rhetorical

---

everyone, Jonah included. This is a satire, and the author deliberately over-draws his scene to highlight the irony of the peevish prophet's totally unexpected success. We are supposed to laugh at the ludicrous picture, precisely because Jonah becomes so upset" (*Irony In The Old Testament*, 49-50).

[212] Miles, "Laughing at the Bible," 177.

[213] Brichto, *Toward a Grammar of Hebrew Poetics*, 77.

[214] Ibid., 79 and 269, n. 22.

[215] In particular by Lohfink (1961), Trible (1963), Landes (1967), Cohn (1969), Magonet (1976), Fretheim (1977), Vanoni (1978), Witzenrath (1978), Soleh (1979), Halpern and Friedman (1980), Simon (1983 & 1992), Craig (1993), and most recently again by Trible (1994).

[216] See the commentaries by Wolff (1986), Sasson (1990), Simon (1992), and Limburg (1993). In his commentary, Allen remarks that the book is a "model of literary artistry, marked by symmetry and balance" (*The Books of Joel, Obadiah, Jonah and Micah*, 197, 200).

techniques to illustrate that the book of Jonah, like the other
stories in our corpus, is indeed a fine work of literary
craftsmanship.[217]

The symmetrical arrangement of the book has been noticed in
particular by Trible, Landes, Cohn, Ben-Menachem, Magonet,
and Simon, who believe that the book displays a special twofold
structural arrangement of content and themes.[218] For example,
both parts start with the phrase "the word of the Lord came to
Jonah" and both parts contain people in trouble appealing to God,
"perhaps the god will be kind to us" (1:6), and "who knows but
that God may turn and relent?" (3:9). This structural arrangement
displays parallelism between narrative sequences and inner
thematic parallelism within the chapters.[219] Thus, for example, all
four chapters have crisis situations, responses to the crisis, and
Yahweh's reaction. The thematic parallels between the two parts
produce a general pattern: call, response, conversion of pagans,
suffering and prayer of Jonah, and response of Yahweh.[220]

The following literary structures have been noticed in the
book: The first two chapters take place in the sea, whereas the last
two take place on dry land. The first and third chapters deal with
non-Israelites (sailors and Ninevites); the second and fourth chapters deal with Jonah. It has been noted that there is an inclusio in

---

[217] Burrows, "The Literary Category of The Book of Jonah," 87. For
attempts to show that the entire book is written in metrical language, see
Duane L. Christensen, "Narrative Poetics and the Interpretation of the Book
of Jonah," 29-48; and Raymond de Hoop, "The Book of Jonah as Poetry,
An Analysis of Jonah 1:1-16," 156-71.

[218] Trible, *Studies in the Book of Jonah*, 186-202; Landes, "Jonah: A
mašal?," 146-47; Cohn, *Das Buch Jona*, 49-61; Ben-Menachem, *Commentary on the Book of Jonah*, 3; Magonet, *Form and Meaning*, 55-63; and
Simon, "Structure and Meaning in The Book of Jonah," 298-316; idem
*Jonah*, 19-23.

[219] Trible, *Studies in the Book of Jonah*, 193-202; and Landes, "The
Kerygma of the Book of Jonah," 26-27.

[220] Carmel McCarthy and William Riley, *The Old Testament Short Story*,

that the book starts with God's words and ends with God having the last word.[221] Magonet has observed a symmetry in the speeches of Jonah and God.[222] This symmetry is so precise that even the number of words both characters speak are symmetrical. Jonah's speech in vv. 2-3 has 39 words, and God's speech in vv. 10-11 has 39 words. God's question to Jonah in v. 9 has 5 words, and Jonah's answer to God in the same verse has 5 words. Finally, God's question to Jonah in v. 4 has 3 words as does Jonah's lament to God in v. 8. Other commentators have noticed various chiastic structures in individual verses and groups of verses.[223] Of the many repetitions of words and phrases, one of the more interesting in the book is the so-called "growing phrase,"[224] whereby each time a phrase is repeated it contains an additional element. One concerns the fear of the sailors: "the sailors feared" (1:5); "these men feared a great fear" (1:10); "these men feared the lord, a great fear" (1:16).[225] Another example concerns the storm on the sea: "there was a great storm on the sea" (1:4); "for the sea continued to rage" (1:11); "for the sea continued to rage against them" (1:13).[226]

The book is characterized by its use of key words.[227] We have already noticed that the word גָּדוֹל 'big' or 'great' is used 12 times as an adjective and twice as a noun.[228] Another key word is

---

135.

[221] Simon, "Structure and Meaning in the Book of Jonah," 316; idem *Jonah*, 86; Warshaw, "The Book of Jonah," 202.

[222] Magonet, *Form and Meaning*, 56-58.

[223] See, for example, the work of Duane L. Christensen, "Anticipatory Paronomasia in Jonah 3:7-8 and Genesis 37:2," 261-63; idem, "The Song of Jonah: A Metrical Analysis," 217-31; idem "Narrative Poetics and the Interpretation of the Book of Jonah," 40-45.

[224] Magonet, *Form and Meaning*, 31-33.

[225] R. Pesch, "Zur konzentrischen Struktur von Jona 1," 578.

[226] Cohn, *Das Buch Jona*, 54.

[227] For a comprehensive survey, see Halpern and Friedman, "Composition and Paronomasia," 80-88.

[228] See p. 101 above.

רָעָה, which occurs 9 times in the book, and which has the added feature of having different nuances for each of its occurrences.[229] There is the 'wickedness'[230] (of the Ninevites, 1:2); the 'misfortune' (of the sailors, 1:7, 8); the 'immoral' way of life of the Ninevites, 3:8, 10); 'punishment' (of God on Nineveh, 3:10; 4:2); 'displeasure' (of Jonah, 4:1); and 'discomfort' (of Jonah, 4:6). We see from this list that רָעָה can be an inherent character-istic (the 'wickedness' or the 'immoral' way of life of the Ninevites), a current condition (the 'misfortune' of the sailors, and the 'displeasure' of Jonah), or an expected condition ('punish-ment' of God on Nineveh, and the 'discomfort' of Jonah). The dif-ferent nuances of the word lend themselves to *double entendres* and plays on meaning. For example, God's changing His mind about רָעָה ('punishment') for the Ninevites is considered a great רָעָה ('displeasure') to Jonah, and רָעָה in 4:6 may be taken in two ways. It is not only to save Jonah from his physical distress, but also to save Jonah from his displeasure (over God's mercy).[231]

Many puns and word plays have been detected in the book. Halpern and Friedman have described the book as "an ornate tapestry of paronomastic techniques."[232] It has even been sug-gested that Jonah's name constitutes a play with Nineveh (נִינְוֵה/יוֹנָה).[233] There is a pun when the sailors ask Jonah:

---

[229] G. I. Davies, "The Uses of *r'' qal* and the Meaning of Jonah iv 1," 105-10; Magonet, *Form and Meaning*, 22-24; Sasson, *Jonah*, 76; and Brichto, *Toward a Grammar of Biblical Poetics*, 82.

[230] Or, according to Goitein, ("Some Observations on Jonah," 63-77), and Abramsky, ("Jonah's Alienation and Return," 377), 'punishment' as in 3:10 and 4:2. When God plans to punish a certain place, it is said he brings a רָעָה "a punishment" on that place (1 Kgs. 14:10; Jer. 18:1, cf. v. 8).

[231] Magonet, *Form and Meaning*, 25; and Halpern and Friedman, "Composition and Paronomasia in the Book of Jonah," 87.

[232] See Halpern and Friedman, "Composition and Paronomasia in the Book of Jonah," 83.

[233] Ibid., 86. Many scholars have noted the resemblance of the first part of Nineveh to the Akkadian and Aramaic words for 'fish' (*nūnu* and נוּנָא). The connection of the city of Nineveh and fish is an ancient one. One of the cuneiform signs for Nineveh is written with a logogram (NINA) that has the

מַה־מְּלַאכְתְּךָ "what is your business?"[234] Jonah does not answer. But the reader knows that Jonah's business, since he is a prophet, is that of a מַלְאָךְ "a messenger (of the Lord)."[235] We have made mention above of the possible word play on נֶהְפָּכֶת "to be over-thrown" in Jonah's oracle.[236] There we observed that the verb נֶהְפַּךְ, as well as meaning physical overthrow, can denote a change of character, "to be transformed." Finally, there is clearly a pun involving the root טעם which, in one sense means 'order', and in another means "to taste." So the king of Nineveh gives 'orders' (מִטַּעַם הַמֶּלֶךְ "by decree of the king") that nobody should 'taste' (אַל־יִטְעֲמוּ) anything (3:7).

The above survey indicates the scope and depth of the rhetorical features present in the book of Jonah. When these are added to the plethora of the other characteristic satirical features: the fantastic events, the distortions, the ironies, the parodies and the ridiculing, there seems little doubt that the book meets all the necessary criteria for a satire. With this in mind, in the next chapter, we shall examine what the implications are of reading the book of Jonah as a satire.

---

syllable ḪA = nūnu 'fish' inside it. See E. A. Speiser, "Nineveh," 552; Sasson, Jonah, 71; and Brichto, Toward a Grammar of Hebrew Poetics, 83. J. Rosenberg has equated the second part of the word with Hebrew נָוֶה 'place', 'habitation', leading to a translation of the town as "fish-place" ("Jonah and the Prophetic Vocation," 25-26, n. 4).

[234] Halpern and Friedman, "Composition and Paronomasia in the Book of Jonah," 87.

[235] Prophets are called 'messengers' in Isa. 63:9 (מַלְאַךְ פָּנָיו); Hag. 1:13 (מַלְאַךְ יְהוָה); Mal. 2:7 (מַלְאַךְ יְהוָה). The very name of the prophet Malachi (מַלְאָכִי) means "my messenger."

[236] See p. 125 above.

# VII

## Implications of a Satirical Reading of Jonah

In the preceding chapter we outlined in detail the satirical elements in the book of Jonah, and we noted that the book has all the
formal requirements of a satire.[1] What then are the implications of
reading the book as satire? In our view, the implications are
threefold: they relate to the interpretation of the book, its genre,
and purpose.

In regard to interpretation, reading the book as a satire helps
explain many details in the story that were formerly considered
problematic.[2] For the very features that were formerly considered
to be problems in the text (absurdities, exaggerations, fantastic
events, and incongruities) can now be attributed to the satirical
nature of the text. For example, obvious absurdities in the story,
like Jonah living in the belly of a big fish for three days, or cattle
fasting and wearing sackcloth, or incongruities such as Jonah
sleeping during a life threatening storm, or waiting outside the city
for a decision which God has already made, can all be accounted
for by the satirical nature of the story.

---

[1] Similarly, Rauber "The author is a comic genius who uses all of the techniques available to him, including wit, irony, satire, exaggeration,
outrageousness--even parody and burlesque" ("Jonah--The Prophet as
Schlemiel," 31).

[2] We thus agree with Ackerman who states that "only satire permits such a
blend of wild improbabilities with ironic incongruities" ("Satire and Sym-

Second, recognition that the book may be a satire helps explain some of the curiosities about the book that we mentioned at the beginning of our discussion:[3] (a) that the book is not a collection of oracles like other prophetic books, but a narrative about an incident in the life of a prophet; (b) that the subject of the book is Nineveh, one of Israel's most despised enemies, hence thought to be an unlikely candidate for receiving God's grace; (c) that the message of the book is not made explicit in the book itself; (d) that Jonah, the prophet of God, is depicted as opposing God; and (e) that Jonah is portrayed as a negative model of prophetic behavior.

Third, recognition that the book may be satire impacts on a historical interpretation of the book. For satire, by its very nature, is deliberate fiction. Curiously, the view that the book is historical still has its adherents among scholars today.[4]

As for the genre of the book, it is, of course, a truism that understanding a book's genre is an important clue to understanding its purpose.[5] In looking at the considerable number of satirical features, which we have documented above, it seems that previous suggestions regarding the book's genre have not adequately taken into account the formal literary characteristics of the book.[6] This applies to all suggestions that the book is a short story with a moral,[7] a prophetical legend,[8] a *midrash* on a biblical verse or

---

bolism in the Book of Jonah," 227).

[3] See pp. 93-94 above.

[4] Its latest champion being Alexander, *Jonah*, 74-77.

[5] M. E. Andrew, "Gattung and Intention of the Book of Jonah," 13; Magonet, *Form and Meaning*, 88 & 112; and T. D. Alexander, "Jonah and Genre," 42-44.

[6] Mather rightly objected to the customary separation of form and content in the book by virtually all commentators ("The Comic Art of the Book of Jonah," 281).

[7] So lately, Wolff, *Obadiah and Jonah*, 83-85; Friedemann W. Golka, "Jonah," 72; and Limburg, *Jonah*, 22-26.

[8] So Kaufmann, *The Religion of Israel*, 284; Ernst Sellin, *Introduction To The Old Testament*, 173; and Jepsen, *Anmerkungen zum Buche Jona*, 299. But the whole point of a legend is to glorify its hero (cf., George M. Landes

verses,[9] or an allegory.[10] In recent years, most commentators have classified the book of Jonah as a parable.[11] Landes sums up the reasoning: It is "a comparatively short, simple, dramatic story, not necessarily historically factual, designed to teach a lesson...."[12] But Jonah is not a simple story. It has at least two parts. And the lesson it is alleged to teach is not at all clear. Furthermore, whereas other parables in the Bible are accompanied by an explicit indication of their meaning (Nathan's rich and poor man, the woman of Tekoah's two sons, and Isaiah's vineyard), the book of Jonah has no such indication.[13] Nor does its being a parable adequately take into account the fantastic elements, the ironies, the ridicule and parody which, as we have seen, dominate the story. On the other hand, these literary characteristics support the contention of those scholars who have previously suggested that the book is a satire.

## The book is a satire

This suggestion was made two hundred years ago by Thomas Paine, who viewed the book as a satire against the malignant

---

"Jonah," 489), and what happens to Jonah is the exact opposite. He is not glorified but ridiculed.

[9] For a summary of the arguments against this suggestion, see A. G. Wright, "The Literary Genre Midrash," 432.

[10] In this view, Jonah symbolizes Israel, Nineveh symbolizes the nations, and the swallowing of Jonah by the great fish represents the Babylonian exile. This view has been advocated in recent years by J. D. Smart, *Jonah*, 874; and Peter R. Ackroyd, *Exile and Restoration*, 244-45. But Jonah does not fit the model of other biblical allegories. Other biblical allegories are characteristically short and contain unmistakeable indications of their allegorical character (Aalders, *The Problem of the Book of Jonah*, 18).

[11] See Landes, "Jonah: A *mašal*?" 137-58.

[12] Landes, "Jonah," 489.

[13] See Benoit Trépanier, "The Story of Jonas," 14; Aalders, *The Problem of the Book of Jonah*, 15-17; Trible, *Studies in the Book of Jonah*, 160-61; and Brichto, *Toward a Grammar of Biblical Poetics*, 80-81.

character of a Bible prophet.[14] It was championed in the first decades of the twentieth century by Arnold B. Ehrlich[15] and Adolphe Lods.[16] Phyllis Trible (1963) revived the idea in her Ph.D. dissertation,[17] and others such as Zalman Shazar (1971),[18] Hans Walter Wolff (1986),[19] Carmel McCarthy and William Riley (1986),[20] Conrad Hyers (1987),[21] and R. P. Carroll (1990),[22] also contend that the book, or part of the book, is satire. In his pioneering work *Irony In The Old Testament* (1965),[23] Edwin M. Good was able to identify a number of satirical elements in the book. Since then, a host of scholars such as D. F. Rauber (1970),[24] Millar Burrows (1970),[25] Thayer S. Warshaw (1974),[26] John A. Miles (1975),[27] Terence E. Fretheim (1977),[28] John C. Holbert (1981),[29] James S. Ackerman (1981),[30] André Lacocque and Pierre-Emmanuel Lacocque (1981),[31] J. Mather (1982),[32]

---

[14] *The Age of Reason*, 2:113-15.

[15] Ehrlich, *Randglossen zur Hebräischen Bibel*, 3: 422-23.

[16] *The Prophets and the Rise of Judaism*, 15-16, 334-35.

[17] Trible, *Studies in the Book of Jonah*, 256, 261.

[18] "The Book of Jonah," 434; idem, "Jonah--Transition from Seer to Prophet," 1-8.

[19] *Obadiah and Jonah*, 84.

[20] *The Old Testament Short Story*, 112-39; 481.

[21] Hyers, *And God Created Laughter*, 94-109.

[22] "Is Humour Among the Prophets?" 181.

[23] Pp. 41-55.

[24] "Jonah--The Prophet as Schlemiel," 29-38.

[25] "The Literary Category of the Book of Jonah," 80-107.

[26] "The Book of Jonah," 191-207.

[27] "Laughing at the Bible," 168-81.

[28] *The Message of Jonah*, passim.

[29] "Satire in the Book of Jonah," 59-81.

[30] "Satire and Symbolism in the Song of Jonah," 213-46.

[31] *The Jonah Complex*, 71.

[32] "The Comic Art of the Book of Jonah," 280-91.

Bruce Vawter (1983),[33] Arnold J. Band (1990),[34] Athalya Brenner (1992)[35] and Willie van Heerden (1992),[36] have all recognized different satirical aspects in the book, many of which we have referred to in our previous chapters.

If the book is satire, then what is the purpose of the satire? This question is not an easy one to answer for a number of reasons. In the first place, no work of satire automatically reveals its true purpose. For to do so, like revealing a punch line of a joke at the wrong place, would ruin the satire. A satirist will try to write so that his work can be taken on two levels (the real and apparent), and by doing so will thus give no hint of his real purpose. In the normal course of events, readers for whom the satire is written are usually well able to comprehend the author's true intention. However, later readers, for whom the names and events mentioned in the satire have lost their meaning, are not always so fortunate. Secondly, while good satire is timeless and universal, the precise targets designated by the author are not always recoverable. This is the situation with the book of Jonah. The literary form tells us that the work is a satire, but we are left to ponder whether the target of the satire is Jonah himself or whether Jonah represents some other person (e.g., another prophet or a type of prophet). Third, we have to consider whether the satire is advocating a particular message by having Jonah act as a foil to the author. That is, whether Jonah is made the representative of a position, belief or ideology which is opposed by the author. Thus, by making Jonah appear ridiculous, the author simultaneously makes Jonah's ideas appear ridiculous.[37]

Let us first consider the possibility that the satire is advocating a particular message. The five principal messages that

---

[33] *Job and Jonah*, 87-117.

[34] "Swallowing Jonah," 177-95.

[35] "Jonah's Poem Out of and Within its Context," 189-90.

[36] "Humour and The Interpretation of The Book of Jonah," 389-401.

[37] Warshaw writes that "the more ridiculous he is made to look, the stronger

scholars have suggested for the book of Jonah can be classified under the following headings: (1) universalism; (2) repentance; (3) prophecy; (4) God's mercy; (5) tension between God's justice and God's mercy, or some combination of these.[38]

## Universalism

The first message, which is thought be the focus of the book, is universalism. God's mercy extends to all peoples who have the opportunity to change their ways and repent. This is said to be exemplified by the case of the Ninevites who did change their ways and, as a result, were saved.[39] Jonah is thought to begrudge[40] or oppose mercy to the Ninevites. Hence he is seen to represent a type of nationalistic or particularist ideology believed to be current in the time of Ezra and Nehemiah. The author, by contrast, is one who upholds universalistic ideals in opposition to the particularist ideas of that time,[41] *so the satire points up the*

---

is the case against the value he represents" ("The Book of Jonah," 196).

[38] Magonet, *Form and Meaning*, 85-112; and Watts, *The Books of Joel, Obadiah, Jonah*, 73.

[39] See the standard commentaries and Introductions, and more particularly, Chayim Gevaryahu, "The Universalism of the Book of Jonah," 20-27, and Day, "The Book of Jonah," 47. For the history of interpretation, see Bickerman, *Four Strange Books of the Bible*, 17-28.

[40] To the 18th century German founders of modern biblical scholarship (Semler, Michaelis, Eichhorn), Jonah exemplified the Jewish fanaticism which begrudged God's mercy to the Gentiles. The book of Jonah was written as an admonition to intolerant Israel. See Bickerman, *Four Strange Books of the Bible*, 25.

[41] Typical statements are those of Bewer "the author wants to teach the narrow, blind, prejudiced, fanatic Jews, of which Jonah is but the type that the love of God is wider than the measures of man's mind" (*A Critical and Exegetical Commentary on Jonah*, 64), and Smart, "The writer of the book gently but sharply exposed in the person of Jonah the absurdity of the attitude which prevailed among so many of his countrymen" (*Jonah*, 872).

*theme of universalism.*[42] However, this theory has been subjected to a number of serious objections, a few of which we mention here. Bickerman has pointed out that "the opposition between Israel and the Gentiles is introduced by commentators who find more than is really there."[43] Clements has shown that the entire story fails to raise any single example of those issues which we know deeply affected the relationships of Jews and non-Jews in the post-exilic period.[44] Lastly, Rofé correctly observed that "nowhere in his tirade does Jonah complain that God is too merciful with gentiles. Neither does he express any particular objection to God's behavior towards Nineveh." Hence we must conclude with him that "it is difficult to find evidence for, or even a hint of, a polemic against Jewish particularism in the Book of Jonah."[45]

## Repentance

Since the Ninevites repent, and are thereby saved from destruction, it is held by some that the main focus of the book therefore has to do with repentance. Israel should be as willing to repent as Nineveh was.[46] Repentance is possible for all mankind, Israelites

---

[42] Burrows, "The Literary Category of the Book of Jonah," 105; Orth, "Genre in Jonah," 276-77. In the book there is a "virtuoso exhibition of the techniques of satire, irony, and ridicule that supports the theme of universalism against a too narrow ethnocentrism" (Warshaw, "The Book of Jonah," 199).

[43] Bickerman, *Four Strange Books of the Bible*, 28.

[44] Thus it does not mention mixed language, mixed marriage, cultic holiness, dietary laws, etc. (Clements, "The Purpose of the Book of Jonah," 19).

[45] Rofé, *Prophetical Stories*, 161-62. See also Trible, *Studies in the Book of Jonah*, 262-65; Landes, "The Kerygma of the Book of Jonah," 9, n. 32; idem, "Jonah," 147; and Brichto, *Toward a Grammar of Biblical Poetics*, 79-80.

[46] Clements, "The Purpose of the Book of Jonah," 21-28; Abramsky, "Jonah's Alienation and Return," 370-95; George M. Landes, "The Canonical Aproach to Introducing the Old Testament: Prodigy and Problems," 39; B. Porten, "Baalshamem and the Date of the Book of Jonah," 237-43.

and non-Israelites alike.[47] If Jonah represents a point of view different from that of the author, then he must be opposed to the possibility of repentance for non-Israelites.[48] *The satire against Jonah would represent a negation of Jonah's point of view* and enable the author to advocate the possibility of repentance for everyone, Israelites and non-Israelites alike.

But it is doubtful whether repentance is the main focus of the book. In the first place, the theme of repentance is not dealt with in the first half of the book, nor is it the subject of its climax. In the first half of the book, the sailors are not depicted as sinners, and Jonah, though he disobeys God, prays but does not repent. Indeed, in His final speech, God does not say Nineveh is spared because of its repentance, but because it is a large city.[49] Also, as has often been noted, if the focus of the book were on repentance then the book could have ended with the third chapter.[50]

## Prophecy

A third popular interpretation of the book of Jonah is that its focus is prophecy. When Jonah's prophecy does not come to pass, it is thought that he is angry[51] because God has made him a false

---

[47] "What the prophets said about God's readiness to forgive repentant sinners and remit the punishment he had threatened was addressed to the people of Israel. In assuming that the same principle applied equally to Israel's enemies the author the book of Jonah took a very advanced position" (Burrows, "The Literary Category of the Book of Jonah," 101).

[48] Fretheim, *The Message of Jonah*, 23. To some, Jonah's opposition is restricted to the nature of Nineveh's crimes. Hence Jonah is thought to be opposed to repentance for Ninevites only because of their reputed wickedness (Aviezer, "The Book of Jonah," 12).

[49] Simon "Structure and Meaning in the Book of Jonah," 291-92; idem, *Jonah*, 86.

[50] See most recently, Walton, "The Object Lesson of Jonah 4:5-7," 50.

[51] Goitein, "Some Observations on Jonah," 72; Clements, "The Purpose of the Book of Jonah," 21; Grace I. Emmerson, "Another Look at Jonah," 87.

prophet,[52] and that he can no longer rely on the absoluteness of God's word.[53] On the other hand, in opposition to Jonah, the author's view is that God's word is conditional and that repentance can effect a change in God's final decree.[54] In other words, prophecy is conditional. The divine decision is not, as Jonah thought, absolute and unalterable.[55] The prophet is no longer just a herald delivering unalterable decrees, but a watchman coming to warn the people and implore them to repent.[56] If necessary, God can change the word given to His prophet.[57] *The satire against Jonah would then be because he*, or other prophets like him,[58] is depicted as one who *believes that,*

---

[52] Burrows, "The Literary Category of the Book of Jonah," 97; Berlin, "A Rejoinder to John A. Miles Jr.," 231; Licht, *Storytelling in the Bible*, 58 & 121.

[53] Jepsen remarks that Jonah's complaint about God is that "He repents and changes His mind. An element of uncertainty is thus introduced into God's ways with His creatures" (*Anmerkungen zum Buche Jona*, 300). Vawter writes, "it is being asserted here that Yahweh can and does reverse his position, change his mind, and confound his devotees by leaving them entirely in the lurch as regards what they have prophesied what he will and will not do" (*Job and Jonah*, 110).

[54] Burrows, "The Literary Category of the Book of Jonah," 98. "If man repents, God may relent from an unfavorable decree" (Clements, "The Purpose of the Book of Jonah," 21).

[55] Abraham J. Heschel, *The Prophets*, 286-87; Brevard S. Childs, "The Canonical Shape of the Book of Jonah," 125; idem, *Introduction to the Old Testament as Scripture*, 424; Shazar, "Jonah--Transition from Seer to Prophet," 1-8; Rofé, *The Prophetical Stories*, 166.

[56] Bickerman, *Four Strange Books of the Bible*, 32-39, 43, 47; Goitein, "Some Observations on Jonah," 64, 71-73; Rofé, *The Prophetical Stories*, 166; J. H. Tigay, "The Book of Jonah and the Days of Awe," 73; Emmerson, "Another Look at Jonah," 86-88.

[57] Rofé, "Classes in the Prophetical Stories," 156; idem, *Prophetical Stories*, 165, 168-69.

[58] According to Ratner, "Jonah typifies the particular group of prophets targeted by the author for reproof and instruction. He intends to chastise his peers for their adamant adherence to an outmoded view of the prophetic role

irrespective of any other consideration (e.g.. repentance), *God's word is absolute* and a prophet's word must come to pass. On the other hand, the author is propounding a new view of prophecy which is that true prophets, paradoxically, do not want their message to come true. A true prophet would prefer to witness genuine repentance rather than see his warnings and prophecies of woe and threatened punishment come to pass.

But it is very dubious whether prophecy is the major focus of a book in which the very word for prophet does not even appear.[59] Nor does the story as a whole lend itself to the view that Jonah believes prophecy to be absolute.[60] Furthermore, the supposed new message of the author that prophecy is conditional is not a very original one,[61] but was known in earlier literature.[62] In any event, it would be meaningless to the book's readers who were aware that Nineveh did actually fall in fulfillment of Jonah's prophecy.[63]

---

and thereby to persuade them not to act like Jonah" ("Jonah, The Runaway Servant," 18).

[59] See the discussion in Magonet, *Form and Meaning*, 90-94.

[60] Cohen makes two good points: (1) If Jonah understood the prophecy as absolute, "why did he not go on the first call, in which case he has no reason to flee?"; (2) "why did he wait outside of the city to see if the inevitable will occur? The account suggests that Jonah is waiting to see *if* the decree will occur" ("The Tragedy of Jonah," 166).

[61] As argued by Freedman, "Did God Play a Dirty Trick on Jonah at the End?," 26-31.

[62] Childs, "The Canonical Shape of the Book of Jonah," 123. The theme of God's repentance may be seen in Gen. 6:6, 7; Exod. 32:14; Judg. 2:18; 1 Sam. 15, 11, 35; 2 Sam. 24:16 (= 1 Chr. 21:15); Jer. 18:7-11; 26:2-3, 19; Amos 7:3, 6; Joel 2:13; and Ps. 106:45 (see Aalders, *The Problem of the Book of Jonah*, 21).

[63] Payne, "Jonah from the Perspective of its Audience," 10.

## God's mercy

A fourth major interpretation of the book is that its focus has to do with God's compassion--which extends to Israelites and foreigners alike. God's mercy is appealed to by the Ninevites, it is referred to by Jonah in his complaint and according to God's final speech, it is the reason, why Nineveh was saved.[64] The lesson of the gourd shows that at times, everyone, even Jonah,[65] can avail himself of God's mercy. And God, should He so desire, can display this mercy even to Ninevites despite their crimes. *The satire would then be against Jonah for not understanding God's mercy.*[66] The message to the reader would be that if a prophet of God does not understand that God's mercy extends also to foreigners, then how much the more does the reader, or community of readers, not understand it! The readers are admonished that perhaps they, like Jonah, do not know the truth about everything. Consequently, they should emulate God's compassion with the Ninevites[67] and exercise more tolerance with people of contrary or different views.

But the story does not bear out the contention that Jonah does not understand God's mercy. He seems to be well aware of it when he prays inside the fish, when he recites the credo, and when he appeals to God to help him when he is languishing outside of Nineveh. Hence, as far as God's mercy is concerned, Jonah does not seem to be in discord with the author. Thus, it is improbable that God's mercy is the cause of the satire.

---

[64] See Leah Fränkel, "'His Mercy Extends to All His Creatures': On the Meaning of the Book of Jonah," 193-207; Licht, *Storytelling in the Bible*, 121; Freedman, "Did God Play a Dirty Trick on Jonah at the End?" 26-31; Walton, "The Object Lesson of Jonah 4:5-7," 55.

[65] Aviezer, "The Book of Jonah," 15.

[66] Trible, *Studies in the Book of Jonah*, 256 & 261; and Murphy, "The Book of Jonah," 481.

[67] Warshaw, "The Book of Jonah," 194.

## Tension between God's justice and God's mercy

In recent times a growing number of scholars have suggested that the main focus of the book has to do with the tension between divine justice and divine mercy.[68] Jonah is portrayed as a champion of divine justice: sin should be punished.[69] In many respects, Jonah's theological problem is similar to Job's. Job deals with the problem of why the righteous suffer and the wicked prosper; Jonah's problem is why the wicked go unpunished.[70] Wicked Nineveh deserves the punishment which has been canceled by an act of divine mercy. To Jonah, like Job, this means there is no justice in this world, and life is "arbitrary and capricious."[71] Jonah sees mercy as a threat to God's order.[72] He would rather die than live in a world where a just God no longer reigns.[73] *The purpose of the satire would be to illustrate the tension between Jonah, the advocate of God's justice, and the author who believes in the supremacy of His mercy.*[74]

Jonah is said to hold a 'justice' point of view on two occasions. The first being on the ship when Jonah acknowledges to the

---

[68] Jepsen, *Anmerkungen zum Buche Jona*, 299; Fretheim, *The Message of Jonah*, 24; idem, "Jonah and Theodicy," 227-37; Simon, "Structure and Meaning in the Book of Jonah," 297-98, 307, 313-16; idem, *Jonah*, 9; Shlomo Bacher, "The Book of Jonah--The Author vs. His Hero," 39-43; Tsmudi, "Jonah's Gourd," 44-48; Levine, "Jonah as a Philosophical Book," 235-45; Aviezer, "The Book of Jonah," 11-15, 50; Nisan Ararat, "On Jonah's Fear of God (Divine Justice)," 85-110; Nurit Arum, "The Purpose of the Book of Jonah," 211-14.

[69] Kaufmann, *The Religion of Israel*, 284-85; Chaim Abramowitz, "Maftir Jonah," *Dor le Dor* 14/1 (1985), 3-9; Tigay, "The Book of Jonah and the Days of Awe," 74-75.

[70] Chayim Lewis, "Jonah--A Parable for Our Time," 160.

[71] Ackerman, "Jonah," 240.

[72] Idem, "Satire and Symbolism in the Song of Jonah," 245.

[73] Idem, "Jonah," 240.

[74] Idem, "Satire and Symbolism in the Song of Jonah," 245. Orth asks: "is the point of the satire that the author is mocking prophetic books for their

sailors his responsibility for the storm and acquiesces in his own punishment. He perceives a cause and effect result: should he be tossed overboard, justice would be served and the storm would stop (1:12).[75] The second is deduced from the reason Jonah gives for refusing God's commission. He knew that God is a god of mercy (4:2), and this 'mercy' is not what Jonah believes should have been in store for the Ninevites. Jonah expresses a wish to die because he perceives the mercy shown to Nineveh as a grievous error, perhaps even a miscarriage of justice. This is so particularly because it is perpetuated by God Himself, the symbol of Absolute Justice.[76] Such a lack of discrimination on God's part is unjust.[77] On the other hand, the author represents the view that God's mercy overrides His justice. The point of God's lesson to Jonah with the plant is designed to belittle Jonah for his 'justice' point of view. Jonah's view is incompatible with human frailty. Everyone needs the benefits of divine consideration and mercy, even when unmerited.[78] As can be seen with the plant episode, even Jonah, the proponent of strict justice, accepts and was extremely pleased with his undeserved favor: "Jonah was very happy with the plant" (4:6).[79]

But this interpretation also has its weaknesses. In the first place, we have no evidence at the beginning of the book that Jonah flees from God because he is a champion of divine justice.[80] Indeed if Jonah were a champion of divine justice, one would

---

simple view of divine justice?" ("Genre in Jonah," 272-73).

[75] Bacher, "The Book of Jonah," 39; Warshaw, "The Book of Jonah," 193.

[76] Aviezer, "The Book of Jonah," 12-13.

[77] Fretheim, "Jonah and Theodicy," 229.

[78] Cohn, *Das Buch Jona*, 88; Aviezer, "The Book of Jonah," 13.

[79] "How can he then be so upset when this favor is withdrawn? Upset enough to even want to die because of it? Jonah has proved unable to live up the standards of integrity he has set for others" (Aviezer, "The Book of Jonah," 14).

[80] Cohen, "The Tragedy of Jonah," 164.

expect that he would not flee God's command. He was told to announce punishment on Nineveh for its wickedness (1:2), a commission which should have eminently suited Jonah's belief in 'justice',[81] yet he refused and fled. Surely one championing a philosophy of 'justice' would not have acted in such a manner. Second, setting Jonah up as a defender of divine justice in opposition to the author's support of divine mercy assumes that such a demarcation of belief existed in ancient Israel. But the theological fact that God was both just and merciful was well known from an early period in Israel.[82] Jonah himself is well aware of God's mercy as is evident from the fact that he recites the coda which glorifies God's mercy. If Jonah were really a champion of divine justice, then it could be expected that he would have quoted a different form of the coda, one that included within it a mention of God's justice.[83] Hence, it is unlikely that the primary message of the book has to do with the tension between divine justice and divine mercy nor, therefore, that the book is a satire on this theme.

**No message is advocated, rather Jonah himself is satirized**

From the foregoing survey it is apparent that none of the above messages is entirely compelling. None of these proposals is explicitly expressed, and all require inductive reasoning from the text. If the author was, as alleged, a staunch exponent of some point of view, one wonders why that point of view is not stated somewhere in the text.[84] It may well be that the book is not

---

[81] Emmerson, "Another Look at Jonah," 86.

[82] Childs, "The Canonical Shape of the Book of Jonah," 123.

[83] For example, he could have cited the oldest version (in Exod. 34;6f) which combines God's mercy with His justice (visitation of the iniquity of the fathers upon the children).

[84] Cohen asks the very same question ("The Tragedy of Jonah," 169).

advocating any particular philosophy or point of view.[85] Indeed, when one reviews the portrayal of Jonah in the book, one has to ask what possible message could warrant the depiction of a prophet in such a fashion? We recall that Jonah is depicted throughout the story as a virtual caricature of a prophet.[86] He is made to look undignified.[87] He is physically placed in compromising situations: sleeping on the ship, tossed overboard, and swallowed by the great fish. He is made to utter statements which are un-prophetic (such as denouncing God for His merciful qualities), hypocritical (attesting his faith in a God from whom he has fled), and inappropriate (the thanksgiving psalm). His agreement to prophesy the second time around is not portrayed as being the result of any conversion on Jonah's part. Rather we are given the impression that Jonah is forced to yield because he cannot resist.[88] Despite all his reluctance, he meets with huge success. Yet he is unhappy even about this! He is made to appear self-centered because of his concern for the קִיקָיוֹן plant,[89] in contrast to his lack of concern for the fate of the tens of thousands of humans and

---

[85] Our view is similar to that of David J. A. Clines who remarks: "If the book is viewed as story, we can sit looser to the idea that we should search for *the* message or point or kerygma of the book....[If the book is regarded as literature]  may not Jonah have nothing in particular to 'teach' but be an imaginative story (traditional or not) in which various serious concerns of the author are lightly and teasingly sketched" ("Story and Poem: The Old Testament as Literature and as Scripture," 119).

[86] Burrows, "The Literary Category of the Book of Jonah," 86; Vanoni, *Das Buch Jona*, 151; Payne, "Jonah from the Perspective of its Audience," 6; Ackerman, "Satire and Symbolism in the Song of Jonah," 217; Vawter, *Job and Jonah*, 98, 101; Payne, "The Prophet Jonah," 131; Ratner, "Jonah," 10-11.

[87] Burrows, "The Literary Category of the Book of Jonah," 94-95; L. H. Brockington, "Jonah," 627; Good, *Irony In The Old Testament*, 41, 49-50.

[88] Vawter, *Job and Jonah*, 104.

[89] Burrows, "Literary Category," 97; Magonet, *Form and Meaning*, 33; Wolff, commenting on Jonah's ego, notes that he uses the first person nine times in two verses (4:2-3) (*Obadiah and Jonah*, 168).

animals in Nineveh.[90] It is our contention that it is this negative portrayal of the prophet, not any ideological message, which is the principal 'message' of the book.[91] What we have here is nothing less than a satire on the prophet himself.[92] It is the behavior of the prophet with which the book is dealing.[93] Jonah is satirized for behavior thought to be unbecoming to a prophet.[94]

Thus this satire is in accord with the two other anti-prophetic satires involving Israelite prophets discussed in the previous chapters. We recall that in these satires the prophets were also satirized, not because of ideological reasons, but for personal behavior. In the satire of the boys and the bald prophet, Elisha is satirized, not for any philosophical or theological message, but for his supposed abuse of prophetic power. The same is true in the satire of the lying prophet, where both the man of God and the old prophet of Bethel are satirized, not for ideological reasons, but for foolishness, lying and concern with petty values. Similarly, Jonah is satirized, not for his philosophical ideas, but for his behavior.

---

[90] Magonet, *Form and Meaning*, 95.

[91] We note that in his pioneering study on Irony in the Hebrew Bible, Good had already anticipated our conclusions: "his [the author's] purpose was not to propose some theological statements for our consideration, but to expose absurdity by the irony of satire" (*Irony In The Old Testament*, 54).

[92] Despite all this evidence, some scholars deny that Jonah is portrayed satirically. For example, Goitein remarks that "the whole tenor of the story is much too earnest for a satire; Jonah is not painted with the brush of mockery or disdain, but drawn with the pencil of deep and sympathetic insight into human weakness" ("Some Observations on Jonah," 73-74). Goitein's opinion is echoed by Magonet, *Form and Meaning*, 86; Emmerson, "Another Look at Jonah," 87, and Abramsky, "Jonah's Alienation and Return," 385-86.

[93] Ackerman observes that "the story has satirized Jonah as a prophet whose piety is out of sync with his behavior" ("Jonah," 240).

[94] Thus Jonah is not, as Fretheim, (*The Message of Jonah*, 29-30, 43) and others believe, a figure used by the author as a vehicle for describing his contemporaries, a type of the author's audience, or a metaphor for Israel.

In the next chapter, we shall sum up what all the satires of our corpus have in common and see if it is possible to identify the prophets who are the objects of our satires. Also we shall offer some suggestions as to when and why these satires may have been written, and how they got accepted into the canon.

# VIII

## Afterword on Anti-prophetic Satire

The four stories that we have discussed in the preceding chapters, Balaam and his donkey (Num. 22:21-35), the boys and the bald prophet (2 Kgs. 2:23-25), the lying prophet (1 Kgs. 13), and the book of Jonah, have a number of features in common. All these stories relate incidents in the life of a prophet, and in all of them the prophet is the center of attention. They are all stories of the kind that is typically found in the Former Prophets. Even the book of Jonah, which is canonically placed with the Latter Prophets, has the same literary form as these stories.[1] But whereas in other biographical stories the prophets are the heroes of the stories told about them, in these stories they are anti-heroes.[2] A striking feature in all four is that the prophets are on the move, they travel somewhere. Balaam, on his donkey, travels from Pitru on the upper Euphrates,[3] to curse Israel at the Moabite border. Elisha is making his way from Jericho to Bethel. The man of God journeys from Judah to Bethel, and is on his way home when the old Bethel prophet meets him. Twice in this story the old prophet has his donkey saddled and rides to meet the Judean man of God. Jonah flees by boat trying to escape to Tarshish, and then travels (by

---

[1] See p. 93 above.
[2] Burrows, "The Literary Category of The Book of Jonah," 86.
[3] See p. 29 above.

foot?) some 600 miles to Nineveh. Keeping the target on the move is a well-known satirical technique, as a means of sustaining narrative interest.[4] Apollonius' *The Golden Ass*, Swift's *Gulliver's Travels*, Voltaire's *Candide*, and many other satires include voyages to distant lands. So the travelling of our prophets is fully in accord with this satirical feature. Another common feature is that in all four stories there are animals who perform some extraordinary feat.[5] Balaam's donkey talks; two she-bears are able to maul forty-two children; the lion only kills, but does not eat the man of God, nor does it touch his donkey; the great fish does not masticate Jonah, but preserves him alive for three days; and the lowly worm is able to attack Jonah's קִיקָיוֹן plant in the short period of time between dawn and sunrise "so that it withered" (4:7). But the most important common characteristic we feel we have identified in these stories is that they all contain sufficient satiric features to be classified as satires. They all have targets (Balaam, Elisha, the man of God, the old Bethel prophet, and Jonah). They all contain a predominance of characteristic satirical features such as unbelievable events, irony, ridicule, parody, and fine rhetorical techniques.

But if these stories are indeed satires against the prophets, a number of questions must now be asked even if we can only speculate on the answers. Who were these prophets? Were they considered false prophets? When and why were these satires written? How did these stories get accepted into the canon?

## Who were these prophets?

Although three of our satires are attributed to known biblical figures (Balaam, Elisha,[6] and Jonah) there can be no certainty as to

---

[4] See Feinberg, *Introduction To Satire*, 229; Worcester, *The Art of Satire*, 102; and Highet, *The Anatomy Of Satire*, 159.

[5] On the motif in these stories of animals being superior to man, see Rofé, *The Book of Balaam*, 53

the identity of the prophets bearing their names. In fact, the very nature of the satiric genre works against identifying them. For example, although Jonah of our story is modelled on a Jonah of the same name in 2 Kgs. 14:25,[7] it is likely that he represents a type of prophet rather than a specific individual. A satirist, in general, tends to use types rather than individuals "because he is usually concerned with Man rather than men, institutions rather than personalities."[8] In satire we find only caricatures, never characters.[9] Sometimes the mere names of characters indicate that the satirist is not attempting to portray rounded individuals. Voltaire uses Candide (literally, 'innocent'); Gogol's chief of police is Rascal-Puffed-up, the school superintendent is Bedbug, and the judge, Bungle-Steal; Evelyn Waugh's characters are named Lady Circumference, Lord Tangent, Lord Outrage, Mrs. Melrose-ape, and so on. According to Highet, the presence of distorted or ridiculous names is always a sure sign of satire.[10] This is often a good clue for detecting satire in the Bible too. We have mentioned in an earlier chapter how the king of Moab is caricatured in the Story of Ehud (Judg. 3). Eglon's name literally means, "King Fatted Calf" or "King Round One."[11] Also in our discussion of ironic elements in the book of Jonah, we observed that Jonah belies his name. Jonah's name (יוֹנָה בֶן־אֲמִתַּי) means "dove, son of faithfulness" or "dove, faithful son," but Jonah

---

[6] Elisha is not actually named in this episode, but it is reasonably certain that he is the subject of the satire (see p. 43 above).

[7] Good speculates on why Jonah was selected: "perhaps Jonah was so obscure a figure that a new story about him would contradict nothing previously known!" (*Irony In The Old Testament*, 41-42).

[8] Feinberg, *Introduction to Satire*, 232. W. O. S. Sutherland has observed that "in personal, political, or literary satire it is accurate to say that the 'object' of satire is actually a symbol" (*The Art of the Satirist*, 19).

[9] Feinberg, *Introduction to Satire*, 234.

[10] *The Anatomy of Satire*, 275.

[11] See p. 19 above.

proves to be unfaithful at the first opportunity.[12] Jonah then would be a type, an "Obedient Dove"! It is likely then that in all our satires the prophets are types rather than specific individuals. Indeed, in all the stories of our corpus there is a certain anonymity: either the name or the designation 'prophet' or "man of God" is missing. In the Balaam story and in the Jonah narrative, neither Balaam nor Jonah is given any designation. In the story of the lying prophet, we have the opposite situation. Designations (the terms 'prophet' and "man of God") occur, but neither is assigned names. Lastly, in the story of the boys and the bald prophet neither Elisha's name nor any term for the prophet occurs. This anonymity makes it likely that these prophets represent types of prophets rather than specific individuals. Balaam is a type of non-Israelite seer, and Elisha, the lying prophet, the old man prophet, and Jonah are types of wayward Israelite prophets.

**Were they false prophets?**

It should be made clear at this point that although the prophets in our stories are satirized for their behavior, their legitimacy is not in doubt. If 'legitimate' prophets can be identified on the grounds that they are God's representatives, that is, they are said to communicate with God and transmit His word, then all of the prophets in our stories are certainly genuine. Balaam, even though he is not an Israelite, communes with God and transmits His word. Elisha curses the boys in the very name of God. In the story of the lying prophet, the Judean prophet is the emissary of God, performs miraculous acts in God's name, and eventually is killed for disobeying God's instructions. Neither is the legitimacy of the prophet from Bethel in doubt although some scholars believe that he was a false prophet attached to an illegitimate sanctuary.[13] Two

---

[12] See pp. 104-5 above.
[13] Klopfenstein, "1. Könige 13," 646; Noth, *Könige*, 300; Jepsen, "Gottesmann und Prophet," 178; Walsh, "The Contexts of 1 Kings xiii,"

details in the story, however, attest to his legitimacy. Firstly, the Bethel prophet receives a genuine divine oracle from God (which results in the death of the Judean man of God) and secondly, three times[14] in the narrative he is characterized as being old. The importance of stressing his age is that it means he must have been a prophet long before the erection of Jeroboam's new sanctuary. The sanctuary, which is new, is considered by the author to be illegitimate and false, but he, the prophet of Bethel, is old (hence his legitimacy is not affected by the sanctuary). In the story we don't have a simple contrast between true and false prophecy. All we can learn from our text with respect to false prophecy is that God may speak through a lying prophet.[15] Finally, as far as Jonah is concerned, we have noted in the previous chapter that some scholars believe the message of the book has to do with false prophecy.[16] We have disputed that point of view primarily on the grounds that we believe it is Jonah's behavior, not any particular message like false prophecy, which is the main focus of the book.[17] Nevertheless, regardless of the interpretation of the book, and despite the fact that we have argued that Jonah does not act the way we think a prophet should act, there can be no doubt that Jonah is a legitimate prophet of God. All the prophets in our stories are legitimate prophets: they are genuine representatives of God, and it is as God's representatives that they are satirized.

---

360.

[14] Vv. 11, 25, & 29.

[15] Van Winkle, "1 Kings XIII: True and False Prophecy," 39; J. L. Crenshaw, *Prophetic Conflict*, 47.

[16] See pp. 150-52 above.

[17] See pp. 156-57 above.

**When and why were these satires written?**

A clue as to when these satires might have been written ought to lie in the date of the documents where the satire occurs. The story of Balaam and his donkey, generally agreed to be an insertion into the Numbers narrative,[18] is commonly assigned to the Yahwist or 'J' author.[19] Unfortunately, neither the date of the Yahwist nor the time of insertion is known. The traditional dating of the Yahwist, that of the 10th or 9th century B.C.E., has been the subject of so much debate that there is now little agreement on its date.[20] According to Rofé, the satire was inserted to answer a problem which troubled later generations: how could it be that a non-Israelite was able to converse with Israel's god?[21] Whereas earlier generations could accept the fact that a non-Israelite seer was able to commune with Israel's god, later generations (like the Deuteronomist and Second Isaiah [6th century]) found this difficult to accept.[22] The tradition that Balaam conversed with God and ultimately blessed Israel was too strong to deny, but they tried to diminish Balaam's stature by emphasizing the fact that he was essentially incompetent, able to operate only with God's help.[23] The purpose of the satire was to demonstrate that Balaam was not a real prophet.[24] If Balaam were to represent a type of non-Israelite seer, then the satire could have been used to demonstrate that all 'Balaams', all non-Israelite seers, were equally incompetent and thus illegitimate sources of the divine word. Such a negative depiction of Baalam would conform to other biblical (Deuteronomistic and Priestly) and post-biblical traditions which

---

[18] See p. 30 above.
[19] Wilson, *Prophecy and Society in Ancient Israel*, 148.
[20] Albert de Pury, "Yahwist ('J') Source," 1015-18.
[21] Rofé, *The Book of Balaam*, 53.
[22] Ibid, 48, 53.
[23] See also Joe Ann Hackett, "Balaam," 570.
[24] Rofé, *The Book of Balaam*, 53.

are critical of him.[25]

Both stories found in the book of Kings (the boys and the bald prophet, and the lying prophet) are attributed to the Deuteronomist or one of his revisors. This means they can be dated anytime in the 7th or 6th centuries B.C.E.[26] As far as the Book of Jonah is concerned, various attempts to date the book ranging from the 8th century B.C.E. (the time of the setting of the book) to the 3rd century B.C.E. have been made.[27] Of all the indicators of date, the only reliable one is language. But this indicator too has been widely debated. The latest consensus is that a 6th or 5th century date seems to be the most reasonable.[28] In his work on prophetical stories, Rofé has suggested that the stories of Balaam, of the lying prophet and of Jonah are closely related in date (beginning of the Second Temple period), and that "they originated in the same circle."[29] It is thus possible that our satires represent a point of view concerning wayward prophets current in the 6th century.[30] Alternatively, our satires may represent a reac-

---

[25] On the two biblical traditions about Balaam that he was a sinner (e.g., Num. 31:8, 16 [P]; Deut. 23:6 [D]; Josh. 13:22 [P]; Neh. 13:2 [= D]; Philo; Josephus; *m. 'Abot* 5:19) or saint (e.g., Num. 22-24; he submits to the will of God; Mic. 6:5 and *Midr. Num. Rab.*), see Milgrom, *Numbers*, 469-71; and Hackett, "Balaam," 569-71.

[26] Steven McKenzie, "Deuteronomistic History," 162-67.

[27] Lacocque and Lacocque believe that the book is a satire and a product of the third century B.C.E., a time of party strife in Judea between the 'Hellenized' (or modernist) Jews, and the Hasidim (or orthodox) strongly opposed to foreign influence on ancestral tradition. Jonah symbolizes the Hasidim and the Ninevites symbolize the Hellenists. The satire would then be a protest against "intellectual provincialism" and "religious fanaticism" of the orthodox party in Judah (*Jonah*, 41).

[28] See George M. Landes, "Linguistic Criteria And the Date of the Book of Jonah," 147*-70*.

[29] *The Book of Balaam*, 52-54; idem, *The Prophetical Stories*, 171.

[30] A post-exilic date is also favored by Burrows, "The Literary Category of the Book of Jonah," 104; Ackerman, "Jonah," 242; Fretheim, *The Message of Jonah*, 36-37, and others.

tion against miracle-working prophets or seers. In this scenario, members of the Deuterononomic school who incorporated these stories within their history, and the author of the book of Jonah, may have used these stories to indicate the contrast of these prophets with contemporaneous (6th century) non-miracle working prophets like Ezekiel and Jeremiah. We do know that in post exilic times there were these kind of prophets around,[31] but we should emphasize that the physical presence of prophets of the type represented by our prophets is not absolutely necessary since, as we have suggested above, it is most likely that these satires really target prophetic types more than real life prophets.[32] If Elisha represents a type of abusive prophet then the satire against him would represent a criticism of the abuse of prophetic power by a prophet who invoked an atrociously severe curse for a seemingly mild offense. If the Judean man of God, the lying prophet, and Jonah are types of wayward prophets then these satires represent a criticism of these prophets for lying, foolishness, concern with petty values, and behaviors unbecoming a prophet. All these satires against the Israelite prophets then lend themselves to be interpreted in a wider sense, as warnings to authority figures[33] not to be like Elisha, Jonah, and the other prophets. Insults on one's person are no excuse for abuse of power even if one is a prophet of God. Authority figures should not lie, nor should they be susceptible to deception, nor should they be concerned with their own selfish interests.

---

[31] See Zechariah (chapter 13), and Nehemiah (chapter 6).

[32] See Miles, "Laughing at the Bible," and Band, "Swallowing Jonah," 183, 192.

[33] So, for example, Robinson draws the message that the Elisha story is "a warning to those who exercise spiritual office not to emulate the petulance and the Prima Donna self-consciousness of Elisha. A leader should attempt to bring sinners to repentance, not to repel them" ("II Kings 2:23-25," 2).

## How did these stories get accepted into the canon?

There is no way of knowing if the canonizers were aware of the satirical elements which we have outlined in this book. Most probably they, like later audiences, were not.[34] Thus the original satiric nature of the stories of the boys and the bald prophet, of the lying prophet, and of Jonah may no longer have been understood as such. The unbelievable elements were taken as typical of stories that featured seer-type prophets, just as the fantastic exploits of Elijah and Elisha were accepted as the norm for that type of prophet. The story of the boys and the bald prophet was incorporated into the Elisha cycle of stories as another of the short wonder stories involving the prophet. The story of the lying prophet was incorporated into the Deuteronomist cycle because it served the didactic purpose of the Deuteronomist to show the illegitimacy of the northern king Jeroboam and of the Bethel sanctuary and its priesthood.[35] The book of Jonah was probably accepted into the canon as a prophetic book because it was taken at face value to be a story about an Elijah or Elisha-type prophet.[36] It dealt with subjects of theological significance such as repentance and God's mercy. Indeed it was the very prominence of these ideas in the book that led to it being inserted first in the Latter Prophets and much later to be chosen to be read as a הַפְטָרָה for the afternoon of the Day of Atonement.[37]

---

[34] So Band, "Swallowing Jonah," 184, 191, 194.

[35] See p. 82 above.

[36] The Song of Songs is another example where the understanding of a book's original meaning is thought to have changed prior to canonization. See Band, "Swallowing Jonah," 193.

[37] The first mention of this custom is found in *b. Meg.* 31a, centuries after the period of canonization. See Sasson, *Jonah*, 28.

## Postscript

Our satires deal with behaviors considered to be unbecoming for prophets in Israel. Elisha is satirized for his cruel curse; the man of God for disobeying God; the old prophet for lying, and being concerned about his own remains; Jonah for disobedience, hypocrisy, and for being concerned with his own physical comfort. Because these stories criticize the imperfections of certain prophets, even though they are only prophetic types, they enable us to see how the writers and their audiences really feel about the standard bearers of prophecy. For satires, by their very nature, reflect a certain conservatism and a desire to uphold the traditions.[38] The satirist uses his art "to shore up the foundations of the established order."[39] Thus when our satires criticize the behavior of the prophets, there lies the unspoken wish of what the proper behavior should be. If prophets are criticized for hypocrisy, foolishness, and abuse of power, then the writers, and their appreciative audiences, are expressing their views, through the satires, that there has been a grievous falling away from proper standards of behavior and an implied wish that the proper standards be restored.

---

[38] So Elliott, *The Power of Satire*, 266. Note Orth's well-taken observation concerning parody that "a by-product of detecting parody in a text is the fact that it means that there must have been some sort of canon at the time the story was written" ("Genre in Jonah," 261).

[39] Elliott, *The Power of Satire*, 273.

# IX

## Works Cited

AALDERS, G. Ch. *The Problem of the Book of Jonah*. London: Tyndale, 1948.

ABRAMOWITZ, Chaim. "Maftir Jonah." *Dor le Dor* 14/1 (1985), 3-9.

ABRAMSKY, Shula. "Jonah's Alienation and Return." *Beth Mikra* 24 (1979), 370-95 [in Hebrew].
_____. "About Casting Lots in Order to Catch a Sinner." *Beth Mikra* 26 (1981), 231-66 [in Hebrew].

ABRAVANEL. = Isaac Abravanel (1437-1508). *Commentary on the Former Prophets*. Repr. with additions. Jerusalem: Torah Vada'at, 1955 [in Hebrew].

ACKERMAN, James S. "Satire And Symbolism in The Song of Jonah." *Traditions in Transformation: Turning Points in Biblical Faith: Frank Moore Cross 60th Birthday Festschrift*. Eds. Baruch Halpern & Jon D. Levenson. Winona Lake, Ind.: Eisenbrauns, 1981, 213-46.
_____. "Jonah." *The Literary Guide to the Bible*. Eds. R. Alter & F. Kermode. Cambridge, Mass.: Harvard University, 1987, 234-43.

ACKROYD, Peter R. *Exile and Restoration: A Study of Hebrew Thought of the Sixth Century B.C.* Philadelphia: Westminster, 1975.

AHARONI, Yohanan. *The Land of the Bible: A Historical Geography.* Rev. & Enlarged ed. Philadelphia: Westminster, 1979 <1967>.

ALEXANDER, T. D. "Jonah and Genre." *Tyndale Bulletin* 36 (1985), 35-59.
_____. *Jonah: An Introduction and Commentary.* Tyndale Old Testament Commentaries 23b. Downers Grove, Ill.: Inter-Varsity, 1988.

ALLEN, Leslie C. *The Books of Joel, Obadiah, Jonah and Micah.* NICOT. Grand Rapids, Mich.: Wm. B. Eerdmans, 1976.

ALTER, Robert. *The Art of Biblical Narrative.* New York: Basic, 1981.
_____. *The Art of Biblical Poetry.* New York: Basic, 1985.
_____. "Language as Theme in The Book of Judges." *The Eleventh Annual Rabbi Louis Feinberg Memorial Lecture in Judaic Studies.* Cincinnati: Judaic Studies Program, University of Cincinnati, 1988.

ALTSCHULER, Yeḥiel Hillel. = Meṣudat David.

AMIT, Yairah. "Hidden Polemic in the Conquest of Dan: Judges xvii-xviii." *VT* 60 (1990), 4-20.

ANDERSEN, Francis, and FREEDMAN, David Noel. *Amos.* AB 24A. Garden City, N.Y.: Doubleday, 1989.

ANDREW, M. E. "Gattung and Intention of the Book of Jonah." *Orita* 1 (1967), 13-18, 78-85.

ARARAT, Nisan. "On Jonah's Fear of God (Divine Justice)." *Beth Mikra* 33 (1987-88), 85-110 [in Hebrew].

_____. "Genesis 11:1-9 as a Satire." *Beth Mikra* 39 (1994), 224-31 [in Hebrew].

ARCHER, G. L., Jr. *A Survey of Old Testament Introduction.* Chicago: Moody, 1964.

ARUM, Nurit. "The Purpose of the Book of Jonah." *Sefer Chayim M. Y. Gevaryahu: Studies in the Bible and Jewish Thought.* Ed. B. Z. Luria. Jerusalem: Qiryat Sefer, 1989, 211-14 [in Hebrew].

AULD, A. Graeme. *I & II Kings.* Philadelphia: Westminster, 1986.

AVIEZER, N. "The Book of Jonah: An Ethical Confrontation between God and Prophet." *Dor le Dor* 14 (1985), 11-15, 50.

BACHER, Shlomo. "The Book of Jonah--The Author vs. His Hero." *Beth Mikra* 28 (1982-1983), 39-43 [in Hebrew].

BAKHTIN, M. *Problems of Dostoevsky's Poetics.* Ann Arbor, Mich.: Ardis, 1973.

BAND, Arnold J. "Swallowing Jonah: The Eclipse of Parody." *Prooftexts* 10/2 (1990), 177-95.

BAUER, J. H. "Drei Tage." *Biblica* 39 (1958), 354-58.

BAXTER, J. Sidlow. *Mark These Men.* London: Marshall, Morgan & Scott, 1949.

BEN MENACHEM, Eliyakim. *Commentary on the Book of Jonah.* Jerusalem: Mosad Harav Kook, 1973 [in Hebrew].

BEN-YOSEF, I. A. "Jonah and the Fish as a Folk Motif." *Semitics* 7 (1980), 102-17.

BERLIN, Adele. "A Rejoinder to John A. Miles Jr., With Some Observations on the Nature of Prophecy." *JQR* 66 (1976), 227-35.

BEWER, Julius A. *A Critical and Exegetical Commentary on Jonah*. ICC. Edinburgh: T. & T. Clark, 1912.
_____. *The Literature of the Old Testament In Its Historical Development*. New York: Columbia University, 1922.

BICKERMAN, E. *Four Strange Books of The Bible. Jonah/Daniel/Koheleth/Esther*. New York: Schocken, 1967.

BOOTH, Wayne C. *A Rhetoric of Irony*. Chicago: University of Chicago, 1974.

BRENNER, Athalya. "Jonah's Poem Out of and Within its Context." *Among the Prophets: Essays on Prophetic Topics*. Eds. P. R. Davies & D. J. A. Clines. JSOTSup 144. Sheffield: JSOT, 1992, 183-92.

BRICHTO, H. C. *Toward a Grammar of Biblical Poetics*. New York: Oxford University, 1992.

BROCKINGTON, L. H. "Jonah." *PCB*, 627-29.

BRONGERS, H. "Some Remarks on the Biblical Particle halo'." *OTS* 21 (1981), 177-89.

BROWN, Michael A. "'Is It Not?' or 'Indeed!': HL in Northwest Semitic." *Maarav* 4/2, (1987), 201-19.

BURROWS, Millar. "The Literary Category of The Book of Jonah." *Translating and Understanding the Old Testament: Essays in Honor of Herbert Gordon May.* Eds. H. T. Frank & W. L. Reed. Nashville: Abingdon, 1970, 80-107.

CARROLL, R. P. *Jeremiah.* OTL. Philadelphia: Westminster, 1986.
_____. "Is Humour Among the Prophets?" *On Humour and the Comic in the Hebrew Bible.* Eds. Y. T. Radday & A. Brenner. JSOTSup 92. Sheffield: Sheffield Academic, 1990, 169-89.

CASSUTO, U. *From Noah to Abraham. A Commentary on the Book of Genesis. Part Two.* Trans. Israel Abrahams. Jerusalem: Magnes, 1964.

CHASE, Mary Ellen. *The Bible and the Common Reader.* Rev. ed. New York: Macmillan, 1952 <1944>.

CHILDS, Brevard S. "The Canonical Shape of the Book of Jonah." *Biblical and Near Eastern Studies. Essays in Honor of William Sanford LaSor.* Ed. G. A. Tuttle. Grand Rapids, Mich.: Eerdmans, 1970, 122-28.
_____. *Introduction to the Old Testament as Scripture.* Philadelphia: Fortress, 1979.

CHRISTENSEN, Duane L. "Anticipatory Paronomasia in Jonah 3:7-8 and Genesis 37:2." *RB* 90 (1983), 261-63.
_____. "The Song of Jonah: A Metrical Analysis." *JBL* 104 (1985), 217-31.
_____. "Narrative Poetics and the Interpretation of the Book of Jonah." *Directions in Biblical Hebrew Poetry.* Ed. E. R. Follis. JSOTSup 40. Sheffield: JSOT, 1987, 29-48.

CLEMENTS, R. E. "The Purpose of the Book of Jonah." *VTSup* 28 (1975), 16-28.

CLINES, David J. A. "Story and Poem: The Old Testament as Literature and as Scripture." *Interpretation* 34 (1980), 115-27.

_____. *The Esther Scroll: The Story of the Story.* JSOTSup 30. Sheffield: JSOT, 1984.

COGAN, Mordechai. "A Technical Term for Exposure." *JNES* 27 (1968), 133-35.

_____, and TADMOR, H. *II Kings.* AB 11. Garden City, N.Y.: Doubleday, 1988.

COHEN, Abraham D. "The Tragedy of Jonah." *Judaism* 21 (1972), 164-75.

COHN, Gabriël H. *Das Buch Jona: im Lichte der biblischen Erzählkunst.* Assen: Van Gorcum, 1969.

COHN, Robert. "Literary Technique in the Jeroboam Narrative." *ZAW* 97 (1985), 23-35.

CONRAD, Lawrence I. "The Biblical Tradition for the Plague of the Philistines." *JAOS* 104 (1984), 281-87.

COOPER, Alan. "In Praise of Divine Caprice: The Significance of the Book of Jonah." *Among the Prophets: Essays on Prophetic Topics.* Eds P. R. Davies & D. J. A. Clines. JSOTSup 144. Sheffield: JSOT, 1992, 144-63.

CRAIG, Kenneth M., Jr. *A Poetics of Jonah: Art in the Service of Ideology.* Columbia, S.C.: University of South Carolina, 1993.

CRENSHAW, J. L. *Prophetic Conflict. Its Effect upon Israelite Religion.* BZAW 124. Berlin: de Gruyter, 1971.

CROUCH, Walter B. "To Question an End, to End a Question: Opening the Closure of the Book of Jonah." *JSOT* 62 [1994], 101-12.

DAICHES, Samuel. "Balaam--a Babylonian bārû." *Hilprecht Anniversary Volume.* Leipzig: J. C. Hinrichs, 1909, 60-70.

DAUBE, David. "Jonah: A Reminiscence." *JJS* 35 (1984), 36-43.

DAVIES, G. I. "The Uses of *r'' qal* and the Meaning of Jonah iv 1." *VT* 27 (1977), 105-10.

DAY, John. "The Book of Jonah." *In Quest of the Past: Studies on Israelite Religion, Literature and Prophetism.* Ed. A. Van der Woude. *OTS* 26. Leiden: E. J. Brill, 1990, 32-47.

DE HOOP, Raymond. "The Book of Jonah as Poetry, An Analysis of Jonah 1:1-16." *The Structural Analysis of Biblical and Canaanite Poetry.* Eds. W. van der Meer & J. C. de Moor. JSOTSup 74. Sheffield: Sheffield Academic, 1988, 156-71.

DENTAN, Robert C. "The Literary Affinities of Exodus xxxiv 6f." *VT* 13 (1963), 34-51.

DE PURY, Albert. "Yahwist ('J') Source." *ABD*, 6:1012-20.

DE VRIES, Simon J. *1 Kings.* Waco, Tex.: Word, 1985.

DOZEMAN, Thomas B. "The Way of the Man of God from Judah:  True and False Prophecy in the Pre-D Legend of 1 Kings 13." *CBQ* 44 (1982), 379-93.
_____. "Inner-Biblical Interpretation of Yahweh's Gracious and Compassionate Character." *JBL* 108 (1989), 207-23.

EBEN-SHOSHAN, Abraham. *Millon Chadash.* 4 vols. Jerusalem: Kiryat Sepher, 1958 [in Hebrew].

EERDMANS, B. D. *The Religion of Israel*. Leiden: Universitaire Pers Leiden, 1947.

EHRLICH, Arnold B. *Mikrä ki-Pheschutö*. 3 vols. Berlin: M. Poppelauer, 1899-1901 [in Hebrew].
_____. *Randglossen zur Hebräischen Bibel*. 5 vols. Hildesheim: Georg Olms, 1968 <1909-14>.

EICHLER, Myron. "The Plague in 1 Samuel 5 and 6." *Dor le Dor* 10 (1982), 157-65.

ELLIOTT, R. C. *The Power of Satire: Magic, Ritual, Art*. Princeton, N.J.: Princeton University, 1960.

EMMERSON, Grace I. "Another Look at Jonah." *ExpTim* 88 (1976), 86-88.

FEINBERG, Leonard. *The Satirist*. Ames, Iowa: Iowa State University, 1963.
_____. *Introduction To Satire*. Ames, Iowa: Iowa State University, 1967.

FENTON, T. L. "Command and Fulfillment in Ugaritic: tqtl: yqtl and qtl: qtl." *JSS* 14 (1969), 34-38.

FEUILLET, A. "Les Sources du Livre de Jonas." *RB* 54 (1947), 161-86.

FISHELOV, David. "The Prophet as Satirist." *Prooftexts* 9/3 (1989), 195-211.

FOKKELMAN, Jan P. *Narrative Art in Genesis: Specimems of Stylistic and Structural Analysis*. 2nd ed. The Biblical Seminar 12. Sheffield: JSOT, 1991 <1975>.

FONTAINE, Carole. "The Deceptive Goddess In Ancient Near Eastern Myth: Inanna and Inarash." *Semeia* 42 (1988), 84-102.

FRÄNKEL, Leah. "'His Mercy Extends to All His Creatures': On the Meaning of the Book of Jonah." *Ma'ayanot* 9 (1967), 193-207 [in Hebrew].

FREEDMAN, David Noel. "Did God Play a Dirty Trick on Jonah at the End?" *Bible Review* 6/4 (1990), 26-31.

FRETHEIM, Terence E. *The Message of Jonah: A Theological Commentary*. Minneapolis: Augsburg, 1977.
_____. "Jonah and Theodicy." *ZAW* 90 (1978), 227-37.

FRYE, Northrop. *Anatomy of Criticism: Four Essays*. Princeton: Princeton University, 1971 <1957>.

GARSIEL, Moshe. *The First Book of Samuel. A Literary Study of Comparative Structures, Analogies, and Parallels*. Ramat Gan: Revivim, 1985.

GASTER, Theodor H. *Myth, Legend, and Custom in The Old Testament*. New York: Harper & Row, 1969.

GEVARYAHU, Chayim. "The Universalism of the Book of Jonah." *Jewish Bible Quarterly: Dor le Dor* 10 (1981), 20-27.

GINSBERG, H. L. "Introduction to Jonah." *The Five Megilloth and Jonah: A New Translation*. Philadephia: JPS, 1969, 114-16.

GOITEIN, S. D. "Some Observations on Jonah." *JPOS* 17 (1937), 63-77.

GOLKA, Friedemann W. "Jonah." *Revelation of God: A Commentary on the Song of Songs and Jonah*. Eds. George A. F. Knight & Friedemann W. Golka. International Theological Commentary. Grand Rapids, Mich.: Eerdmans, 1988, 65-136.

GOOD, Edwin M. *Irony In The Old Testament*. Philadelphia: Westminster, 1965.

GORDIS, Robert. *The Biblical Text in the Making. A Study of the Kethib-Qere*. New York: Ktav, 1971 [1937]).

GORDON, Cyrus. *Introduction to Old Testament Times*. Ventnor, N.J.: Ventnor, 1953.

GORDON, S. L. *The Book of Second Kings*. Tel Aviv: Massada, 1956 [in Hebrew].

GOTTWALD, Norman K. *The Hebrew Bible: A Socio-Literary Introduction*. Philadelphia: Fortress, 1985.

GRAY, John Gray. *I & II Kings*. 2nd rev. ed. OTL. Philadelphia: Westminster, 1970.

GREENSTEIN, Edward L. "Deconstruction and Biblical Narrative." *Prooftexts* 9/1 (1989), 43-71.
_____. "A Jewish Reading of Esther." *Judaic Prespectives On Ancient Israel*. Eds. Jacob Neusner, Baruch A. Levine & Ernest S. Frerichs. Philadelphia: Fortress, 1987, 225-43.

GREENSTONE, Julius H. *Numbers with Commentary*. The Holy Scriptures. Philadelphia: JPS, 1939.

GROSS, Walter Gross. "Lying Prophet and Disobedient Man of God in 1 Kings 13: Role Analysis as an Instrument of Theological Interpretation of an OT Narrative Text." *Semeia* 15 (1979), 97-135.

HAAS, W. E. "Some Characteristics of Satire." *Satire News Letter* 3/1 (1965), 1-3.

HACKETT, Joe Ann. "Balaam." *ABD*, 1:569-72.

HALLPIKE, Christopher R. "Hair." *The Encyclopedia of Religion*. Ed. Mircea Eliade. New York: Macmillan, 1987, 6:154.

HALPERN, Baruch. *The First Historians: The Hebrew Bible and History*. San Francisco: Harper & Row, 1988.
_____. "The Assassination of Eglon---The First Locked-Room Murder Mystery." *Bible Review* 4 (1988), 32-41, 44.
_____, and FRIEDMAN, Richard Elliott. "Composition and Paronomasia in the Book of Jonah." *HAR* 4 (1980), 79-92.

HANNOOSH, M. *Parody and Decadence: Laforgue's 'Moralites Legendaires'*. Columbus, Ohio: Ohio State University, 1989.

HARAN, Menachem. *Temples and Temple Service in Ancient Israel*. Oxford: Clarendon, 1978.

HARRIS, W. V. *Dictionary of Concepts in Literary Criticism and Theory*. New York: Greenwood, 1992.

HARTOUM, A. *The Book of Kings*. Tel Aviv: Yavneh, 1960 [in Hebrew].

HAUSER, Allan John. "Jonah: In Pursuit of the Dove." *JBL* 104 (1985), 21-37.

HELD, Moshe. "The Action-Result (Factitive-Passive) Sequence of Identical Verbs in Biblical Hebrew and Ugaritic." *JBL* 84 (1965), 272-82.

_____. "Two Philological Notes on Enuma Elish." *Cuneiform Studies in Honor of Samuel Noah Kramer.* Ed. B. L. Eichler. AOAT 25. Neukirchen-Vluyn: Neukirchener, 1976, 231-39.

HENDRICKSON, G. L. "*Satura Tota Nostra Est.*" *Classical Philology* 22 (January, 1927), 46-60. Repr. in *Satire: Modern Essays in Criticism.* Ed. R. Paulson. Englewood Cliffs, N.J.: Prentice-Hall, 1971, 37-51.

HESCHEL, Abraham J. *The Prophets.* New York: JPS, 1962.

HIGHET, Gilbert. *The Anatomy of Satire.* Princeton, N.J.: Princeton University, 1962.

HODGART, Matthew. *Satire.* World University Library. New York: McGraw-Hill, 1969.

HOLBERT, John C. "'Deliverance Belongs to Yahweh!': Satire in The Book of Jonah." *JSOT* 21 (1981), 59-81.

HOLLADAY, Carl R. "Biblical Criticism." *HBD*, 129-33.

HYERS, Conrad. *And God Created Laughter: The Bible As Divine Comedy.* Atlanta: John Knox, 1987.

JEMIELITY, Thomas. *Satire in the Hebrew Prophets.* Louisville, Ky.: Westminster/John Knox, 1990.

JENKS, William. *Comprehensive Commentary.* Philadelphia: J. B. Lippincott, 1849.

JEPSEN, Alfred. "Anmerkungen zum Buche Jona." *Wort-Gebot-Glaube: Walter Eichrodt Zum 80. Geburtstag.* Eds. J. J. Stamm, E. Jenni & H. J. Stoebe. ATANT 59. Zürich: Zwingli, 1970, 297-305.

_____. "Gottesmann und Prophet: Anmerkungen zum Kapital 1. Könige 13." *Problem biblischer Theologie: Gerhard Von Rad zum 70. Geburtstag.* Ed. H. W. Wolff. München: Chr. Kaiser, 1971, 171-82.

JOHNSON, Edgar. *A Treasury of Satire.* New York: Simon & Schuster, 1945.

JOÜON, P., and MURAOKA, T. *A Grammar of Biblical Hebrew.* Subsidia Biblica 14/I-II. Rome: Biblical Institute, 1991.

KAUFMANN, Yehezkel. *The Religion of Israel: From the Beginnings to the Babylonian Exile.* Trans. M. Greenberg. New York: Schocken, 1972.

KEEL, Yehuda. *Book of Kings.* Jerusalem: Mosad Harav Kook, 1989 [in Hebrew].

KEIL, Carl Friedrich. *The Twelve Minor Prophets.* 2 vols. Trans. J. Martin. Biblical Commentary on the Old Testament. Edinburgh: T. & T. Clark, 1871.

_____, and DELITZSCH, Franz. *The Books of the Kings.* Biblical Commentary on the Old Testament. Edinburgh: T. and T. Clark, 1872.

KERNAN, A. B. *The Plot of Satire.* New Haven & London: Yale University, 1965.

KIMḤI. = David Kimḥi (1160-1235). Commentary in *Miqra'ot Gedolot.*

KIRK, E. P. *Menippean Satire. An Annotated Catalogue of Texts and Criticism.* New York: Garland, 1980.

KISSANE, Edward J. *The Book of Isaiah.* Vol. 1. Dublin: Browne & Nolan, 1941.

KLOPFENSTEIN, Martin A. "1. Könige 13." *Parreseia: Karl Barth zum achtzigsten geburststag am 10. Mai 1966.* Zürich: EVZ, 1966, 639-72.

KNOX, Norman. "On the Classification of Ironies." *Modern Philology* 70 (1972), 53-62.

KNOX, Ronald A. "On Humour and Satire." *Essays in Satire.* London: Sheed & Ward, 1928. Repr. in *Satire: Modern Essays in Criticism.* Ed. R. Paulson. Englewood Cliffs, N.J.: Prentice-Hall, 1971, 52-65.

KRAELING, E. G. *Daniel - Malachi.* Commentary on The Prophets, 2. Camden, N.J.: Thomas Nelson, 1966.

LACOCQUE, André, and LACOCQUE, Pierre-Emmanuel. *The Jonah Complex.* Atlanta: John Knox, 1981.
_____. *Jonah: A Psycho-Religious Approach to the Prophet.* Studies on Personalities of the Old Testament. Columbus: University of South Carolina, 1990.

LANDES, George M. "The Kerygma of the Book of Jonah: The Contextual Interpretation of the Jonah Psalm." *Interpretation* 21 (1967), 3-31.
_____. "The 'Three Days and Three Nights' Motif in Jonah 2:1." *JBL* 86 (1967), 446-50.
_____. "Jonah." *IDBSup*, 488-91.

_____. "Jonah: A *mašal*?" *Israelite Wisdom: Theological and Literary Essays in Honor of Samuel Terrien.* Eds. G. Gammie, W. A. Brueggemann, W. L. Humphreys, & J. M. War. Missoula, Mont.: Scholars, 1978, 137-58.

_____. "The Canonical Aproach to Introducing the Old Testament: Prodigy and Problems." *JSOT* 16 (1980), 32-39.

_____. "Linguistic Criteria And the Date of the Book of Jonah." *Eretz-Israel* 16 (1982), 147*-70*.

_____. "Review of Lacocque and Lacocque, *Jonah: A Psycho-Religious Approach.*" *JBL* 111/1 (1992), 130-34.

LANDY, Francis. "Humour as a Tool for Biblical Exegesis." *On Humour and the Comic in the Hebrew Bible.* Eds. Y. T. Radday & A. Brenner. JSOTSup 92. Sheffield: Sheffield Academic, 1990, 99-115.

LARGEMENT, René. "Les oracles des Bile'am et la mantique Suméro-Akkadienne." *Mémorial du Cinquantenaire de l'École des langues orientales anciennes de l'Institute Catholique de Paris.* Paris: Bloud & Gay, 1964, 37-50.

LASINE, Stuart. "Guest and Host in Judges 19: Lot's Hospitality in an Inverted World." *JSOT* 29 (1984), 37-59.

LEE, G. *Allusion, Parody and Imitation.* Hull: University of Hull, 1971.

LEMKE, Werner E. "The Way of Obedience: 1 Kings 13 and the Structure of the Deuteronomistic History." *Magnalia Dei The Mighty Acts of God: Essays on the Bible and Archaeology in Memory of G. Ernest Wright.* Eds. F. M. Cross, W. E. Lemke, & P. D. Miller, Jr. Garden City, N.Y.: Doubleday, 1976, 301-26.

LEVINE, Etan. "Jonah as a Philosophical Book." *ZAW* 96 (1984), 235-45.

LEWIS, Chayim. "Jonah--A Parable for Our Time." *Judaism* 21 (1972), 159-63.

LICHT, Jacob. *Storytelling in the Bible.* Jerusalem: Magnes, 1978.

LIMBURG, James. *Jonah.* OTL. Louisville, Ky.: Westminster/ John Knox, 1993.

LINDBLOM, Johannes. *Prophecy in Ancient Israel.* Philadelphia: Fortress, 1962.

LODS, Adolphe. *The Prophets and the Rise of Judaism.* Trans. S. H. Hooke. New York: E. P. Dutton, 1937.

LOHFINK, N. "Jona ging zur Stadt hinaus (Jona 4,5)." *Biblische Notizen* 5 (1961), 185-203.

LONG, Burke O. *1 Kings With An Introduction to Historical Literature.* Grand Rapids, Mich.: Eerdmans, 1984.

LUBECK, R. J. "Prophetic Sabotage: A Look at Jonah 3:2-4." *Trinity Journal* 9 (1988), 37-46.

LUMBY, J. Rawson. *The First and Second Book of the Kings.* Cambridge: Cambridge University, 1903.

MCALPINE, T. H. *Sleep, Divine and Human in the Old Testament.* JSOTSup 38. Sheffield: JSOT, 1987.

MCCARTHY, Carmel, and RILEY, William. *The Old Testament Short Story: Explorations into Narrative Spirituality.* Message of Biblical Spirituality 7. Wilmington, Del: Glazier, 1986.

MACDONALD, Dwight, ed. *Parodies: An Anthology from Chaucer to Berbohm--and After*. New York: Random House, 1960.

MCKENZIE, John L. *The World Of The Judges*. Englewood Cliffs, N.J.: Prentice-Hall, 1966.

MCKENZIE, Steven. "Deuteronomistic History." *ABD*, 2:160-68.

MAGONET, Jonathan. *Form And Meaning. Studies in Literary Techniques in The Book of Jonah*. Bible And Literature Series 8. Sheffield: Almond, 1983 <1976>.

MALBIM. = Meir Loeb ben Yehiel Michal (1809-1879). Commentary in *Miqra'ot Gedolot*. Repr. Jerusalem/Lublin: Miqra'ot Gedolot, 1964 [in Hebrew].

MALUL, Meir. "Adoption of Foundlings in the Bible and Mesopotamian Documents: A Study of Some Legal Metaphors in Ezekiel 16:1-7." *JSOT* 46 (1990), 97-126.

MARCUS, David. "Some Antiphrastic Euphemisms for a Blind Person in Akkadian and Other Semitic Languages." *JAOS* 100 (1980), 307-10.
_____. "Juvenile Delinquency in The Bible and the Ancient Near East." *JANES* 13 (1981), 31-52.
_____. "In Defence of Micah: Judges 17:2: He Was Not a Thief." *Shofar* 6 (1988), 72-80.
_____. "Ridiculing the Ephraimites: The Shibboleth Incident (Judges 12:6)." *Let Your Colleagues Praise You: Studies in Memory of Stanley Gevirtz. Maarav* 7-8. Eds. R. J. Ratner, L. M. Barth, M. L. Gevirtz & B. Zuckerman. Rolling Hills Estates, Calif.: Western Academic, 1993, 95-105.

MATHER, J. "The Comic Art of the Book of Jonah." *Soundings* 65 (1982), 280-91.

MAYES, A. D. H. *Judges*. Old Testament Guides. Sheffield, JSOT, 1985.

MESLIN, Michel. "Eye." *The Encyclopedia of Religion*. Ed. Mircea Eliade. New York: Macmillan, 1987, 5:236-39.

MESSNER, Richard G. "Elisha and the Bears." *Grace Journal* 3/2 (1962), 12-24.

MEṢUDAT DAVID. = Yeḥiel Hillel Altschuler. Commentary in *Miqra'ot Gedolot*.

MEYERS, Eric M. *Jewish Ossuaries: Reburial and Rebirth*. BibOr. Rome: Biblical Institute, 1971.

MILES, John A. "Laughing at the Bible: Jonah as Parody." *JQR* 65 (1975), 168-81.

MILGROM, Jacob. *Numbers: The Traditional Hebrew Text with the New JPS Translation*. JPS Torah Commentary. Philadelphia: JPS, 1990.

MIQRA'OT GEDOLOT. Rabbinic Bible containing commentaries by Rashi (Solomon ben Isaac), Radak (David Kimḥi), Meṣudat David (Yeḥiel Hillel Altschuler). New York: Pardes, 1951 < 1524/5 > [in Hebrew].

MONTGOMERY, James A. *A Critical and Exegetical Commentary on The Books of Kings*. ICC. Edinburgh: T. & T. Clark, 1960 < 1951 >.

MOORE, George Foot. *A Criticial and Exegetical Commentary on Judges*. ICC. 2nd ed. Edinburgh, T. & T. Clark, 1976 <1895>.

MUECKE, Douglas Colin. *The Compass of Irony*. London/New York: Metheun, 1969.
_____. *Irony: The Critical Idiom*. London/New York: Methuen, 1970.

MUFFS, Y. *Love & Joy: Law, Language and Religion in Ancient Israel*. New York: Jewish Theological Seminary, 1992.

MURPHY, R. E. "The Book of Jonah." *The Interpreter's One Volume Commentary on the Bible*. Ed. C. M. Laymon. Nashville: Abingdon, 1971.

NA'AMAN, Nadav. "Beth-Aven, Bethel and Early Israelite Sanctuaries." *ZDPV* 103 (1987), 13-21.

NOTH, Martin. *Numbers*. OTL. Philadelphia: Westminster, 1968.
_____. *Könige*. BKAT IX/1. Neukirchen-Vluyn: Neukirchener, 1968.

ORLINSKY, H. M. "Nationalism-Universalism and Internationalism in Ancient Israel." *Translating and Understanding the Old Testament: Essays in Honor of Herbert Gordon May*. Eds. H. T. Frank & W. L. Reed. Nashville: Abingdon, 1970, 206-36. Repr. in Orlinsky, *Essays in Biblical Culture*, 78-116.
_____. *Essays in Biblical Culture and Bible Translation*. New York: Ktav, 1974.

ORTH, M. "Genre in Jonah: The Effects of Parody in the Book of Jonah." *The Bible in the Light of Cuneiform Literature: Scripture in Context III.* Eds. W. W. Hallo, B. W. Jones, & G. L. Mattingly. Ancient Near Eastern Texts and Studies 8. Lewiston, N.Y.: Mellen, 1990, 257-81.

OTTO, Rudolf. *The Idea of The Holy: An Inquiry into The Non-Rational Factor in The Idea of The Divine and Its Relation to The Rational.* London: Oxford University, 1958 <1923>.

OXFORD ENGLISH DICTIONARY. 2nd ed. Oxford: Oxford University, 1989 <1933>.

PAINE, Thomas. *The Age of Reason. The Theological Works of Thomas Paine.* Vol II. Chicago: Belford, Clarke & Co, 1882 <1794>.

PARKER, Simon B. "The Birth Announcement." *Ascribe to the Lord. Biblical and Other Studies in Memory of Peter C. Craigie.* Eds. L. Eslinger & G. Taylor. JSOT Supp 67. Sheffield: JSOT, 1988, 133-49.

PAULSON, Ronald. "The Fictions of Satire." *Satire: Modern Essays in Criticism.* Englewood Cliffs, N.J.: Prentice-Hall, 1971 <1967>, 340-59.
_____, ed. *Satire: Modern Essays in Criticism.* Englewood Cliffs, N.J.: Prentice-Hall, 1971.

PAYNE, David F. "Jonah from the Perspective of its Audience." *JSOT* 13 (1979), 3-12.

PAYNE, Robin. "The Prophet Jonah: Reluctant Messenger and Intercessor." *ExpTim* 100 (1989), 131-34.

PELLI, M. "The Literary Art of Jonah." *Hebrew Studies* 20-21 (1979-1980), 18-28.

PESCH, R. "Zur konzentrischen Struktur von Jona 1." *Biblica* 47 (1966), 577-81.

PHELPS, William Lyon. *Human Nature in the Bible*. New York: Scribner's, 1923.

PINKUS, Philip. "An Impossible Task? Review of Leonard Feinberg's *Introduction to Satire*." *Satire News Letter* 5/2 (Spring, 1968), 164-67.

PORTEN, B. "Baalshamem and the Date of the Book of Jonah." *De la Tôrah au Messie*. Eds. M. Carrez, J. Doré, & P. Grelot. Paris: Desclée, 1981, 237-44.

PRICE, Martin. *Swift's Rhetorical Art: A Study in Structure and Meaning*. New Haven: Yale University, 1953.

RABINOWITZ, Chayim D. *The Haftarot Arranged According to the Books of the Prophets*. Vol. 2. Jerusalem: Daat Yisrael, 1985 [in Hebrew].

RADAK. = Rabbi David Kimḥi (1160-1235). Commentary in *Miqra'ot Gedolot*.

RADDAY, Yehuda T. "On Missing The Humour in the Bible: An Introduction." *On Humour and the Comic in the Hebrew Bible*. Eds. Y. T. Radday & A. Brenner. JSOTSup 92. Sheffield: Sheffield Academic, 1990, 21-38.
_____. "Esther With Humour." Ibid., 295-313.

RANDALL, C. Corydon. "An Approach to Biblical Satire." *The Psalms and Other Studies on the Old Testament Present to Joseph I. Hunt*. Eds. J. C. Knight & L. A. Sinclair. Nashotah, Wis.: Nashotah House Seminary, 1990, 132-44.

RANDOLPH, M. C. "The Structural Design of the Formal Verse Satire." *Philological Quarterly* 21 (1942), 368-84. Repr. in *Satire: Modern Essays in Criticism.* Ed. R. Paulson. Englewood Cliffs, N.J.: Prentice-Hall, 1971, 171-89.

RASHI. = Rabbi Solomon ben Isaac (1040-1105). Commentary in *Miqra'ot Gedolot.*

RATNER, Robert J. "*Derek*: Morpho-Syntactical Considerations." *JAOS* 107 (1987), 471-73.

_____. "Jonah: Toward the Re-education of the Prophets." *Jewish Bible Quarterly: Dor le Dor* 17/1 (1988-1989), 10-18.

_____. "Jonah, The Runaway Servant." *Sopher Mahir: Northwest Semitic Studies Presented to Stanislav Segert. Maarav* 5-6. Ed. E. M. Cook. Santa Monica, Cal.: Western Academic, 1990, 281-305.

RAUBER, D. F. "Jonah--the Prophet as Schlemiel." *The Bible Today* 49 (1970), 29-38.

RAWLINSON, George. *II Kings.* The Pulpit Commentary. London: Kegan Paul, 1890.

RENDSBURG, Gary A. "The Mock of Baal in 1 Kings 18:27." *CBQ* 50 (1988), 414-17.

ROBINSON, Bernard P. "II Kings 2:23-25. Elisha and the She-bears." *Scripture Bulletin* 14 (1983), 2-3.

_____. "Jonah's Qiqayon Plant." *ZAW* 97 (1985), 390-403.

ROBINSON, J. *The First Book of Kings.* CBC. Cambridge: Cambridge University, 1972.

_____. *The Second Book of Kings.* CBC. Cambridge: Cambridge University, 1976.

ROFÉ, Alexander. "Classes in the Prophetical Stories: Didactic Legenda and Parable." *VTSup* 26 (1974), 143-64.

_____. *The Book of Balaam.* Jerusalem Biblical Studies 1. Tel Aviv: Simor, 1979 [in Hebrew].

_____. *The Prophetical Stories: The Narratives About the Prophets in the Hebrew Bible--Their Literary Types and History.* Jerusalem: Magnes, 1988.

ROSE, Margaret A. *Parody//Meta-Fiction: An Analysis of Parody as a Critical Mirror to the Writing and Reception of Fiction.* London: Croom Helm, 1979.

_____. *Parody: Ancient, Modern, and Post-Modern.* Literature, Culture, Theory 5. Cambridge: Cambridge University, 1993.

ROSENBERG, J. "Jonah and the Prophetic Vocation." *Response* 22 (1974), 23-26.

ROSENHEIM, Edward. *Swift and the Satirist's Art.* Chicago: University of Chicago, 1963.

RUDOLPH, Wilhelm. "Jona." *Archäologie und Altest Testament: Festschrift für Kurt Galling zum 8. Januar 1970.* Eds. A. Kuschke & E. Kutsch. Tübingen: J. C. B. Mohr (Paul Siebeck), 1970, 233-39.

SAFREN, Jonathan D. "Balaam and Abraham." *VT* 38 (1988), 105-13.

ŠANDA, A. *Die Bücher der Könige.* EHAT 9. Münster i. Westf.: Aschendorffsche, 1911.

SANDMEL, Samuel. *The Enjoyment of Scripture.* New York: Oxford University, 1972.

SASSON, Jack M. *Jonah: A New Translation with Introduction, Commentary, and Interpretation.* AB 24B. Garden City, N.Y.: Doubleday, 1990.

SELLIN, Ernst. *Introduction To The Old Testament.* Rev. Georg Fohrer. Nashville: Abingdon, 1968.

SHAZAR, Zalman. "The Book of Jonah." *Beth Mikra* 47/4 (1971), 432-37. Repr. in *Studies in the Minor Prophets.* Ed. B. Z. Luria. Jerusalem: Qiryat Sefer, 1981, 247-52 [in Hebrew].
_____. "Jonah--Transition from Seer to Prophet." *Dor le Dor* 7/1 (1978), 1-8.

SIMON, Uriel. "1 Kings 13: A Prophetic Sign--Denial and Persistence." *HUCA* 47 (1976), 81-117.
_____. "Structure And Meaning in The Book of Jonah." *Isaac Leo Seeligmann Volume: Essays on the Bible and the Ancient World.* Vol. 2. Eds. A. Rofé & Y. Zakovitch. Jerusalem: E. Rubinstein, 1983, 291-318 [in Hebrew].
_____. *Jonah: Introduction and Commentary.* Mikra Leyisra'el. Jerusalem: Magnes, 1992 [in Hebrew].

SMART, J. D. *Jonah. IB* 6:871-74.

SNAITH, Norman H. *II Kings, Exegesis.* Ed. G. A. Buttrick. IB 3. Nashville: Abingdon, 1954, 187-338.

SOLEH, Aryeh. "The Story of Jonah's Reflective Adventures." *Beth Mikra* 24 (1979), 406-20 [in Hebrew].

SPACKS, P. M. "Some Reflections on Satire." *Genre* 1 (1968), 13-20. Repr. in *Satire: Modern Essays in Criticism.* Ed. R. Paulson. Englewood Cliffs, N.J.: Prentice-Hall, 1971, 360-78.

SPEISER, E. A. "Nineveh." *IDB* 3: 551-53.

STECK, J. H. "The Meaning of The Book of Jonah." *Calvin Theological Journal* 4 (1969), 23-50.

STINESPRING, W. F. "Irony and Satire." *IDB* 2:726-28.

STUART, Douglas. *Hosea-Jonah*. WBC 31. Waco, Tex.: Word, 1987.

STURDY, John. *Numbers*. CBC. Cambridge: Cambridge University, 1976.

SUTHERLAND, W. O. S. *The Art of the Satirist*. Austin: University of Texas, 1965.

TIGAY, J. H. "The Book of Jonah and the Days of Awe." *Conservative Judaism* 38 (1985-1986), 67-76.

TRÉPANIER, Benoit. "The Story of Jonas." *CBQ* 19 (1951), 8-16.

TRIBLE, Phyllis L. *Studies in the Book of Jonah*. Ph.D. Columbia University. Ann Arbor: University Microfilm, 1963.
_____. *Rhetorical Criticism: Context, Method, and the Book of Jonah*. Guides to Biblical Scholarship, Old Testament Series. Minneapolis: Fortress, 1994.

TSMUDI, J. "Jonah's Gourd." *Beth Mikra* 29 (1982), 44-48 [in Hebrew].

UFFENHEIMER, B. *Ancient Prophecy in Israel*. Jerusalem: Magnes, 1973 [in Hebrew].

VANONI, G. *Das Buch Jona. Liter- und formkritische Untersuchung.* Münchener Universitätsschriften. Arbeiten zu Text und Sprache im Alten Testament 7. St. Ottilien: Eos, 1978.

VAN HEERDEN, Willie. Humour and The Interpretation of the Book of Jonah. *Old Testament Essays* 5 (1992), 389-401.

VAN WINKLE, D. W. "1 Kings xiii: True and False Prophecy." *VT* 29 (1989), 31-43.

VAWTER, Bruce. *Job and Jonah: Questioning the Hidden God.* New York/Ramsey: Paulist, 1983.

WALSH, Jerome T. "The Contexts of 1 Kings xiii." *VT* 39 (1989), 355-70.

WALTKE, Bruce K., and O'CONNOR, M. *An Introduction to Biblical Hebrew Syntax.* Winona Lake, Ind.: Eisenbrauns, 1990.

WALTON, John H. "The Object Lesson of Jonah 4:5-7 and The Purpose of The Book of Jonah." *Bulletin For Biblical Research* 2 (1992), 47-57.

WARSHAW, Thayer S. "The Book of Jonah." *Literary Interpretations of Biblical Narratives.* Eds., K. R. R. Gros Louis, J. S. Ackerman & T. S. Warshaw. New York: Abingdon, 1974, 191-207.

WATSON, W. G. E. *Classical Hebrew Poetry: A Guide to Its Techniques.* Sheffield: JSOT, 1983.

WATTS, John D. W. *The Books of Joel, Obadiah, Jonah, Nahum, Habakkuk and Zephaniah.* Cambridge Bible Commentary. Cambridge: Cambridge University, 1975.

WEBB, Barry G. *The Book of Judges: An Integrated Reading.* JSOTSup 46. Sheffield: JSOT, 1987.

WENHAM, Gordon J. *Numbers.* Tyndale Old Testament Commentaries. Downers Grove, Ill.: Inter-Varsity, 1981.

WILSON, John Ambrose. "The Sign of the Prophet Jonah." *Princeton Theological Review* 25 (1927), 630-42.

WILSON, Robert R. *Prophecy and Society in Ancient Israel.* Philadelphia: Fortress, 1980.

WINTON THOMAS, D. "A Consideration of Some Unusual Ways of Expressing the Superlative in Hebrew." *VT* 3 (1953), 209-24.

WISEMAN, D. J. "Jonah's Nineveh." *Tyndale Bulletin* 30 (1979), 29-51.

WITZENRATH, H. *Das Buch Jona: Eine Literature wissenschaftliche Untersuchung.* Münchener Universitätsschriften. Arbeiten zu Text und Sprache im Alten Testament 6. St. Ottilien: Eos, 1978.

WOLFF, Hans Walter. *Obadiah and Jonah.* Augsburg Continental Commentaries. Minneapolis: Fortress, 1986.

WORCESTER, D. *The Art of Satire.* New York: Russell & Russell, 1960 <1940>.

WORTLEY, W. Victor. "Some Rabelaisian Satiric Techniques." *Satire News Letter* 5/1 (1967), 8-15.

WRIGHT, A. G. "The Literary Genre Midrash." *CBQ* 28 (1962), 431-32.

WÜRTHWEIN, Ernst. "Die Erzählung vom Gottesmann aus Juda in Bethel." *Wort und Geschichte: Festschrift für Karl Elliger zum 70. Geburtstag*. Eds. H. Gese & H. P. Rüger. AOAT 18. Neukirchen-Vluyn: Neukirchener, 1973, 181-89.

_____. *Das Erste Buch der Könige, Kapitel 1-16*. ATD 11/1. Göttingen: Vandenhoeck & Ruprecht, 1977.

ZAKOVITCH, Yair. *The Pattern of the Numerical Sequence Three-Four in the Bible*. Jerusalem: Hebrew University Ph.D. Dissertation, 1977 [in Hebrew].

_____. "Get up Baldy! Get up Baldy!" *Jerusalem Studies in Hebrew Literature* 8 (1985), 7-23 [in Hebrew].

_____. *The Concept of the Miracle in the Bible*. Tel-Aviv: MOD Books, 1991 [in Hebrew].

_____. "'Elisha Died...He Came to Life and Stood Up' (2 Kings 13:20-21): A Short 'Short Story' in Exegetical Circles." *Shaarei Talmon: Studies in the Bible, Qumran, and the Ancient Near East Presented to Shemaryahu Talmon*. Eds. Michael Fishbane & Emanuel Tov. Winona Lake, Ind.: Eisenbrauns, 1991, 53*-62* [in Hebrew].

_____. "Through the Looking Glass: Reflections/Inversions of Genesis Stories in the Bible." *Biblical Interpretation* 1/2 (1993), 139-52.

ZLOTOWITZ, M. *Yonah/Jonah: A New Translation with a Commentary Anthologized from Midrashic And Rabbinic Sources*. Brooklyn, N.Y.: Mesorah, 1980.

# General Index

# Brown Judaic Studies

| 140291 | *The Babylonian Esther Midrash, Vol. 1* | Eliezer Segal |
| 140292 | *The Babylonian Esther Midrash, Vol. 2* | Eliezer Segal |
| 140293 | *The Babylonian Esther Midrash, Vol. 3* | Eliezer Segal |
| 140294 | *The Talmud of Babylonia: An American Translation* | |
| | *V. A: Tractate Yoma Chapters 1 and 2* | Jacob Neusner |
| 140295 | *The Talmud of Babylonia: An American Translation* | |
| | *V. B: Tractate Yoma Chapters 3-5* | Jacob Neusner |
| 140296 | *The Talmud of Babylonia: An American Translation* | |
| | *V. C: Tractate Yoma Chapters 6-8* | Jacob Neusner |
| 140297 | *The Talmud of Babylonia: An American Translation* | |
| | *XXII.D: Tractate Baba Batra Chapters Seven and Eight* | Jacob Neusner |
| 140298 | *The Talmud of Babylonia: An American Translation* | |
| | *XXII.E: Tractate Baba Batra Chapters Nine and Ten* | Jacob Neusner |
| 140299 | *The Studia Philonica Annual, 1994* | David T. Runia |
| 140300 | *Sages, Stories, Authors, and Editors in Rabbinic Judaism* | Richard Kalmin |
| 140301 | *From Balaam to Jonah: Anti-prophetic Satire in the Hebrew Bible* | David Marcus |

## Brown Studies on Jews and Their Societies

| 145001 | *American Jewish Fertility* | Calvin Goldscheider |
| 145002 | *The Impact of Religious Schooling: The Effects of Jewish Education Upon Religious Involvement* | Harold S. Himmelfarb |
| 145003 | *The American Jewish Community* | Calvin Goldscheider |
| 145004 | *The Naturalized Jews of the Grand Duchy of Posen in 1834 and 1835* | Edward David Luft |
| 145005 | *Suburban Communities: The Jewishness of American Reform Jews* | Gerald L. Showstack |
| 145007 | *Ethnic Survival in America* | David Schoem |
| 145008 | *American Jews in the 21st Century: A Leadership Challenge* | Earl Raab |

## Brown Studies in Religion

| 147001 | *Religious Writings and Religious Systems I* | Jacob Neusner, et al |
| 147002 | *Religious Writings and Religious Systems II* | Jacob Neusner, et al |
| 147003 | *Religion and the Social Sciences* | Robert Segal |